On Silver Wings

A Life Reconstructed

by

Kristin Noreen

To Sonja –
Happy Trails!
Kristin Noreen

On Silver Wings. A Life Reconstructed

Copyright © 2015 Kristin P. Noreen

First published by Kristin P. Noreen, Bellingham, Washington, in 2015.

Some names and identifying details have been changed to protect the privacy of individuals.

ISBN: 978-09861836-0-7
LCCN: 2015934644

Library of Congress Cataloging-in-Publications Data has been applied for.

Book and cover design and production by Kathleen Weisel, (weiselcreative.com)

Cover photo by Sarah Pree.

Photos of Nimby and Kristin by Jill Bates.

Winged bike graphic: © Kirill Smalugov | Dreamstime.com

Permission to quote from the song, *By Way of Sorrow*, granted by Julie Miller via Vector Management.

Permission to quote from the song, *You Are Here*, granted by Ruth Moody of the Wailin' Jennys.

Permission to quote from the song, *The One Who Knows*, from Dar Williams, via MCT Management.

In Memory of

Paul W. Noreen Jr.
1935-2013
Best Dad Ever

and

Nimby Tyson Noreen
2005-2014
Best Friend Ever

and

In Honor of

Dorothy Noreen
Best Mom Ever

*"Take it easy with the new lease on life.
That shit's hard to maintain."*

~ Nurse Jackie

Introduction

August 2008

So these were *poffertjes*, these glorious round puffs of griddled dough, sprinkled with powdered sugar and drizzled with honey butter. Heaven on a paper plate! They were so sweet, the roof of my mouth tickled as I chewed. It was worth every minute of the long wait in line. Now that I had experienced the highlight of the Northwest Washington Fair, it was time to go to the Whatcom Humane Society outreach booth where I was scheduled to volunteer with Andy Clay, the president of the board at the time. I hadn't met her yet and I was a little intimidated by the idea of working with the board president, but I was an enthusiastic new volunteer and I was ready for just about anything. I pushed through the crowd to the second row of booths and looked for the purple Whatcom Humane Society logo.

Andy greeted me with such a pleasant smile, I forgot all about being intimidated. In between greeting guests to the booth, signing up new members, selling pet supplies and taking donations, we started chatting. I told her how I had just returned from riding my bicycle from my house in Bellingham, Washington to my best friend's house in Eugene, Oregon. Like everyone, Andy asked "Who did you go with?" I rode alone. I stayed with friends and relatives along the way, with the exception of one night in a hostel and one night in a KOA cabin. I prefer to ride alone and socialize in the evening. Like everyone, Andy was impressed that I did it alone, but unlike everyone else, she didn't seem to think it was odd, just gutsy.

The evening started winding down and there weren't many people at our outreach booth. Andy invited me to visit her other booth, the one for the school she founded with her husband in Kenya. I went and learned about this amazing place where the villagers were given the tools to lift themselves out of poverty and disease. I admired the handcrafts from the village that were sold to help finance the school. I went back to the Humane Society booth and asked Andy how she came to have a school on the other side of the world.

Andy seemed to size me up for a minute, then told me how her third son had been killed when his small plane crashed in the mountains. Andy had lapsed into paralyzing depression. She had planned to climb Mt. Kilimanjaro with her son, and she decided to make the climb on her own as a way to say good-bye and do the impossible—let go. Andy did climb Mt. Kilimanjaro, and her way back down, she met a man who invited her to his village. The people there were anxious to improve their own lot and only needed help getting started. Andy had the energy, the time, and the family money to help. Her new purpose was found. As I listened to her story, I saw the way her feet met the ground and her energy radiated from her proud, straight spine, and I knew this woman would never be fragile again.

At the end of the evening, I said good-night and that it was an honor to meet her. Andy said, "Oh, the honor is all mine."

I laughed and asked, "How does that work?"

Andy smiled knowingly and said, "You just found out what you're made of. Now I get to know you while we find out who you're going to become."

I walked away thinking, "I did just find out what I'm made of. I'm a tough lady too." I thought of the Seinfeld episode in which Babu the restaurant owner tells Jerry, "You are a very, very good man," and Jerry thinks smugly, "I *am* a good man," and laughed and got over myself. After all, I had only gotten a glimpse of what I'm made of. I really had no idea how tough I was going to have to find out I am.

WHUMP.

August 23, 2010

4:00. A gorgeous sunny August day. I had been at my desk working all day, barely even stopping for lunch. My report was due to my client by Friday and I had reams of review comments to sift through before then. But in northwest Washington, one doesn't take a perfect 72-degree sunny day for granted. To waste such a day sitting indoors at a desk is a sin.

Lucky for me (though not so much at the time), I had lost my "real job" a year ago and was working out of my home for two friends who had voluntarily left the same company and started their own ventures. I had found that by charging an independent consultant's fee, I could work part-time and have enough time for the volunteer work I loved, animal rescue with the Whatcom Humane Society. Working at home also meant no one would know if I took off a little early to get a quick 10-mile bike ride in before dinner. I would ride a country loop that swung by my favorite Thai restaurant, where I would load up on take-out to feed me for the rest of the long work week.

My legs wanted a ride. My first love is bicycle touring, and I had just returned from a six-day, 235-mile loop that started with an annual day ride with friends on the Hood Canal, then I went north to Port Townsend, west to Port Angeles, and across on the ferry to Victoria, BC. The first three days had been cold, rainy and miserable. At one point, shivering in the wind and slapping cold rain at the bottom of a mountain pass, I tried to call a friend to come get me. There was no reception. I soldiered on to Port Townsend, where I figured I could get to my night stop faster than I could be bailed out. The next day started out promising, but I only made it a few miles before rain pelted me all the way to Port Angeles. In the bathroom at the ferry terminal, I changed into an outlandish outfit composed of the only dry things in my bag, a sleeveless pool cover-up I use as a night shirt with a pair of wool tights, covered by my muddy rain jacket. A woman jerked her child away from me as if I were a deranged vagrant. On the ferry, my bike was buffeted miserably in the wind and rain; the bike rack was on the deck toward the bow. At one point I had to go out on the deck and reorient the bike to keep the wheel from twisting in the wind. When the ferry pulled into Victoria, the sun came out with a giant double rainbow and I enjoyed three perfect days exploring the city, and the wonderful network of bike trails around Vancouver Island. Just as the fun was getting started, it was time to go home and back to work. After a week of confinement at my desk, I couldn't stand any more.

Not only was I swamped with work, I was preparing for my parents to visit for the first time in three years. I was proud of my two-bedroom condo and of the fact that I hadn't missed a mortgage payment since losing my job. My condo didn't really have the capacity to absorb the contents of my large office, so I was busy de-junking the place to make it presentable. As I went to get my cycling shoes, I wove around piles of stuff waiting to be carried off for donation or disposal, and thought, "Thank God my parents will never see *this* mess." My enormous brown tabby cat, Nimby (for Not In My Back Yard), followed me outside and nattered at me not to go. "I'll be home in an hour, Boo, I promise," I said as he head-butted my cycling glove.

The joy as I pushed off from the curb! My legs surged with anticipation and my skin warmed with the delightful touch of the late afternoon sun. "Hi, Silver," I said to my vintage high-end Schwinn touring bike. Silver was indeed silver when I bought her new 30 years ago. The bike had fallen into disuse over the years as she wore out part by part. I had been shopping for a new bike for some time but didn't like the modern bikes with their thick tubing and visible weld marks. I preferred the old slim steel alloy frames with the handcrafted lug work. They're not that much heavier and they're graceful and ride comfortably for the long hours that touring demands. After unsuccessfully attempting an organized ride from Seattle to Portland (the STP) on a mountain bike I bought from a friend, I realized I had my dream bike hanging in my shed already, I just needed to rebuild it. Now repainted "Wineberry Pearl" with contrasting "Indigo Frost" lugs, Silver was simply gorgeous. The only mark on her was the original silver Schwinn medallion on the head tube. Converted from a 10-speed to a triple crankset, her hill-climbing capacity was boundless and she handled gracefully with a load. No SUV-supported group tours for me; I ride alone and carry my own gear.

As I rode along the bike lane on hilly Smith Road, I relived my recent trek through the Vancouver Island countryside. I remembered the evenings in the hostel drinking tea with my new friend Loretta from California, the small urban market where we found everything we could ever want to eat in single portions, the walk through narrow Fan Tan Alley in Chinatown where I bought Chinese trinkets for my friends back home. I turned onto Hannegan Road, a country arterial where traffic whizzed by doing 45 mph. Hannegan Road has a wide paved shoulder and I had never thought of it as especially dangerous, despite the head-shaking of my non-cyclist friends. Bike touring means using busy roads and highways sometimes, and you learn to handle yourself.

Hannegan Road is full of turns and hills, usually in combination. I crested the last of the hills and coasted down the straightaway toward the DIY strip mall—a cluster of plumbing and lumber shops on the outskirts of town where I could pull over and phone in my order to the Thai House so it would be ready to grab and go. The strip mall was about a mile ahead and while it looked like the road kept going slightly downhill, I was always surprised by how much I needed to pedal along that stretch.

Anyone who rides will know what I mean when I say that a squirrelly vibe made me look up. I scanned the road for danger signals and found a young man in a boxy white Scion, driving too fast for conditions, an expression of inattention on his face. The innermost lane of oncoming cars stopped behind someone making a left turn. The young man smacked right into a silver Dodge Durango at the tail of the line. I watched in disbelief as the vehicles collided, then time slammed into slow motion as the Scion ricocheted directly toward me. My brain frantically calculated and rejected escape routes until I computed impossibly that the car was *going* to hit me, then WHUMP.

I remember the air being forced from my lungs and an especially sharp pain from my right hand, then being thrown with impossible force and rolling downhill with a momentum that snapped bones as I went. I remember thinking "no one could survive this impact" before I blacked out.

•

I love afternoon naps. There is nothing like waking up from a good nap all refreshed and easing back into the day. Everything was bathed in gold and glowing warm. There is a common recurring dream people have in which you are underwater and find you can breathe just fine. I had that sensation of gulping deeply of the air when I shouldn't be able to breathe. A man's voice kept talking to me from far away, getting closer until he was right there next to me. I opened my eyes and suddenly I couldn't breathe at all, every harsh gasp brought incredible pain. The voice urged me to take slow, deep breaths. That was impossible, why couldn't I tell him so? It started flooding back, the impact and flying through the air, then hurtling downhill. Oh God, how could I still be alive? Did I wake up just to feel myself die? I tried wiggling my toes. Yes, I could feel them moving. Where was my right shoe? Why couldn't I move anything else? The man's voice again. "Can you tell me your name?"

It took several tries to gasp it out over two breaths. "Kris—tin."

"Good, Kristin, I need you to take deep, slow breaths." (damn you, I can't!) "We called 911 and help is on the way. Is there anyone I can call for you?"

My family is all out of state and while I have lots of friends in town, only one friend would know how to reach everyone else—my ex-husband in Seattle. I managed to gasp Kenn's name and it took three gasps per digit to get his phone number out.

I heard sirens. "Kristin, you need to breathe in deep, slow breaths. Can you do that for me?" (No, I really can't, why don't you get that?) The membrane between the worlds was thin, all I would have to do was think about letting go and I'd be gone. A gentle falling sensation tempted me and I fought it. Nimby! My wonderful twenty-one-pound tabby cat who I had adopted from the Whatcom Humane Society only three years before. Nimby with his unique temperament and his own set of house rules. He would be abandoned again and no one could understand him like I did. His blossoming in my care would be undone.

No! I was going to hang on. I saw my parents getting the news of my death and refused the image. And my work at the Humane Society, who would care for the cats? I loved my life. I finally got it exactly right and now this. This is only supposed to happen to people who need a wake-up call because they're doing something they shouldn't be or not doing something they should.

The image flashed through my mind of the night two summers ago at the Lynden Fair when Andy Clay said, "You just found out what you're made of. Now I get to know you while we find out who you're going to become." *I* wanted to know who I was going to become! I felt my potential and knew that something huge was about to be lost. No. I would not be lost. A siren was getting louder, then it stopped. The paramedics were here. I still couldn't breathe; could they help me in time?

A collar was placed around my neck, locking it into the uncomfortable angle I landed in. I was lifted onto a back board. Oh God, can this much pain even be possible? Crushing pain in my spine and chest and every limb. It felt like my right hand was stuck in a bonfire. Everything seemed to be getting dark. No air. The membrane getting thinner yet. I had to hang on, I mustn't let go, even though the emptiness beckoned with the promise of comfort like a soft blanket. I was vaguely aware of being placed in the ambulance. Voices around me, relaying my condition to dispatch. I had watched enough "ER" to know that what I was hearing was not good. "Abdomen hard and distended," "collapsed lungs," and most alarmingly, "partial amputation of the right hand."

Two medics were arguing over whether to put in a chest tube there or wait until they got to the hospital. Protocol dictated they wait. The other medic said there wasn't time, I needed air now. I knew what a chest tube was—they jam it between your ribs right into your chest. It wasn't done to conscious people, surely they'd put me out. Oh God, no, they didn't! A moment of incredible stabbing pain, then a sweet rush of air. I was *breathing*. Well, not so much, but I wasn't suffocating any more. I realized that no matter what it took to recover from this, that chest tube was probably the worst thing that was going to happen. The worst is over, it all gets better from here. If I can only hang on...

We arrived at the hospital. As I was whisked into the ER, a woman's face appeared close to mine. She wore round wire-rimmed glasses and had long salt-and-pepper braids. She introduced herself and said there would be a lot of people working on me and I needed to just lie back and let them do their jobs. They would probably put me out soon so I shouldn't try too hard to hold on to consciousness, it would be better to just let go. I couldn't let go, that would mean dying. But at some point it all just stopped and I went into stasis while a squad of doctors took over the job of keeping me alive.

ICU

White. Everything white. White ceiling, white walls, white sheets, white table by the bed. Enough bustling about to know this was a hospital room and not some notion of heaven. The ICU, to be exact. My God, did this mean I was still alive? I made it out of the ER? A nurse in navy scrubs appeared in my blurred vision, a brown-skinned man who introduced himself as Mike. "Do you know where you are?" he asked. I wondered how I was supposed to respond, as I couldn't move anything, my arms seemed to be tied down, and there was a tube in my mouth. Mike explained that I was in the ICU and I was badly hurt but I was going to be okay. Time passed, I drifted through it and suddenly Kenn was there. He knew the first thing I needed to hear—that Nimby was being cared for. Then he explained that I had fourteen fractures. Well, fractures heal, I thought. The injuries that are hardest to recover from are the ones where the bones don't give and it's all soft tissue damage. I knew a bit too much about that already. Fractures heal. Maybe these injuries wouldn't be as lasting the ones I'd had before.

I thought of Silver, lying crumpled by the side of the road and the grief was too much. There would be time to mourn her later; my number one priority was surviving until they took me off the respirator. It felt impossibly confining; I just had to stay sane until that part was over. Everything in me wanted to melt down and freak out; I willed myself to breathe slowly and stay calm. At least breathing slowly was possible now.

Two more nurses announced it was time to take a chest x-ray. They slid the hard film tiles under my back and the pain was unbearable. I vomited and they quickly suctioned it away.

More drifting, asleep and awake. Saliva kept

pooling in my throat around the breathing tube and I felt like it would choke me. I tried to communicate this but without my hands, it was impossible. Mike the nurse knew I needed something but couldn't tell what. Kenn asked if he could try. I stuck my left thumb out for yes. "Lights?" he asked, knowing I'm hypersensitive to light and too-bright lights make me crazy. I tried to turn my thumb down and couldn't rotate my wrist. How to indicate no? I extended my middle finger. Kenn and Mike both nearly fell to the floor laughing. Yeah, yeah, I'm cute but I'm choking here! A little help? Finally Kenn wrote the alphabet on a note pad with a Sharpie and pointed to each letter until I gave the thumb-up. S-U-C—Suction, Kenn guessed! Thumb up! Mike suctioned around the tube and explained that the saliva can't actually get into the tube. That didn't matter, I just damn near suffocated by the side of the road and I couldn't bear the sensation of anything like it.

Time drifted along and suddenly my parents were there, both with tears in their eyes. And my sister Kathy! If Kathy was here, I must have really been badly hurt. Beth's absence meant they hadn't come here expecting to say good-bye. Or maybe just that it takes longer to get here from Florida than Minnesota.

I woke up again and it was late at night. The lights were low but it was plenty noisy. An elderly woman was next to me, I could hear her labored breathing and whimpering. A young woman cursed and said she wanted a different nurse. The nurse, another man, sighed and said she'd gone through the whole staff and there was no one left. The woman went on a diatribe about how she knew she was a drug addict but she was sick of everyone judging her. I laid there and thought about how I didn't care what she did with the drugs but I judged her for being a loudmouth and felt bad for the old lady who was forced to hear angry, foul language in what might be her last moments of life.

My own drugs caused me to see endless repeating patterns of incredible beauty. The colors and textures were mesmerizing. Lush fields of stylized grain blowing in the wind gave way to blue-green circles that broke apart into waves. I watched the patterns and reconciled myself to the impossibility of sleep in the ICU.

Morning came and a doctor announced that he was going to see if I could breathe on my own. This was the first awareness I had that I *wasn't* breathing on my own. I knew about the respirator but just hadn't connected the dots. I didn't really feel anything change when he disconnected the tube at a point outside my mouth. I guess I breathed all right, but my oxygen level started falling after 10 minutes so he reconnected the tube. This exercise repeated several times over the next day until finally the doctor decided I was ready to go without the tube. He told me to cough hard as he pulled on the tube. It felt like it expanded to three times its width as he drew it out. Every cough ripped through my chest like a rusty knife. Then it was out and I kept on coughing while they suctioned out gobs of goop. I couldn't keep from swallowing some of it. There was a feeding tube in my nose so they stuck an oxygen cannula up the other nostril and taped it in place, and I wondered how this was better than the tube.

By this time it was decided that I was ready to hear the inventory of fractures and wounds. Nine ribs, my skull, spine, and sacrum (lower spine), my left scapula (shoulder "wing" bone) and humerus (upper arm bone), which was shattered. My right hand had for all practical purposes been amputated; all the nerves and blood vessels were severed and two surgeons had labored for four hours to reattach it all. My lungs had collapsed, which I knew, and my liver and spleen were lacerated. My blood was closely monitored while they waited it out to see if the lacerations would heal naturally. I was told I would need surgery on my arm and shoulder, but I had to stabilize before that could happen. What about my legs? I asked. Miraculously, my legs were fine. A few bruises and cuts, but nothing major. *Excellent*, I thought. I will ride again. A picture formed in my mind of a photo I had seen online of a resort with hanging treehouses on Vancouver Island, within bicycle touring distance. It was on my list of "someday" places. I promised myself I would go next summer. I had a goal. The doctor smiled patronizingly and said maybe someday I could do that. He did not know that the way to ensure I will do something is to tell me I can't, or in this case, patronize me. My fate was sealed; as of that moment I was in training for my next bike trip, to the Free Spirit Spheres in Qualicum Beach, BC.

I Meet My Invisible Roommate

At specified intervals, a pump on my IV stand would pop the lid out of a pre-loaded can of Ensure and pump it down the feeding tube in my nose to my stomach. There was no warning when feeding time would be, I just became aware of the sensation of cold wet concrete glurping down my nose.

At least I could talk, though I didn't much want to for the first day after they took out the breathing tube. The chest x-rays seemed to happen at three-hour intervals, though I'm sure it was longer than that. They used a portable unit and slid the hard films under my back. Every time they tilted me to slide the film under, my breath was cut off. They would tell me over and over not to hold my breath and I would gasp when it was over and explain that for whatever reason, I could not breathe while I was tilted like that. The x-rays made me feel panicky, like I was back in the ditch again.

My family members came in one at a time and stayed a few minutes each time. Every time I asked for my glasses and every time they sighed and said they forgot. They didn't understand why this upset me. I was completely helpless and could not influence my environment in any way; the least I could ask was to be able to see it, and the faces of the people who were caring for me. They don't need their glasses all the time; they didn't get that I was blind in there.

I said to my mom, "I suppose I'm going to miss the Dog Days festival." This major Whatcom Humane Society event is the highlight of summer for us volunteers. I was going to have a booth this year to sell the jewelry I make and I'd been working for weeks to get ready. My mom blinked and said the festival had happened two days ago. I had been in and out of consciousness while they went and met all my friends.

One afternoon there was a flurry of energy outside my room and my friend Sue appeared, flanked by security guards. She grabbed my feet and hung on as if she expected to be dragged out and said, "Hi, sweetie!" One guard asked if I was okay with her being here and I said yes, absolutely. He gave her five minutes and stood disapprovingly, his arms crossed over his chest. Sue is my Realtor; she sold me my condo and we made friends in the process. Sue is effervescent and fun and fills every room she's in. We talked a few minutes, then the guard said her time was up and escorted her out. My dad blinked a few times and said, "She was only here five minutes and I'm exhausted." I was just so happy that she came.

The next day I was told I would be moved to a room on the third floor, the pre-surgical unit. The nurses explained that my bed was actually a movable gurney that could be hooked up to a suspension system in the ceiling, much like a basket that hangs from a rescue chopper. As soon as the bed lifted, my breathing stopped just like it did for the X-rays. Apparently the gurney curved just enough to put me at that bad angle. I had no way to signal my plight to the nurses; fortunately one was paying attention and saw my panicked look. The nurses conferred and decided that they could slide me along the track, into the elevator, and into my new room quickly enough so it wouldn't be dangerous if I did stop breathing, but they attached a hard backboard to the bottom of the gurney to try to prevent the curvature first. My breathing caught a few times as they ran me along the track, but resumed after a few seconds each time. All I could see was the blurred track in the ceiling as we turned corners and elevator doors opened and closed. Then I was deposited in my new room. There was a big window to my right; I liked that. There was a poster on the wall that I couldn't see clearly. I had an idea that there was another half of the room to my left and there was a roommate there, but it seemed that I couldn't turn my head to look. I didn't know it at the time, but my stroke had left me with "left neglect," the inability to perceive anything on my left side. I could in fact look at the left side of the room, but I didn't see anything and couldn't process the resulting confusion.

Because I was at a high risk for developing blood clots, my legs were wrapped in sleeves that joined with Velcro strips and were similar to blood pressure cuffs. They inflated with warm air at regular intervals, maintained pressure for a time, then deflated to promote fluid movement that is normally stimulated by moving around. The cuffs were not uncomfortable, I even liked it some of the time. It felt a little like having heavy Nimby curled up on my legs. The cuffs had a maddening tendency for the Velcro to come apart under pressure and the nurses were forever coming in to reattach them.

A physical therapist came to see me twice a day. I was asked to sit up, which was terribly difficult and painful, and move my legs in ways that promoted circulation. They also did respiratory therapy. I was given a device called an aspiration spirometer that measured how forcefully I could inhale, which is much harder than blowing. My goal was to reach the 1500-cc mark, about 2½ inches up the column, but my first attempts barely moved the ball indicator. I also got a percussor, known as the "pickle," which looked just like a big green pickle with a mouthpiece on one end. The pickle caused a blowback into the lung that felt like a drumbeat and made me cough uncontrollably. This, evidently, was good, despite the searing pain from my damaged lungs and broken ribs. I was expected to use the devices every hour between therapy sessions, but I couldn't pick them up myself, or even hold them in my hands, so unless someone came by to help me with them, they sat on the bedside table.

I liked all the therapists immensely, but Cheryl was my favorite. She radiated life and energy. She told me how a serious bike accident in her youth had inspired her to become a physical therapist. I confided my plan to visit the Free Spirit Spheres on my bike as soon as I was able to. She stepped back, looked me over, and said, "Your legs are fine. You may need an adaptation to your bike if your right hand can't take your weight on the handlebar, but we have a guy at the rehab center who can hook that up. Maybe not next summer, but the summer after for sure." I loved Cheryl for taking my plan seriously and telling me she thought it was possible. I didn't tell many people because I couldn't bear their pity and patronizing looks. If Cheryl had asked me to run laps around the ward, I'd have tried to do it for her. What she did ask of me seemed just as impossible.

Mary, Nancy and Sandy were also a welcome sight, even though they made me sore and tired. One day Sandy appeared in my doorway just as I'd drifted off to a much-needed nap. I felt her presence and opened one eye, and the look in hers was so challenging, I actually heard the OK Corral music in my head. I absolutely did not want to rise to the occasion, but I forced myself awake. After the session, Sandy praised me for trying and not fighting her.

There was talk of transferring me to a rehab center after my arm surgery. The best facility was the one run by the hospital, in another part of town. Chances were my insurance was going to shunt me to a conventional nursing home where I wouldn't get the aggressive therapy I needed. I begged my doctors to fight my insurance company; I wanted to go to South Campus. The program there was notoriously tough; patients signed a contract promising to spend a minimum of three hours a day in one-on-one therapy and relinquish their bed to another patient if they couldn't keep up. My thought was, "how am I going to get better if I'm only working three hours a day? I wonder if they allow overtime." Finally Mary brought me word that I got into the program. She said the staff there had objected to my coming because my injuries made it impossible for me to use a walker or propel my own wheelchair, and it would be hard to integrate me with the other patients who all used walkers. Mary had advocated for me, saying that just because my set of injuries didn't fit into their box, I shouldn't be denied care, and if they couldn't respond to a challenge, what were they there for anyway? I nearly wept with gratitude. It was going to be a long time before I went home, but at least I was headed to the one facility that would give me a chance to get as much back as I could.

You Are Here

Around this time, as they backed down my opiates somewhat, I started to think I was going to wake up and find myself back in my regular life. My daily routine started to come back to me and I would get confused. Later, the psychologist told me this was normal. The brain can't process that sudden a change in life circumstances; it takes about four to six weeks to fully comprehend, and another several months to accept.

My catheter was removed and I was expected to get up and use the commode—literally a chair with a toilet seat placed near the bed, with a removable tank under the seat. I had no use of my arms at all, and my ribs and shoulder were so shattered that the nurses couldn't give me a hand to help me forward. The best they could do was raise my bed until I was almost sitting up, which was excruciating all by itself, then I had to use my stomach muscles to rise out of bed. I would hold it as long as I could bear to before I would get up. I couldn't even reach for the nurse call button; the nurse would rest it under my right hand before she left so I could push down on it with one finger when I needed to. Often the button would slip away and I couldn't reach it, and I had to lie there waiting until a nurse happened by. On that busy floor, nurses rarely *happened by*. Once I had to go to the bathroom so badly, I could barely keep from wetting myself as I got up. I was in tears by the time the nurse came along, and she tied the call button to my forearm with a strip of gauze. After that, I always had my call button secured to me somehow.

One day my IV stand started beeping and wouldn't stop. At first it was because it was feeding time and there was no waiting bottle of Ensure. The nurse popped in a bottle and I asked, "Wait, is that fresh out of the refrig—" It was. As the icy mass glurped down my feeding tube, I had the worst ice-cream headache of my life.

No sooner had the nurse left than the stand started beeping again. No one could make it stop. My parents actually left to go run errands and my sister stayed with the horrendously annoying sound. After more than two hours of it, I hit the call button and sobbed into the microphone, "You have to make it fucking stop!" Finally someone realized that one of the batteries was low and that was the problem. It seems to me that a low-battery alert sound would drain the battery even faster, but that's how it was done.

Late one night I was trying to sleep and an east Indian family was gathered in the hall outside a patient's room. There had to be two dozen people, the women in bright saris and the men in somber suits, all of them talking at full party volume. I put up with it for more than an hour. When my nurse came by, she asked if the noise was bothering me and I said yes, and she herded most of them to the lobby, asked the rest of them to use "indoor voice," and closed the door to my room. The nurse asked why I hadn't complained and I said I was just at the mercy of the noise level around there and had given up hope of any kind of normal sleeping schedule.

One night I had a restless dream of being at my sister's house in Minneapolis and living in her garage. I woke up with a sticky sensation all over and buzzed for the nurse. It wasn't my imagination; my feeding tube had come out of my nose and I was drenched with an entire container of Ensure that had been pumped onto my chest where the tube landed. The nurse who came looked exactly like my niece, Sara, and having come from the dream of living in the garage of her house, I was really confused. The nurse's name was Michelle and she had a new bed rolled in for me and cleaned me up some before and after the transfer. She left the feeding tube out and decided to consult with the doctor in the morning to see if it needed to be put back in. I was grateful when they decided it didn't, but this brought a new complication.

I couldn't feed myself. The nurses had to feed me like a baby. This is a terribly intimate thing and no one was comfortable with it. Agnes, a young CNA from Poland, was the best at it. She was attentive to when I was ready for another bite without being too much in my space. I started requesting Agnes at feeding time. I could tell this pained her somewhat, but she was a good sport and always came if she was on duty. One day Agnes got a little snippy with me and I didn't handle it very well myself. An hour later, she came to my door with an in-bed hair wash kit and offered to wash my hair. The kit left a sticky residue in my hair and I didn't feel any cleaner, but it felt good to be cared for and I felt a human connection with Agnes after that. Anyone can have a bad day, it takes a great nurse to come back and try to make it right.

Another nurse, Josh, tried feeding me and he jabbed the fork at me so I reared back. I teased him, saying "it's a fork, not the Hammer of Thor!" I called him Thor after that. Thor redeemed himself, though, when he solved another problem I was having. It took nineteen pillows to prop my body in a neutral position that didn't make me miserable. I sweated profusely all the time and the doctor thought this was because of the opiates. Thor suggested that the mechanical bed could be adjusted in such a way that I only needed three pillows. The sweating was greatly reduced as soon as all those pillows were taken away, and the firmer support made me more comfortable all around. I told the nursing supervisor about that to make sure he got recognized for it.

I had to spend a few hours each day sitting in a

recliner; the risk of blood clots was lower if I sat up part of the time. For the first hour up, I would look out the window and watch the sky, and I was flooded with a sense of well being. My window looked out on the hospital grounds, with the helipad on the lawn. Beyond the helipad, the forest abutting Cornwall Park provided a peaceful view. After an hour of staring at the clouds above the tree line, the pain set in and I would want to lie back down. I usually wasn't allowed to before at least three hours were up. I kept having confusing thoughts as I tried to backtrack to the time this all started and change it. This had to be a dream; I would have to wake up and be back in my real life again. Nimby was waiting, I had to get back!

The strains of a song I had heard once at a Wailin' Jennys show in Vancouver came back to me, in gorgeous 3-part harmony led by Ruth Moody:

> *And there's no making cases*
> *For getting out or trading places*
> *And there's no turning back, no,*
> *You are here...*

The group introduced the song at their show at the Chan Center at the University of British Columbia, an acoustically brilliant venue on one of the most beautiful university campuses in the world, where manicured Chinese gardens compete for attention with snow-peaked mountains rising sharply across the water. I went with the band's promoter, who invited me as a guest of the Wailin' Jennys. Earlier that summer I had posted a note on their blog saying how my Nimby would joy-roll every time I turned on their music, and I posted a photo of Nimby on his back, paws curled. The Jennys are big cat lovers and asked Jamie to let me know they got a kick out of my post. I had tickets to their show in a nearby town the following month. Jamie asked me to point myself out to him then so he could introduce me to the ladies. I wasn't able to point myself out because I had to leave the show early. I had an allergic reaction to some medication I had just started taking and had to leave at intermission. Jamie and the Jennys thought this was such a shame, they offered me the best seats in the house in Vancouver a few weeks later, and Jamie gave me a ride up. Naturally, I became an ardent fan of the band. This one song stuck in my mind and I was able to remember the lyrics even though I couldn't remember other, more immediate things. I played the refrain over and over in my mind and it helped cement me in the present.

The three-part harmony of the Wailin' Jennys is incredibly beautiful, and anything they told me had to be true and okay. I kept listening to the song over and over in my mind, not even sure if I remembered it right. When the CD was released a few months later, I found that I remembered it perfectly.

Scary Stuff

I tried to avoid thinking about the stroke; that was too scary and my mind just rejected that it had even happened. By this time, physical therapists were visiting twice a day and it was apparent that my left side was affected. My left arm hung useless and shattered. I kept forgetting it was there. I felt nothing and most of the time had no concept of it. The therapists suggested that I suffered from "left neglect." This was reinforced by the fact that I continued to be surprised that I had no roommate on the left side of the room each time I was turned to face that side directly. I couldn't see the left side or relate to it while lying in my bed, but I assumed that a roommate existed behind a curtain. There was no curtain and no roommate.

There was a poster at the foot of the bed that I continually tried to make sense of. My brain couldn't conceptualize that I was unable to read it, but the left neglect alternately blanked out the left half of the poster and the left half of the letters, and what I could see made no sense by itself.

My sister brought me a binder full of printed e-mails from people who logged on to my Caring Bridge web site. Caring Bridge is a social network site where people going through medical issues can post notices of their progress and receive messages from people who check the site. Kathy had set me up on a page and I looked with interest at the photos, but said I was too tired to read the e-mails. I tried to, but the words swam and made no sense. Again, I could not read them and my brain had no way to process that fact. The clock was another mystery; there was one on my wall and it looked perfectly normal, but I looked at it again and again and never knew what time it was. I could even tell the nurses what number the big and little hands were on, but I couldn't tell them what time it was. It felt like there was an equation in there I needed to translate that information into a time of day.

The dressing on my hand and wrist had to be changed daily. The nurses did this with my hand down by my side and I couldn't see anything. I felt the air hit the wound and it stung like a thousand hornets every time. One day Dr. Bachman, a fun woman with a larger-than-life presence, asked to see my hand when the dressing was changed. Dr. Bachman had presided over my initial surgery in the ER and was curious to see how the wound was healing. My mom was there and wanted to see it too. The nurse peeled the last of the bandages off and there it was, a mass of stitches and discolored steri-strips circling my wrist. The heel of my hand was still almost black with bruising where it had peeled away from the bone. Sections of skin looked like spent chewing gum where they had been stretched back into place. My stomach felt hollow. Dr. Bachman exclaimed, "Oh, that's beautiful work!" My mom sat there mute with shock, tears filling her eyes. I looked at Dr. Bachman and said accusingly, "You made my mom cry!" That broke the tension and we all laughed, but I wasn't laughing inside. That hand terrified me. I am an artist; what chance did I have of ever picking up beads again with that brutalized hand? How would I hold a handlebar with it? Well, Cheryl the therapist was all over that, but fine craft work was another thing altogether. Would I even be able to hold a pen? Would my handwriting look anything like itself? I remembered watching my grandma lose control of her hands from Parkinson's disease and the resignation with which she put away her needlework. Back then I wondered what life would be worth without being able to express my talent. I still wondered.

One night I was feeling weepy and weak, and the nurse told me she didn't like my numbers. My oxygen was too low and my red blood count was through the floor. A blood transfusion had been ordered, two units of whole blood. Because my blood was filled with allergic antibodies and hard to cross-match, the blood was being brought down from a blood bank in Surrey, B.C. At least it was Canadian blood... Still, the idea of a blood transfusion terrified me. I got the nurse to dial my mom on the room phone. My mom was a retired medical technologist; I just wanted her to know this was happening. At 3:00 AM, she and my dad slept right through my loud and annoying ringer. I left a message, which my mom would have no idea how to retrieve. After I got home more than a month later, I listened to that message and was shocked by how weak I sounded. The nurse heard me leave the message and raised her eyebrows as I spoke. When she took the phone from me, she said, "Honey, you severed your radial artery. People kill themselves that way. Do you think this is the first blood you've been given? You went through as much blood in the ER as a gunshot victim."

The nurse hung the blood and connected the bag to my three-port "pick line" IV, which was routed to my subclavian vein. This line had been installed during my first surgery in the ER. As soon as the blood started going in, I felt the energy of it, like life itself flowing into my body. I remembered my Tai Chi training and consciously accepted the blood. Over the next hour, I felt steadily better. Soon I fell into a deep and restful sleep, my first really good night of sleep in the hospital.

More Surgery

Now that I was more or less stable, I was scheduled for surgery to repair my arm and shoulder. To prepare for this, my surgeon came to visit, one Dr. Van Hofwegen, accompanied by Dr. Hoekema, the orthopedic surgeon who reconnected the nerves in my right hand. Dr. Hoekema did a follow-up visit to see what kind of movement I had in my fingers. I could tell he was really surprised by how much I had, and a little rightfully pleased with himself. Later, Dr. Van Hofwegen told me that Dr. Hoekema really came along because they were afraid I'd be so depressed and depressing, they thought I'd pull it together a little better if there were two of them.

The two men entered my room in humble blue scrubs, but they were clearly golden boys. Both radiated competence and something more— that ornery vibe I thrived on. They were a comedy tag team and I set them both on their ears. I don't even remember what we made small talk about, but I laughed so hard I had to ask for more pain killer for my aching ribs. Dr. Van Hofwegen described the surgical procedures, one to pin my scapula back together and one to remove the shattered remains of my humerus bone and replace it with a plate attached to the intact ends. To install the plate, he would have to dissect the bicep muscle, which separates like the segments of an orange, but takes about two years to fully fuse back together. The scapula procedure looked even more painful. Fortunately, by the time my surgery date came, the X-rays showed that I didn't need the scapula surgery; the bone had drifted into place correctly on its own and seemed to be staying there.

The night before my surgery, the dietitian asked if I had any special meal request. I was a little alarmed by the similarity to the last meal on death row, but I said I wanted the Thai meal I had been on my way to get when this happened. I sent my parents to the Thai House and they returned with my swimming rama, fried tofu in spiced peanut sauce served over lightly seared spinach leaves and rice. My parents, unfamiliar with Thai food and used to bland Midwestern fare, went to Wendy's. Agnes fed me my swimming rama.

The morning of my surgery, I was taken downstairs on a gurney and two prep nurses helped to calm my nerves. Really, I was kind of resigned to the whole thing because it wasn't like I could say no and get dressed and go home. There was nothing to be done but lie there and get through it. I did just about lose it when they had to postpone the surgery two hours because someone hadn't turned off my heparin drip. I was surprised that it would only take two hours to metabolize the heparin and regain my clotting ability. The hours dragged by. The prep nurses, who reminded me very much of my friends Karen and Jill, did their best to keep me sane. They learned quickly that the way to do that was to tease me nonstop and let me sling it back.

Finally it was time to roll me back into surgery. Dr. Van Hofwegen stood quietly in the corner of the room, flexing his fingers, rising on his toes, and breathing deeply. I realized that he was getting in the zone for me! This man respected his work and me enough to get on top of his game and give himself over fully to the work of repairing my arm. I went under anesthesia with the certainty that everything was going to be all right.

I woke up in an enormous bike shop. Bicycles hung from the ceiling and stood in rows on the floor. Mechanics in white coats bustled about. I stopped one and asked if my bike was ready. "Her name is Silver," I said. He laughed and said I was in the recovery room and my surgery was done. I said, "Really? This isn't a bike shop? Then why are there bikes everywhere?" The orderly said I should give it a minute and the bikes would go away. Sure enough, after a few minutes I didn't see any bikes. Still, as they rolled me back to my room, I asked if they were sure I hadn't been in a bike shop while I was out.

The bike shop hallucination just showed how bonded I was to Silver. I was waiting for her to come out of surgery too. I assumed I would have to get a new bike and was already planning to take the train to Walnut Creek, California to buy a Rivendell—the only bike made after 1985 that I would consider buying. There was a little anticipation of meeting my new bike; I visualized her as being poolwater blue. But the sadness over Silver was too deep. I was bonded to Silver like a cowboy to his horse and I couldn't bear to lose her. In all my years of riding, I had never seen a bike I would rather have than my own. I asked Kenn how badly her frame was bent and he said not too badly, but her wheels were mangled. If the forks were okay, there was still hope. I asked him to bring the poor wrecked bike to Pedal Dynamics in Seattle, where Dean and Chad rebuilt her for me in 2004, to see if she could be saved.

Meanwhile, even though my arm was now bound to my side with a large sling, it was no longer hanging shattered by my side and I could try to use my right arm a little. My fingers were still pretty useless, but I had therapy exercises for them now that consisted of wiggling one at a time, and I could at least reach my call button if it hadn't skittered more than a foot out of range. Life was a little more bearable. As they wheeled me back into my old room, I exclaimed over how nice it was to be transferred to a private room. The nurses looked at each other and rolled their eyes.

Visitors!

After I was transferred out of the ICU, a few visitors braved the surgical ward. Most were waiting for me to be transferred to the rehab center, which was more visitor-friendly. My first night in the surgical ward, I got a surprise visit from Laura Clark, the Executive Director of the Whatcom Humane Society. Laura has been one of my favorite people since the day we met, when I adopted Nimby. In fact, it was my desire to have people like Laura for friends that got me started volunteering.

It just so happened that Petwatch, the monthly program produced by WHS, started at 6:30 and I had asked for it to be turned on. Petwatch represented my real life, the one I was supposed to wake back up in any minute. Laura stood in the doorway to my room as the Petwatch theme song played and said, "You've *got* to be kidding me." She came over to my bedside and looked for a safe place to touch. She settled on my foot, which she squeezed, then held as she sat down on the bed. Laura has seen so much in her animal rescue career, even seeing me like this didn't creep her out. With tears in her eyes, she told me how much everyone missed me at the Dog Days festival. She stayed as the new episode of Petwatch played out its 30-minute slot, and at the end I saw her on TV, sending her love and dedicating the festival to me. I was speechless and in tears. Laura just squeezed my foot again and said she and the cats couldn't wait for me to come back.

The day after surgery, I was forced to start walking around the ward. The nurse held my gait belt, a canvas belt that felt a bit like a leash, and pushed my IV stand for me. The IV stand was a beast, it had a large oxygen container the size of a propane tank mounted at the bottom and looked like something out of

M*A*S*H. I made it to the door of my room and back the first time, breathless with the effort to stay upright. Because of the stroke, I didn't have much muscle memory of walking; I figured it out as I went along. The day after that, I had to make it to the lobby and back. When I returned to the room, my friends Judith and Jo from the Humane Society were there. Jo has multiple sclerosis and often walks with a cane, and I'm sure she really didn't like being in the hospital when she didn't have to be. It was so good to see them.

The next day, when I made it all the way around the floor loop, I came back to find Lauren and Kris, one former and one current board member of the Humane Society. They brought me rooibos tea and a New Yorker magazine, which to my relief I could read for a few minutes at a time. All at once, the poster on the wall made sense too. The clock continued to elude me.

My favorite visitor was there when I returned from another walk. Emily Bertino, the Outreach Director at the Humane Society, had been there about a year and during that time had become my best friend there. I worked with Emily often at events and saw her every Monday when I came in to visit the shelter cats. Emily was the busiest staff person at the Humane Society. I was so excited to see her! She brought me gourmet brownies and a bottle of lavender oil. I remember about two weeks after she gave me the lavender oil, when I had been transferred to the rehab center, I was finally able to remove the cap by myself and smell it. To this day, the scent of lavender makes me feel a surge of triumph.

The loop around the floor seemed to take an eternity and I was sure it was longer than the quarter-mile loop walk to my mailbox at home. Recently, while visiting a friend at the hospital, I went around the loop looking for a bathroom and was shocked at how short the hallway actually was.

Lawyering Up

It is hard to lawyer up in the hospital. I strongly recommend that you research some personal injury lawyers on your own and have some names in your back pocket if the need ever arises. I was certain that I wanted to nail the guy who hit me but had no idea how to go about it. Brad, my "boss" (I was technically self-employed but contracted to his firm), recommended an attorney he'd had a good experience with. The attorney did personal injury law but his main focus was employment law, which is what he did for Brad. I know now that a person may be very good in one area and not necessarily another. I scheduled an interview for Keith Beckstrom[1].

My parents and sister were there for the interview; Kathy took notes. I was propped up in my recliner, a blanket over my hospital gown, a fleece pad between the shoulder strap of my sling and my neck, which it rubbed raw. An oxygen cannula ran into my nose and my large IV stand stood by the chair. Not the most dignified position, but I was determined to be in charge and ask the questions.

Keith interviewed well. He was not especially handsome or stylish, but he dressed well and had an unassuming demeanor I liked.

I quickly came to regret outsourcing to Seattle; a local attorney would have been much more convenient. I also had no idea that in Seattle there was an attorney who does nothing but cycling law cases. Eventually I had him render a second opinion on my case.

At the time it felt like I was on the way to collecting damages and being set for life. I looked forward to being a philanthropist like Andy Clay and to being the volunteer who made our new shelter building happen.

---

1 Name changed

We were working in third-world conditions at our existing facility and I wanted to be the one to change that.

I also assumed I would be out of my small, noisy condo soon and on to something without shared walls, and that working would be optional for at least a few years. You read about large awards for much less injury; to walk away broke from this was inconceivable. I had been grievously injured, even maimed, through no fault of my own. Surely I was going to be free of financial worries, at least.

The Rehab Center

A week after my arm surgery, it was time to transfer to the rehab center. I envisioned a place with lots of open space for mobility-challenged people to get about, a place where I might be able to set up a cubicle and work a little. I envisioned wearing real clothes and effortlessly using my phone. I was about a mile ahead of myself!

I wanted to stop at home and see Nimby before going to the rehab center. It would have been out of the way but not impossible. I just wanted to let him know I was alive. It was terribly stressful knowing that he didn't understand why I never came home from my ride and I couldn't bear the thought that he might think I'd abandoned him. Because I was still on oxygen, they decided to transfer me in a hospital van rather than my own car. That knocked out the possibility of making any stops along the way.

The day of transfer seemed to drag on forever. First there were more x-rays, for which I had to stand up. Standing was still hard to do, though it was easier to stand from a sitting position in a wheelchair than to sit from lying down in bed. The technician broke down in tears and told me she had done my first set on the portable x-ray in the emergency room, and she hadn't ever expected to see me stand for an x-ray.

Then there were hours of sitting up in my room, and I wanted to lie down but they kept telling me it wouldn't be much longer. By the time they finally came for me, I was so exhausted I was cranky and no longer ready for a change of venue. Waiting for tomorrow was not an option.

A nurse wheeled me out to a waiting van. Fresh air! The first I'd smelled in a month. It was dizzying, the smell of grass and flowers and even the funk of garbage in the air. I felt like a cat reading a message left by another cat on a shrub (known to us animal folks as "P-mail.") I still had the oxygen line and the nurse rolled a portable tank alongside my chair.

The van had a wheelchair lift and I thought of the recurring dreams I'd had where I was using a wheelchair and didn't really need to, and was afraid people would find out. Now I was using one for real. The van lurched along the three miles to the rehab center, the chair straining against the brake and threatening to roll forward and backward at every stop. It tired me out just trying to stay upright in the chair. Then we were in the entry for the rehab center. I'd ridden by it on my bike a thousand times, always mildly curious about what went on there but never imagining I'd find out this way. I was wheeled into an elevator, taken to the third floor, and deposited in a small room with two high beds. This time I really did have a roommate. I was momentarily horrified, but wondered how bad it could be if I'd had an imaginary roommate for the last three weeks already. A blonde nurse about my age with pigtails and round glasses introduced herself as Kathy. She exuded an impossibly strong energy and I imagined she was typical of the Outward Bound mentality of this place. Kathy introduced me to Joan, my roommate, an older woman who had suffered a stroke. Joan was still pretty incapacitated and muttered when I said hello. Well, as long as Joan didn't watch constant loud TV, we'd get along fine. Another nurse came by and introduced himself. Johnnie looked and sounded like George Carlin. Johnnie was also impossibly energetic. I started to wonder if I could survive meeting everyone.

Kathy disconnected my portable oxygen tank and hooked me up to a generator that sounded like a lawn mower. I asked if I could stay on the portable tanks and she said no, they were too expensive. I thought of all the older people I see wheeling them around town and wondered how expensive they could be. Kathy showed me around the floor—a common room with a big-screen TV, a kitchen where ambulatory patients were allowed to come fix their own snacks, and a bunch more rooms just like mine, some with three or four patients. We went back to my room and Kathy asked if I'd like the window open. Would I! A real window that opens! And it opened out onto Ellis Avenue, just south of Holly Street, a road I'd cycled hundreds of times. I liked being in a familiar part of town.

Dinner was served in the room and my parents came to visit. My left arm was still strapped to my chest to avoid the external rotation movement that could dislodge the metal plate, but I could feed myself with some difficulty using the fingers of my right hand that protruded from the bandage, and that was so nice. The noise from the oxygen generator was making me crazy and I wondered how Joan could stand it. My mom brought my hostel ear plugs, but I couldn't put them in my ears myself and didn't want to ask a nurse to stuff them in.

It was a long, hot night in the new room with my noisy generator. At 7:00 a nurse came to wake me up and give me my schedule for the day, which she pinned on a cork board by the window. The clock was still troublesome so I was often surprised when my appointment times arrived. Michelle, an occupational therapist, came to help me get dressed. My parents had not brought clothes for my therapy sessions, so I wore my hospital gown with a pair of borrowed shorts. They gave me two pair, hot pink and yellow heavy knit polyester, both many sizes too large. I felt like a kid on the first day of school who didn't come prepared with the things on the shopping list and had to use the school's wide-ruled paper that shredded under a pencil point.

Breakfast arrived at 8. They expected me to pack

down a ridiculous amount of food. Because I'm allergic to eggs and cured meats, my meal included these dreadful protein shakes that tasted like chalk mixed with pool water. When the dietician visited a few days later, I asked for a natural alternative and got something better. Not great, still loaded with sugar and soybean oil, but at least it didn't taste like a chunk of drywall stuck in a blender. I refused to eat junk food in the hospital; my body needed real nutrients to rebuild itself. I struggled with the mountain of food on my tray but my morning nurse assured me that they were going to work me so hard, I'd be ravenous again by lunchtime.

That first morning, there was no coffee on my tray. The nurse said I was on the cardiac list and couldn't get real coffee, but he could bring me decaf if I liked. I said I didn't belong on the cardiac list, and even if I did, I was exercising my right to refuse a treatment by insisting on my coffee. I brandished my bandaged right hand and told him there was a steel brace under the gauze, and he scuttled out and returned with a steaming cup of the real thing.

At 9:00 my first physical therapist arrived. Ian wore pale blue scrubs, Birkenstocks with wool socks, and the unkempt curly red hair and beard of the quintessential Bellingham hippie. He exuded a calm, Zen-like energy. I adored him on the spot. Ian walked me to the door of the room and decided we'd use a wheelchair to get down to the therapy gym. About a half dozen wheelchairs were folded against the wall in the hallway, and Ian asked me to choose my horse. There was one wine-red chair that reminded me of Silver. I had him put a name tape on it so it would be mine for the rest of my stay. I pulled the horrible generator alongside the chair as Ian pushed me. When we got downstairs, the first thing I noticed was an enormous black Labrador retriever sitting on an idle treadmill. If there was a dog down here, how bad could it be? Ian stopped by Llano so I could get acquainted. It was so wonderful to touch an animal after missing Nimby for so long. Llano tried to lick my right hand but I pulled it away; it still had to be kept sterile. Llano backed off and then gently rested his chin on top of my hand and gave me a look of such compassion, I knew he understood exactly how much it hurt and exactly how scared I was that it might never work right again.

Ian rolled me on toward a stationary exercise bike. "I thought we'd try a little biking today," he said brightly. He had to be kidding. How could I even get on the damn thing? Ian waited for me to try and I started to get angry. Then my pride kicked in. Was I really going to ask this guy to show *me* how to get on a *bike*? I struggled upright using the fingers of my right hand on the handlebar, grateful that the bike was bolted to the floor. I gave Ian a cold stare and said, "Tell no one I mounted a bike from the right." Then I hefted my stroke-affected left leg over the pedals and used my right foot to lift up onto the seat. Ian adjusted the seat height and secured my feet to the pedals with rubber straps, and I started to turn them slowly. I was riding! Ian watched my oxygen monitor as I kept going for about ten minutes. Finally he said, "You did a mile and your oxygen sats are great. We can take you off oxygen." He switched off that godawful generator and everyone, even the dog, seemed to sigh with relief. I grinned and said, "I'm doing another mile."

The rest of my therapy session passed in a blur. I felt so free without the oxygen hose attached to my head. I had ridden two miles! That put me two miles closer to getting back on a real bike; two miles closer to the Free Spirit Spheres. I was on my way.

My Bloodstream, the Superfund Site

My daily barrage of pills was unbelievable. I took everything unquestioningly until one morning in rehab when Kathy the nurse came with my pills in their bar-coded plastic bag. I asked what each one was and found out that all patients were given omeprazole, the generic of Nexium, the trendy acid reflux pill. "But I've never had acid reflux," I protested. Kathy said that the other meds I was on were likely to cause acid reflux and it was a preventive measure. More like a pharmaceutical company kickback, I thought. I said I would not take it unless I actually developed a problem. Kathy protested, but I said it was my right as a patient to refuse any medication. I went down the list in this fashion and cut my med load in half. I'm chemically hypersensitive under the best of conditions and I started to sweat less as I reduced the medicine overload.

Shortly after being admitted to rehab, I started swelling. I gained thirty pounds of water weight and my ankles were fat stumps leading to giant lumps of foot that wouldn't fit in my shoes. My hands swelled badly and the nurses put a compression glove on my left hand. My right was still covered in stitches that strained against my waterlogged flesh, threatening all the reconstructive surgery. I could barely walk, it was like wearing concrete boots. My therapy sessions were adjusted to short shuffles around the floor in slipper socks with non-slip soles, because I could barely lift my feet. The onslaught of diuretics did nothing. I began to crave the sparkling water I drink at home, flavored but not sweetened. I had many bottles of the stuff at home and asked my mom to bring me some. The nurses reluctantly allowed me to try a glass with a meal. As soon as I started drinking it, I started to deflate.

Over three days I literally pissed away thirty pounds. The nurses were worried that I was bouncing back too fast and I could throw my electrolytes out of balance and have a seizure. Something about that sparkling water set my balance right and solved the problem. I continued to drink it while I was there. When I ran out, it was hard to get more; I knew what to shop for but my mom didn't. Other brands were not comparable; they had sugar or Splenda and when it's already fruit flavored, why does it have to be *sweetened*? I had my mom take the empty bottle to the store with her and ask for more of the exact same thing. There was a soda fountain in the hallway and we could have as much of any Pepsi product that we liked. Sometimes I had a little Diet Pepsi as a treat, but most of the time I insisted on my sparkling water and the nurses gamely fetched it in a lidded hospital mug with ice.

In addition to the pills, the IV "pick line" and each of the three ports had to be flushed every eight hours when it wasn't in active use. While no fluid was supposed to be released into me during the flushing, there was always a metallic taste in my mouth during the process. The nurses said about one in four people could taste metal when their lines were flushed, and no one understood the phenomenon, but enough people experienced it that no nurse tried to refute it either. The pick line entered just above my elbow on the right inner arm. This made it a little less inconvenient than an IV in the hand, but I still didn't like it. The ports extended on three-inch tubes with plugs at the end that flopped about when I moved my arm.

I only had IV fluid delivery for a week after I arrived at rehab, but they had to leave the pick line in for my frequent injections, and in case I needed emergency surgery. I was still at high risk of throwing another blood clot, or heavy bleeding from my damaged internal organs. It reminded me that only a fine line separated me from Joan in the next bed.

Dorm Life Revisited

My roommate, Joan, didn't do much in the beginning. Her husband, Dave, spent hours by her side and I started chatting with him. I liked him, mainly because of his devotion to Joan and his unshakeable faith that she would get better.

One afternoon I came back from therapy to find the TV on. Joan was watching Curious George. I am extremely irritated by TV when I'm not watching it, but it was her room too and I decided not to get upset until around 9 or so, when I need to wind down for bed. Tired from my session, I sat back on the bed and watched. Curious George was delightful! Joan and I laughed together, our first connection. We watched two episodes and when the program changed, Joan turned it off. The evening passed in companionable silence. When Crystal, the night nurse, came in to check on us, she sensed the change. "Are you two making friends?" Joan and I smiled at each other.

Late that night, I heard the loud male voice of the nurse on duty, in conversation with a much quieter partner. I could not tune him out. My earplugs were in a drawer, out of reach. Joan thrashed in her bed, unable to express her disturbance any other way. I buzzed for the nurse and he came to take me to the bathroom. When I got back to bed, I asked if he could keep his voice down. I said it was bothering Joan. The nurse got defensive and in an even louder voice, said he was in his workplace and he didn't keep his voice down at work. I said, "Well, you're in our bedroom now and we're asking you to use Indoor Voice. Is that so hard?" No response, but the floor got much quieter and stayed that way.

After a few days, Joan started making progress. The speech therapist tried to free her voice by having her fill her lungs and shout. As she started to produce sound, the therapist encouraged her to shout swear words. This helps stroke patients to dissipate some of their anger at being trapped in an unresponsive body. It also reminds the patient's brain how to gather and release air in the process of speaking. One day a nurse wheeled Joan back to the room and before she got back in bed, the nurse said that Joan had something to say to Dave. She huffed and she puffed, and shouted, "God! Dammit! I! Love! You!" I don't think there was a dry eye in the room.

When my parents visited every evening, they drew Joan into the conversations and patiently waited for her to struggle through each word. I started getting to know Joan, and how more than anything, she missed her two cats at home. I told her about my Nimby and we cried together. Joan didn't stop crying; she broke into wrenching sobs and I cried in sympathy. Soon she spiraled into grief for all she'd lost and there was no reaching her. I was in my bed and couldn't go to her. My mom moved close to her bed and held her hand, and then put an arm around her and held her close.

It didn't take Joan's fighting spirit long to come back. Twice a day we both had to take Heparin shots in the stomach. Heparin shots are terribly painful. They come in spring-loaded syringes that snap the needle in like an Epi-pen allergy injector. The nurses love them for the convenience and the fact that they require no finesse to use. You just position it over a pinch of stomach fat and jab with it. After that needle springs in, the Heparin burns like acid and the injection site aches and stings for about an hour, and feels bruised for the rest of the day. I asked how long I had to take the shots and the nurse said when my daily blood testing revealed the right number, I could switch to oral Warfarin. One great morning, Kelli, the bubbly happy nurse I adored, said this was my last shot and

I was going oral that evening. I was ecstatic. That evening, Kathy came with a shot and I said no, I was on oral meds now. Kathy said, "Well, I unwrapped the syringe already. Let's just do it one last time." Oh, I don't think so!

"I'm going to exercise my right as a patient and refuse this shot," I said. "Joan needs the shot, why don't you give it to her?" Joan's left arm extended from the bed, trembling, and she laboriously extended her middle finger and smiled faintly. There was definitely someone in there worth getting to know.

Joan's eighty-first birthday came while she was in the rehab center. The nurses planned a small party and my parents brought flowers. Dave was there with her all day as usual, and Joan's daughter came in the evening. I think Joan was kind of blown away by the big deal we made of her birthday.

Most of my visitors ignored Joan. I felt bad for her because I had so many visitors. My friend Alice and her husband Russ always took care to draw Joan into our conversation and waited patiently for her to form her words, without trying to finish her sentences for her. One night Alice and Russ were visiting and they laughed over Joan's and my identical electric toothbrushes, labeled to make sure we used the right ones. I remarked on how much I missed flossing, and Russ ran out to the drug store and got me a bag of prestrung floss picks that I could manage with one hand. That night I almost wept with joy to be able to floss my own teeth.

The hospital food was surprisingly good and they got their vegetables from Joe's Garden, a local farm. They got a deal on a bumper crop of carrots and started serving them with every meal. We all got mightily sick of carrots, especially when they reached the bottom of the barrel and started serving slices of giant, overripe boiled carrots like small tree trunks. Every evening we got menus to fill out with check marks next to the items we wanted for each meal. I filled out Joan's for her, laboriously making check marks with my bandaged hand. One night Joan asked me to write on her menu card, "No more fucking carrots!" In shaking printed block letters, using the adapted Y-shaped pen I was learning to use in therapy, I copied her exact words. She grinned when I held up the completed menu card.

Down in the therapy gym one morning, Ian was helping me down from my triumphant 4-mile ride when Joan's therapist wheeled her into the gym. This was Joan's first meeting with Llano. When she saw the dog, she urged her therapist to wheel her over to him. Llano trotted over to her, sensing her delight. Joan stretched out a trembling hand to pat his head but she couldn't quite reach him. Llano moved his head under her hand and nuzzled it, simulating a petting motion. The look on Joan's face was pure bliss. Ian and I boarded the elevator with tears in our eyes.

I really missed my Netflix. I still ordered the red envelopes that come in the mail; I saw no reason to upgrade my home electronics while the old ones still worked and the DVDs were still available. The hospital TV didn't have a DVD player, plus I didn't want to inflict Buffy the Vampire Slayer on Joan. I am an ardent Buffy fan; normally I have no use at all for vampire stories, but Buffy is schlocky and fun and makes some real points about friendship and honor. One day Kenn brought me his personal DVD player that he uses on airplanes, along with my stock of Netflix from home. I struggled to position the ear buds and operate the machine with one hand but finally got it going. Kenn went to the bathroom and came back to find me in tears. He asked what was wrong and I said, "Buffy's at the mall with her mom. I'm so happy!" It was a piece of my old life back.

The Block of Torment

Ian and I worked on walking, endurance, and balance. Michelle, the occupational therapist, was in charge of my arm and hand. My arm was still bound to my chest most of the time with a sling to prevent the dreaded external rotation movement that could dislodge the plate. (Put your arm down by your side, then bend at the elbow so your lower arm is across your stomach. Move your hand out toward your side while keeping your elbow pinned to your side. That is external rotation.) To keep my muscles and connective tissue flexible enough to move again, Michelle fitted my sling with a giant padded block that rested just below my breasts, and my arm rested on the outer-facing side of the block. It pushed my arm out from my body a bit, inducing a constant stretch, while keeping it still. That block was the most uncomfortable thing I encountered in my entire time at the hospital, and that's saying something.

After a few hours with my arm on the block, I couldn't bear it any more. I was allowed occasional breaks from it when I was lying down. It was such a production to get the block back in place with the Velcro strips and all, it was almost not worth it to take it off. I hated that block with a ferocity reserved for bullies and animal abusers. I came to equate it with the "Elizabethan collar" or "cone of shame" that Nimby dreaded.

Every day I had two sessions with Michelle. We would remove the sling (joy!) and I would lie down with my arm by my side. I would attempt to raise my arm as high as I could. It took three sessions for my hand to clear my hip. I would pant and drip sweat from the effort it took to do that much. Then Michelle would take my hand at the top of its arc and pull on it gently, raising it a few inches higher until the stifled scream escaped. The pain was unbelievable, like being slashed from my shoulder to my wrist, and again from shoulder to hip. At the end of my session, when Michelle packed my arm back into the sling and installed the dreaded block, I was just about weeping with relief. Still, I loved Michelle. She was so compassionate and she told me funny stories to distract me from the pain. As Joan and I bonded, Michelle drew her into my sessions and let her work on her speech. Listening for Joan's next word was also a great distraction from pain.

Mornings were brutal. We were woken up at 7:00 and had until 8:00 to dress for breakfast. An hour may seem like plenty of time to you. The occupational therapists came around and "helped" us dress. This was mainly a supervisory function. Getting up was getting easier, especially when the nurse would raise the back on my bed to help me sit upright. I would lurch toward my assigned cupboard on morning-blurred legs and open the door with the exposed fingers of my right hand, then laboriously pull out each item, nearly tipping over as I leaned forward without my left arm to steady me.

My mom had gone to Old Navy and bought me an assortment of flannel lounging pants and matching t-shirts, so at least I didn't have to wear the lost-and-found-box shorts any more. The t-shirts were oversized to allow my awkward arms to get through, and I wore a coordinating stretch tank top underneath to avoid dealing with a bra. Getting my t-shirt on was unbearably painful. Michelle would make me do as much as I could on my own before stepping in to help. Socks and shoes were a nightmare. I was happy to have my familiar Smartwool socks and my Keen sport sandals, but they were so hard to get on with the heel loop in back. Even the nurses had trouble helping me on with my shoes. My mom kept trying to make me wear stretchier nylon socks and lace-up shoes, but I had to have stable footing for therapy. Slippery socks and unfamiliar shoes would make things easier for them, but much harder for me. Ian agreed that stable footing was worth whatever trouble it caused, and he offered to help me get my shoes on for therapy.

My sessions with Ian were a welcome break. I made fast progress with him and it was good to have something be comparatively easy. One morning I woke up miserably constipated. With the volume of opiates I was taking, this was expected to happen. Among the barrage of pills I had to take, there was a laxative with every meal. This was not optional; the opiates caused serious constipation problems. Evidently the natural senna they dispensed wasn't getting it done, because I woke up feeling like I was sitting on a barber pole. Kelli, the morning nurse, brought me a stronger laxative and a can of prune juice. Nothing. I sat on the toilet, straining and pouring sweat. Eventually 10:00 came and Ian arrived for our session. I struggled with simple balance exercises and didn't respond to Ian's friendly chatter. Halfway through the session, he stopped and asked if something was wrong. Embarrassed, I told him how miserably constipated I was. He said of course I couldn't work like that, and he was going to have the nurse give me the dreaded suppository and come back later. Because of my hand, I couldn't even insert the suppository myself. They left me on the toilet for the twenty minutes it took to work. Oh, the joy when it did!

I asked Kelli, my favorite nurse, how she could stand dealing with an issue like that, and having to wipe my bum all the time. Kelli came around to face me and said, "I'll tell you how. Every time I wipe your bum, you say 'thank you' and you mean it. Honest to God, I would rather wipe your bum than serve peaches to anyone else on this floor. You are far and away my favorite patient."

I was drenched with sweat from my ordeal and I slept soundly until Michelle came at 2:00. At 4:00 Ian returned. He was off work and therapy was officially done for the day, but he stayed late to give me a make-up session. He rewarded me for rising to the occasion by letting me play therapeutic games on the Wii in the common room. I stood on a balance board and raced him through a narrow canyon, riding inside a bubble that burst if I touched the sides. It was a blast, I didn't even feel how hard I was working to balance, and we played until 5:30. It showed me that they were committed to making me work for my recovery, but that they were willing to work with me too. Ian knew my attitude in the morning session wasn't typical and he took the time to figure out what was behind it, and he sacrificed his own time off to help me. Ian took on heroic dimensions in my mind.

Late that night, the suppository was still working. I got up to use the bathroom, a slow and laborious process. Audra, the night nurse, a southern woman who felt like everyone's mom, helped me to the bathroom, but I only made it a few steps before I made a mess all over myself and the floor. I was so humiliated I cried, but Audra said, "You're among friends, honey, it's all right," and she cleaned me up and helped me back into bed before mopping the floor, all the while saying that it happened to all of us at one time or another and it was okay. She really did make me feel like it was okay. Audra was the most amazing of all the nurses I met, and I met a lot of amazing nurses!

My hand began to show signs of infection after a few days in rehab. A special wound care nurse, Harjit, was brought in to care for my hand. Harjit was from India and wore beautiful, elaborate gold earrings. She applied a topical antiseptic salve to my hand and managed the antibiotic regime. She put me on extremely strong antibiotics because the circulation was still poor in my hand and she wanted to be sure to knock out the infection. I did not realize at the time that Harjit was specially called in for me; she had a patient rotation just like the other nurses and she usually had to work the night shift.

One night the ward was understaffed and I had to use the bathroom so badly I was nearly in tears. I wanted to go to bed and wasn't allowed, or yet able, to get ready on my own. Joan needed help with the bathroom too, and she buzzed and buzzed and no one came. Finally she lost it and had a bowel movement in the bed. Judging from the look on her face, she got some passive-aggressive satisfaction from that. I wasn't especially patient or forgiving when Harjit finally came.

A few days later I found out that Harjit had accepted a position at a birth center in town; it paid much better and gave her better hours. I was glad to see any nurse take a step up. Janet, the nurse who told me about Harjit's new job, asked if I knew she had been called in from the main hospital just to care for my hand. I had no idea. Before her last day, I apologized to Harjit for being short with her the night they were understaffed and said I understood it wasn't her fault. I wished her well with her new job. That poor woman couldn't get out of there fast enough.

My hand throbbed constantly because of the infection, then it itched when the antibiotics started working. My profuse sweating caught up with me again in the form of a skin yeast infection, an angry raised rash that started under my breasts and spread into my armpits. I was told that this is common among hospital patients and they treated it with medicated powder. The itching and stinging, combined with the hand infection and the Block of Torment, just about put me over the edge.

More Visitors

It was kind of a shock to realize how popular I was. At one time, I had so many visitors in my room that I melted down from the chaos and the nurses shooed everyone out, gave me twenty minutes to decompress, then let people in one party at a time. I let my old friends Julie and Phil come in first, since they'd driven all the way from Olympia, with Julie's sister Helen and her husband John. Then came Lauren, my dear friend from my old job, and her fiancé, Josh (who now holds my old job). Josh is an avid cyclist and he said I inspired him to finally wear a helmet. "You weren't wearing a helmet already, you dumbass?" I sputtered. A nurse was in the room at the time and she looked at Josh and said, "Yeah, what she said!"

Lauren is the daughter of the managing partner at my old company and you would think we wouldn't be friends after what happened, but she has always been the steadiest, most loyal friend anyone could have. The twenty-year difference in our ages didn't matter a bit.

When Kenn called Lauren to tell her about my crash, she drove straight to Bellingham to do what she could. She had a key to my place; we'd exchanged keys long ago and designated each other "our person," like Meredith and Cristina on Grey's Anatomy. The person you call for emergencies, the one person you can count on for absolutely everything. Lauren found Kenn already at my place and Nimby, her godson, well in hand. Without missing a beat, she went to the grocery store and bought a full kitchenload of groceries. She knew that with my food allergies, I didn't stock the things that middle Americans typically eat, like bread, eggs, and orange juice. Lauren prepared my home for the arrival of my parents, washing and changing sheets, she thought of everything. My parents were stunned to find "white people's food" in my kitchen.

A huge bouquet arrived from my old office, signed by everyone but my former boss. I wondered why he didn't sign; if he felt weird about it, if they even gave him the chance to sign. I thought for sure the fact that I was nearly killed would break the year-long silence between us. Derek was a close friend until that sunny Friday morning in June when I came in to find one of the partners' cars, a new Porsche, parked in the handicapped spot, at an angle as if for quick escape. Every Friday morning we all had pastries together, and everyone had gathered in the conference room as I was escorted from the building. *No pastries for you.* Our friendship can't recover from that, but I expected him to reach out in some way.

I had so many flowers that one of my nurses had an asthma attack. I arranged for most of the flowers to be taken to my house; there were just too many for my room.

Josh (another Josh), who serves with me on my condo board, came with a big tropical plant and almost immediately burst into tears. He told me how he was on his way to a party on Van Wyck Road the afternoon I was hit. As he approached the turn, an ambulance was speeding away. Police officers still swarmed the scene, and as an Emergency Medical Technician, Josh knew he was seeing the investigation procedures for a fatality. Because it was uncertain whether or not I'd survive, they did investigate the scene as a fatality. Josh recognized my unmistakable bike lying with twisted wheels by the side of the road and turned back home, where he grieved for me until Jeff, our board president and the Fire Department dispatcher on duty that day, called him to tell him I was alive in the ICU.

My friend Meredith, a fellow Humane Society volunteer, visited and asked what comfort food she could bring. Meredith has lupus and lives on disability income. Still, she brought me a nine-dollar bowl of African peanut soup from the Colophon Café, all three times she visited, and she brought me a new book of puzzles to exercise my injured brain. Meredith is an intensely private person and hard to get to know, and her visits meant a lot to me.

One afternoon I was napping on my bed and a hand gently squeezed my foot. I looked up to see my dear friend Chris holding a gorgeous potted orchid. Chris and I used to work together at my old company; he had the sense to get out on his own before the mergers. When Chris left, he said I wouldn't be far behind; that I was only marginally more employable than he was. Chris is an independent thinker and free spirit. We had the two upstairs offices on the mezzanine in our old building; Chris had to walk through my office in order to get to his. He usually left his door open so we could chat throughout the day. He listened to CBC, Canadian public radio, and one afternoon during Canadian campaign season, a politician was railing against "big gas." It sounded to us like "big ass" and we giggled like ten-year-old girls. I had more fun working with Chris than I've ever had with anyone, and it was so good to see him!

My weekly trivia tournament team visited, including my friend Craig, who brought me lattes and eagerly ate my hospital dinners so I could order in. My cat sitter, Karen, who had become my friend by then, and of course Alice came almost every day. I met Alice on my trivia team and found out quickly that our lives intersected at almost every point. Alice and Lauren went to the Greek festival at St. Sophia's and brought me comfort food. What I had asked for wasn't on any menu there, but when they explained that it was for their friend in the hospital, one of those wonderful Greek mothers-to-all made it up special.

One day Mike Schulz came; he was my cousin Mike

to me. My parents' best friends, the Roys and the Schulzes, were around more than our actual relatives growing up, and I thought of them all as aunts, uncles, and cousins. Years ago when Stephanie came to work with me at St. Mary Lodge and I proudly introduced my cousin, I learned that they didn't all feel that way. But when handsome Mike arrived, and my nurse asked how we were related, Mike smiled and said, "We were raised as cousins." I was so grateful that he felt the same bond. We hadn't seen each other in years, but it didn't matter, we were family.

Brad, my boss, came up from Seattle several times. Brad also left our old company before the mergers and he started his own. Because Brad is a decent human being who never lies, yells at anyone, or manufactures drama, people didn't think he was going to make it on his own. When he heard I had been fired, he took me on as a contract employee, along with our friend Paul who had also been "let go." One time when Brad came up, I had ordered Thai food for dinner and forgotten to cancel my hospital meal. Brad scarfed my salmon dinner with gusto, carrots and all.

I was happily surprised when Simon, my favorite colleague, came up from Seattle. Simon works for Manson Construction, a large marine construction company with an excellent reputation. When I worked at my old company, Simon was forever calling me with small-client jobs that no one else at my company wanted. I loved those jobs because I got to know my clients, and I knew the work I did helped them solve real problems. I liked working with Simon because he's such a gentleman. He's a construction foreman who respects women and never tells off-color jokes. Simon liked working with me because we were comfortable with each other and could be direct about things when we needed to, without any drama.

After I got fired, Simon called my old company to

get me to work on a small job at Pier 57 on the Seattle waterfront. When he found out I wasn't there and I hadn't left voluntarily, he tracked me down at home, undeterred by my unlisted number. By then I was working for Brad and I went down and interviewed for the Pier 57 job on behalf of Northwest Environmental Consulting. I, who was deemed "not rainmaker material" by my old company.

I obtained permits for a maintenance and repair plan for the pier, and during the inspection for that project, Simon found parts of the pier that were sagging dangerously. I got permits for emergency repairs for those areas—no small feat. It's just about impossible to get an emergency repair permit in Seattle. After all that was finished, I discovered that they wanted to put a giant Ferris wheel on the pier. I thought they were crazy, but I was willing to give it my best shot, as I genuinely liked them and they'd proven to be prompt payers. We were just about to submit the permit applications for the Ferris wheel when I got hit.

When Simon came to see me, I was up and "dressed" and waiting in a regular chair in the kitchen, trying not to be too pathetic. Simon stayed long enough to walk me around a bit and his visit was huge for me. I hadn't cared if I ever went back to work before that, but it was looking like the Ferris wheel might actually happen, and I wanted to be on the crew responsible for it if it did.

Preparing to Go Home

Every day I was visited by a physiatrist (not a psychiatrist, though I had one of those too), a specialist in long-term trauma care and pain control. You only learn what a physiatrist is if you need one. On alternate days, I saw glamorous Dr. Sakahara, who walked right off the pages of the Sundance catalog, and earthy, fun Dr. Ouellette who you could hear laughing three rooms down. Their down-to-earth sensibility made me feel like what had happened to me wasn't so overwhelming. The physiatrist tracked my progress overall and participated in the weekly evaluation conference where patients would receive a new weekly treatment plan, be discharged for nonparticipation, or discharged for being ready to go home and transition to outpatient treatment plans. The physiatrist visits were a good time to bring up concerns and issues to someone with a holistic viewpoint. I continue to see Dr. Ouellette every six months or so.

My progress in rehab was faster than anyone anticipated. When I wasn't in a therapy session, I was doing my finger exercises and began feeding myself with ease. Every visitor was forced to take me for a walk, usually to the mailbox to drop off my Netflix, which I watched on the portable DVD player every night. I loved stepping outside for even a few minutes.

Ian worked with me on balance and stability. I did endless exercises with different colored disks he threw on the floor and I would have to step to the color he called out, like a Twister game. He had me work on the practice steps, a four-step wooden staircase with rails shoulder width apart, and when I got good at those, we went to the real steps and I had to climb the stairs back to my room instead of taking the elevator. He started walking me outside, so he could have me walk on grass and experience uneven ground and crumbling concrete steps with shaky metal rails. After two weeks, I passed the balance test with a perfect score.

On Ian's day off, Christine, my friend Jeff's wife, who is also a physical therapist at the rehab center, took me for a walk outside. I wore my therapy uniform of flannel lounging pants with a big t-shirt and she secured my gait belt (a leashlike device that allows the therapist to grab from behind and keep a patient from falling over) for our marathon walk. Christine's goal was to see if I could walk a full mile. We did it! I was dizzy and exhausted and napped for hours when we were done, but I did the whole walk. While we were outside walking the streets of downtown, I said I used to be a respected professional in this town, and here I am being walked on a leash in my pajamas. But really, I was so proud to be walking on a real sidewalk, I didn't care who saw me like that.

The therapists conferred and decided they couldn't justify keeping me much longer unless they gave me a job. I couldn't believe it; I was still so weak! But I was allowed to walk on my own now and I freely went to the soda fountain and the community room. Showering was still an ordeal; I had to cover all my wounds and surgical scars with special plastic sleeves and sit on a wheelchair transfer bench with a handheld shower. I had to be helped in and out, and washed and dried. Michelle ordered me a transfer bench to use at home and asked that my mom be included in our sessions so she could take over my therapy at home.

The trouble started immediately. My mom came to help with dressing time and she went to the cupboard to grab my things. Michelle patiently explained that I must get the clothes myself. My mom watched me totter in the closet doorway like a Doberman being told to stay while being tempted with bacon, and Michelle looked almost eager to yank the choke chain. When I started to dress, my mom held out my underpants with the legs ready to step into. Mortified, I took them from her and put them on with difficulty. My mom was so anxious to help, and she had to be taught not to help unless I asked her to.

At the occupational therapy session, my mom was reluctant to hurt me by pulling hard enough on my arm. I had to browbeat her into pulling, and when my tears came, she always let go even though that was when she needed to hang on and maintain the pressure. That had to be scary; I don't know if I could have done it to someone else, wondering if I might be doing real harm. That threshold is something only a trained therapist could be expected to know. Michelle talked with me privately and we agreed that my mom would never be able to hurt me enough to be effective with the arm exercises. She taught me to induce the pressure myself by grabbing the back of a chair and using my body weight to produce the pulling motion. I found I was quite capable of making myself cry, knowing the alternative was to stay like this forever.

Two nights before I was to go home, I was reveling in my newly issued permission to walk in my room unsupervised. I brushed my teeth, then sat in my recliner to read a bit. My recliner was always covered with a bed sheet, tucked in at the chair's seams. As I got up from reading, I caught a stray corner of white sheet trailing on the floor out of the corner of my eye. It was too late to correct; my ankle was already tangled in the sheet. I fell to the floor, unable to put out my arms to break my fall. My head took the brunt of the fall as it caught the corner of Joan's bed table on my way down. I sat there, hurting everywhere but especially in my right elbow and head, and waited in terror for another stroke. My head settled down and no one came; I thought I made a loud enough crash to attract attention. I shouted for help and Janet the night nurse came running. She called for backup and one of the men came to help. I couldn't get up by myself and they couldn't pull me up by my injured arms, so they helped me onto my knees and placed folded towels on the floor in a succession of steps. When I got up high enough to stand with help, they put a gait belt on me and pulled gently on my waist, and I was back upright. They put me to bed, where I despaired of going home in two days. They'd never let me go after a fall like this. Ironically, there was an autumn leaf taped to my room door to indicate a fall risk; it was for Joan.

The next morning Michelle came and asked about my fall. She had Ian put me through the balance test another time and I passed it with a perfect score again. They decided the fall was a freak accident because the sheet had come untucked, and that I wasn't hurt badly enough to justify keeping me there longer. I almost wept with relief, I'd still be holding Nimby tomorrow!

I still wasn't able to wipe my own bum and that was going to be a problem at home. Michelle brought me a tool called a "Bottom Buddy," a long plastic rod with a clamp on one end to hold a wad of toilet paper. Michelle demonstrated the device and Joan and I both got church giggles until we were in helpless tears.

My last day in rehab, Kathy removed my pick line. The line snaked all the way to my subclavian vein and had to be pulled back out. It was by far the creepiest of all the inpatient experiences. Kathy pulled it out slowly and gently, and as I was lying there on the bed, sweating and gritting my teeth, she said she was done. My skin didn't stop crawling for hours.

It's amazing how much crap I had in the room; it took many trips to the car with big plastic hospital bags to move me out. Then it was time to say goodbye to Joan. I bent to hug her and she grabbed my hands and kissed them again and again while tears streamed down her face. I promised to visit her, and I did, many times before she left a month later. I mailed her a bracelet I made with two cat charms on it but never heard back from her; I hope it got to her.

NIMBY!

Finally it was time to get in the car and go home. It felt weird seeing the sights on the way home, like you feel coming back from a long vacation, but mine was no vacation. And it was weird having my dad drive my car. I realized they must have been using it the whole time they'd been here; I just hadn't thought about it. We pulled up in front of my building and Nimby ran out from his watch point in the bushes to greet us. When they started to help me out, his eyes went round with surprise and a bit of trepidation. That was Mom, but it was clear that Mom wasn't right. I moved slowly and clumsily and I must have just reeked of the hospital. He followed me watchfully as he absorbed this different Mom.

I barely recognized my house. My family had been living in it for six weeks and they'd moved things around to suit them. I don't eat much bar-coded food, so my small kitchen has always been more than adequate for food storage. What I saw shocked me—about sixteen different kinds of packaged snack foods spilled out onto my countertops. Paper grocery bags of backstock stood under the martini table in my dining nook. A big black toaster oven stood in the corner where my small white one used to be, and what happened to my lovely steel IKEA countertop dish drainer? "That ugly thing is in the shed," I was told, and the Rubbermaid rack that took up an entire half of the double sink was there to stay until they left.

The storage shed where I kept my bike was full of flower vases and all the natural, locally made "suspect" household products I used, which had been replaced with trusted chemical-laden national brands. (There were even paper napkins in a plastic package on top of my basket of neatly folded cloth ones.) My stoneware dishes were replaced by lightweight plastic ones that I could manage. Even my cookware was replaced. My dish cabinet was already filled to capacity so all this new stuff was sitting on the stove and countertops.

And remember my stacks of things to be carted away and gotten rid of? The mess I was so relieved that my family would never see? They helpfully *put all that stuff away*. Of course it wasn't in the places it would have belonged if it hadn't been crap I was getting rid of. A lot of it was in the shed. All of it was taking up space that was needed for actively used things. After finally de-junking my place before this happened, I was under unbearable stress.

It got worse when I went into the bedrooms. Card tables and the ironing board were placed in front of closets and my family used these for their own stuff. I only had a few clothes I could put on myself, and these were stacked on the ironing board. I wasn't able to access the closets for anything that wasn't already out. My own bed was too low to get in and out of comfortably, plus my parents needed the double, so I set up camp in my cluttered office with its high day bed.

Finally I sat in my recliner, exhausted, and realized I couldn't lean it back. I asked Kenn to help and he suggested that I bring my knees up and use my outer thighs to press against the chair arms. After a few tries, I did lean it back myself. Nimby kept his distance for a bit, but finally jumped on my lap, burrowed in and purred loudly. I wept with relief.

A knock on the door startled Nimby into jumping down. My sister and her husband had arrived from Florida. I sat in my living-room chair, absolutely bewildered, as five family members converged on my space and I contemplated how it could be that I was not the host of this gathering in my home.

That evening I had to ask for my DVDs to be changed and I struggled to work the remote. I went to bed in my office while Nimby paced back and forth between rooms, unsure of where to sleep. Yes, I'd been released from the hospital, but I was still a long way from being home.

The New Routines

Being a household run by a cat, ours depended on its routines. Poor Nimby's routines had been blown for two months already. If he expected a return to normalcy when I got home, he was disappointed. I wasn't right at all, I was slow and weak and clumsy and I smelled of all kinds of unfamiliar things. His grandma continued to feed him, I couldn't bend enough to do it yet.

My second night home, I was lying in my office day bed and heard my dad get up to use the bathroom. My dad hardly heard a thing without his hearing aids and he took them out at bedtime. He went back to bed and I heard Nimby's galloping paws on the carpet as he came up behind my dad, knocked him hard against the legs (which can trip you if you're not expecting it), and jumped up on the bed, body-blocking my dad's way back in. I started laughing out loud as I heard him say, "Dorothy, what do I do? I can't make him move." There wasn't a thing I could do to help; he couldn't hear me and I couldn't get up before he resolved it on his own. My dad must have done what I did, which was gymnastically contort around the cat until he gives me enough room to lie down. Picking him up was never an option. "Good boy, Nimby," I whispered.

Sitting up in bed was still hard, and Nimby came to help me up in the mornings. He would walk around behind me and brace his forehead against my back, and push with all his furry might. He's pretty strong and that actually did help, if for no other reason than it made me determined not to fall backwards on him. After he helped me up, I hugged and praised him, and this became our morning routine for years after I was able to get up on my own.

After a few days, my dad flew back to Minneapolis

to care for their cat, Emma, while my mom stayed for a 3-week shift. Kathy went back too.

I used a wheelchair transfer bench to get into the shower and I had to be bathed. This chore fell to my mom. I was embarrassed by my lumpy post-crash body and determined to learn to shower on my own before my dad's shift started. A full-sized towel was too much for me but I could dry myself with a stack of hand towels. Pay attention some time when you dry yourself off after a shower; there are a lot of intricate motions involved.

To ride in the car, I had to be belted in because I couldn't do my own seat belt. I rode with a pillow under my left arm to protect it from jarring, especially on the profusion of speed bumps in my condo complex. When we got to our destination, I had to wait to be unbelted and helped out of the car. I am normally one to get right out of the car when I get there; the dawdling pace of other people makes me crazy. To have to be the last one out was torture.

Once at the mall, my mom and sister went right in and left me sitting there. I laboriously texted my sister, "Let me out of the fucking car!" She came running back out before I finished the text.

Going to the mall is part of Midwestern life. My mom and sister go several times a week. I live two miles from the mall and had been there maybe four times in five years. Old Navy was where I got my flannel lounge pants and stretch t-shirts that I could put on myself, so to the mall we went. My family probably knows that mall better than I do now.

The next new routine was occupational therapy. I had to go three times a week. The sessions were 45 minutes long but I arrived early or stayed late to do a few miles on the exercise bike. Getting ready took a good hour, and after I got home I had to shower because I got drenched in sweat. Going to therapy was an all-day project.

My first day as an outpatient, I was introduced to Ken Eastham, a quiet, unassuming man. It didn't take long to figure out that under the cool exterior lurked an incredibly snarky wit. Ken asked about my therapy goals; he wanted to know what I hoped to achieve. He said some people just want to be able to go back to work, while others want to return to their pre-injury activities if they can. I told Ken I wanted it all back and he needed to push me hard. He said that he would have to push me to the very limit and I said, "I'm in." We looked each other in the eye and the deal was sealed.

Ken spent the first ten minutes of each session warming me up, either with an ultrasound treatment or a manual massage. Then he used all kinds of devices to force my arm to stretch. The sessions were horrifically painful but Ken made sure to note every degree of progress and keep me moving ahead. We worked on my hand too, stimulating the nerves with various textures. Sometimes I put my hand in a box of warm blowing corn husk dust and grabbed the objects blowing around inside. My job was to identify by touch what I was holding. Ken threw in chess pieces, action figures, office supplies, all kinds of weird things. He made a game out of mystifying me.

I told him how I used to crochet cat blankets for the animal shelter and he said I should try to do that again. Surely my hand was too ruined for that? He said, "Pick up your hook and try. If it takes two hours to do a row, so be it. Only quit if it hurts." I tried it, and it did take an hour to do a row, but I got steadily faster at it. In the evening I had to hang a soup can in a sock from my hand and let the weight bend my wrist backward, stretching the scar tissue painfully. When I watched TV, I busily finger-spelled as much of the dialogue as I could, using the manual alphabet from American Sign Language, to rewire the motor nerves in my hand.

I read an incredible number of books; the library was my salvation. My parents buy their books and I read everything they got too. I had recently read Heather Lende's "Look After the Garden and the Dogs," the memoir of her own bike crash and recovery, and I asked my mom to get me a copy while I was in the hospital. She said she'd get it at Barnes & Noble, near the mall. Local shopper that I am, I arranged for Kenn to be driving her around so she would be forced to buy it at Village Books, the local independent book- store that anchors the Fairhaven shopping district. It helped to relive Heather Lende's recovery journey with her; there was much to relate to.

Back home, I often woke up in the middle of the night in too much pain to stay in bed. I would get up at 3:00, close the door to the bedroom where my mom was sleeping, and go read in the living room. Nimby usual- ly joined me when I did this, a little consternated that I wasn't following the routine, but anxious to help.

My mom tends to be a light sleeper and would of- ten wake up if I even had to go to the bathroom in the middle of the night. I do not like bright lights turned on suddenly; I'm hypersensitive that way. Normally I never turn on the light when using the bathroom at night. My mom would get up and light up the house like a former East German guard tower. There was no hope of getting back to sleep after that. I finally put my foot down and said no lights will be turned on un- less I do it myself. We compromised by putting a night light in the foyer.

One day I had to go to the lab near the hospital for a blood draw. My mom took me, and I extended my arm for the needle with a sigh of resignation. The res- ignation turned to annoyance when the technician

failed to get a vein after five attempts. Other techni-
cians tried and failed. As a retired medical technologist, my mom was mystified; she had been known for
being able to get the toughest patients. She suggested a hot water bottle to warm the vein. Still no luck. I
drank two large glasses of water in the hope that that
would "puff up" my veins. This went on for two hours
before I broke down in tears and said I couldn't do it
any longer. This was the first time I'd lost it since I'd
been hit. My mom agreed, I couldn't be tormented any
more. The lab technician called over to the hospital
and I had to be readmitted, then a nurse used an ultrasound to locate my vein, holding it in view on the
screen while another nurse expertly pierced it on the
first try. I was so grateful for it to be over, I couldn't
stop crying. It wasn't so much that the twenty-plus
needle stabs had been traumatic, I was just burning
out on all this lack of control over my own body, of everything being so much bother and drama.

In December I decided I wanted to go back to my
weekly trivia tournament. We met at a seedy bar on
the outskirts of downtown every Sunday night for our
two-hour match. It was where Alice and I did most of
our socializing. We also did a Tuesday night match
at an upscale bar downtown, but that one was very
crowded and high-energy, and I decided to sit it out
for a while. The Sunday night game with Quizmaster
James was just my speed. Besides, my dad was an avid
trivia buff himself and I wanted him to experience the
local pub trivia scene.

I entered the bar dressed in drawstring lounging
pants and a sweatshirt, carrying my Bottom Buddy in
a canvas grocery bag. My parents buttressed a chair
with pillows as I went to greet James. James hugged
me with tears in his eyes. Before the game started,
James announced my return and everyone applauded
wildly. We had more than the maximum six players, so

my visiting niece, Sara, gamely joined a team of students and gave us a serious challenge. I was fogged on pain meds, but still had a blast. Thanks to Alice and my dad, our team placed respectably.

The bathroom was a nightmare. The toilet paper rolls were on those flat skewers that stretch the roll out of shape so it can't turn, and the paper itself was impossibly thin one-ply that tore off one square at a time. To effectively use the Bottom Buddy, you need at least a continuous three-foot strip of two-ply, or about nine feet of commercial one-ply. It took me nearly half an hour just to wipe myself. Bathrooms in general were problematic. In one Mexican restaurant where I had lunch with my dad, the door stuck and was so heavy I couldn't get it open. With both arms weakened and a recent sacral fracture, there was no part of my body I could hit it with. I ended up knocking on the door from the inside until my dad came to find out what was wrong.

Dad's Shift

Kathy came back out for a week, just before my mom went home. My mom flew out of Seattle and my dad arrived later that day. Kenn picked him up and drove him up to my place. I was excited to see my dad and got dressed in cat-print therapy pants and a big sweater so I could walk outside to greet him. When he arrived, he seemed completely disoriented by what he saw. Evidently from talking with my mom, he expected me to be much more incapacitated. He was stunned to see me up walking steadily and doing basic household chores.

The first thing we did was line up our Netflix queue for classic movies he wanted me to see, and new movies I wanted him to see. The list was heavier on the classics, but that was okay. We watched the movies and stopped the DVD to discuss them any time we wanted. I put on the closed captioning so my dad didn't miss any of the dialogue. I found it helped my tired brain as well. I was either processing what I heard or what I saw; rarely the two concurrently.

I started typing with my left hand and returning e-mails from work. I was working with my client who owns a historic pier on the Seattle waterfront, to put in a giant Ferris wheel. There was already an antique carousel there and gaming arcade, a Ferris wheel was a natural next step. There is nothing simple about permitting a 175-foot tall Ferris wheel on a dock in the Puget Sound.

Brad, the friend I contract to, had taken over while I was gone and submitted the permit applications to the local, state, and federal agencies. The applications were rife with errors and had to be resubmitted. This was not Brad's fault; only someone who knew the project inside out could have correctly completed those applications. Still, they needed me back at work, and without any kind of disability pay, I needed to work in order to keep from losing my condo. As it was, Kenn was bailing me out with mortgage payments.

I was not allowed to return to work without a full neurological exam. This was scheduled at a psychologist's office on the waterfront and the appointment was to take four hours. For the first time, I used the Whatcom Transit Authority's paratransit service. My driver, Lisa, was wonderful. She introduced everyone on the bus as each new person got on. My impairment wasn't obvious at first, so I explained that I had a severe head injury and damage to both arms. Lisa thanked me but said I never had to explain; if I was on their roster, I was eligible to ride.

I saw Dr. Fitz, the same psychologist who saw me at the hospital. Dr. Fitz had been concerned when I was in the rehab center, because I remembered the crash in such detail. Most people don't have much memory of the trauma. I was able to recount everything, but with flat affect, as if it had happened to someone else. Dr. Fitz was concerned that processing the incident was going to be difficult and the worst was yet to come. Because of this, I was scheduled for mandatory counseling sessions with another doctor after my testing session.

Dr. Fitz gave me a battery of tests with breaks of just a few minutes in between. I assembled puzzles, completed drawings from memory, and did the classic word list tests that Alzheimer's patients do. One test in particular was difficult; I had to transcribe a list of symbols from one sheet of paper to another. My damaged hand was on fire after I finished with that one. I went home and slept for hours, completely drained.

A week later I went back to discuss the test results. I did very well on all the tests but the transcription one, and Dr. Fitz was concerned. I held up my scarred hand and asked how much better he thought he could do with that hand. He conceded that I might be at a disadvantage for that test. He said, "I don't know what you were like before you got hit, but you're MENSA material today." I had almost wished he would tell me I couldn't go back to work. I wasn't ready.

My first day back in my home office for real, I went to the bathroom. I still had to use the toilet device to wipe myself and it took a long time in there. The phone rang and my dad answered it. We hadn't talked about how to answer my business phone and he simply said "hello." I always answer it with a professional greeting for my clients so they know they've reached a business. My dad came to the bathroom door and yelled that it was Kyle, my Ferris wheel client. I called through the door that I would call him back. My dad was hard of hearing so I had to practically scream. I heard my dad say, "She's in the bathroom, she'll call you back." I think "mortified to hell" would not be an exaggeration for how I felt. I talked with my dad about only answering my phone if the call display said it was someone he knew; he could let it go to voice mail for my clients. When I called Kyle back, he thought the whole thing was hilarious.

I felt bad leaving my dad alone while I was working, but I think he loved sitting in my living-room chair, reading and enjoying Nimby and his little girlfriend Kali from two doors down, who visited every day. Those cats put on their own little Benny Hill show for him every morning.

My morning apple was a labor of love for Dad. Cutting up an apple did not come naturally to him. Every morning he would get up and leave his own toast to get cold (despite my protests), and struggle with that apple, ultimately handing me a bowl full of mangled chunks with random seeds and core fragments. It's amazing that he never cut himself. For

Christmas the following year, I found a brass apple at Paws Awhile and bought it to show him that I'll never forget him bringing me my morning apple with such effort.

Alice and Russ brought us food every Friday evening; first they unpacked the hot dinner we all ate together, then Alice filled my freezer with containers. That way we didn't have to eat out so much, and I cooked a little too. I was very excited when I got my vegetable-phobic dad to eat my Thai-style green beans.

If I felt up to going out, we would consult the list I'd made of restaurants I hadn't yet tried but wanted to, and we'd pick one that suited our mood. One day we went to lunch at the Grace Café, a little mom-and-pop in the Sunset neighborhood, which I call the "retail gigaplex." It sat precariously between the parking lot for Office Depot and an Applebees. My dad asked if we were expected to say grace there, and the lady at the counter said nobody was *expected* to do anything, but if we wanted to say grace, we were encouraged to. My dad wanted to say grace, so we did, and we felt like we were doing something reckless and fun.

One Saturday we went to the Museum of Radio and Electricity. I had always been curious about it and my dad was into it, so we went. I had no idea what a great day it going to be. The museum was full of early electrical devices, Victrolas with wax cylinders and elaborate antique music boxes, early radios and some futuristic exhibits too. My dad saw the things he grew up with and he was absolutely enchanted. We must have spent three hours in there. I had about five minutes in my legs, so I kept finding straight-backed chairs to sit in. Once I sat on a flight of steps to rest. By the time we left, I was in horrific pain, but I was so happy to have given my dad a worthwhile thing to do, it didn't matter. I bought him a t-shirt.

My dad is a retired world-class distance runner,

and I learned the routine of daily training from him. He always wanted me to run; I hated to run but you couldn't get me off my bike. Growing up, I always felt like my athleticism was unnoticed. I was terrible at team sports and actually had to take remedial gym class in summer school one awful summer, so nobody noticed that I excelled in cycling; I could keep riding forever without stopping. I didn't have any proper sporting equipment until I was old enough to work and buy cycling shoes and trade in my thick cotton sweats for proper wicking fabrics. I did my first 100-mile "century" bike ride when I was seventeen, on a 38-pound tank of a bike. That same day, my dad ran a marathon in Iowa. My mom arranged to pick me up at the finish line, then we would go to the airport to pick up Dad. I felt like my ride was an annoyance that got in the way of Dad's "real" event. I finished the ride at 7:00, and was stunned to see my dad at the finish line. I laid the bike down in the grass and flopped on my back, panting, and he laid a dozen roses in my arms. He said he took an earlier flight when he realized that I was doing something just as big as he was that day. I wore my ride t-shirt and one of the roses pinned to the t-shirt to school the next day. I wore that rose until it was good and dead.

My dad understood why I had to get back on my bike and tour again. I think he would have supported whatever I chose, but he wouldn't have respected me as much if I had hung up my wheels.

Humane Society Gala

The Whatcom Humane Society holds an annual fundraiser "masquerade ball." There isn't any dancing (except for the years we ran the afterparty for big donors willing to pay $200), but we have a formal dinner and silent and live auctions.

I had always worked the silent auction rooms, missing most of the presentation while I packed up the items people had bought. It was exhausting, backbreaking (but really fun) work, and I was not up for that this year. I wasn't really up for anything, but they made me a job so I could come. I was to guard the valuable items on display for the high-end silent auction table. Most of the job consisted of guarding a precious-stone ring, the only item easily carried off.

Dressing up was still hard and I had to wear my sport sandals in order to be steady on my feet, so I wore a fleece half-zip pullover emblazoned with pawprints, with a long Indian skirt that covered my inappropriate shoes. I stood near the items while everyone came to see how I was doing and lavished attention on me. If my dad hadn't been there with me, it's entirely possible that someone may have walked off with the gemstone ring, which my friend Sue won. The auction was finished just after dinner and before the main presentation, so I got to stand in the dining room and see Laura address the crowd for the first time.

Every year we have a featured animal who has recovered from a stunning abuse case, and in Whatcom County there is no shortage of animals to choose from. Our county is that college-town mix of artists, hippies, and rednecks, and our rednecks could give any Appalachian county a run for its money. The featured animal's story is told with a presentation full of heartbreaking "before" pictures, then the animal is brought out healthy and happy, and people's pockets practically turn themselves inside out. That year's featured animal was Laura's own recently acquired dog, Zane. Zane had been nearly starved to death as a pawn in a nasty breakup scenario. The Animal Control officers on the scene loaded the seemingly lifeless dog into the truck and called the police to arrest the owner for animal cruelty. In the truck, one officer noticed that Zane moved ever so slightly, even though they had not detected a heartbeat. Immediately she started an IV. Slowly, over a period of days, Zane came around.

Laura's presentation showed photos of Zane as a dog skeleton—horrifying pictures that made it hard to keep our dinners down. Then the Animal Control officers who rescued Zane brought him out, bounding against his leash, bursting with exuberant energy. Even my dad had tears streaming down his face. In ten minutes, we raised over $50,000 in donations.

I was so proud to have my dad see that and know what the work I do is all about. Every year before, I had been one of the last four people to leave the venue. That year I left as soon as the banquet ended; I was in too much pain to keep holding it together. It would still be three more months before I came back to work at my volunteer jobs.

Sara's Turn

My niece, Sara, came out for a week so my mom and dad could spend some time together. Sara is a veterinary student who is learning up-to-date medical treatment philosophies. Sara didn't need to be told that she should let me do things myself unless I asked for help. The first thing Sara did when she arrived was help make my space my own again. Under my direction, and sometimes with my help, Sara took down the tables and ironing board from in front of the closets, condensed the contents of the kitchen, and rearranged cabinets yet again that my parents had rearranged to suit their own needs. Now it finally felt like I was home.

Sara arrived a couple days before my dad left, so we had the chance to do some things together. WeSnip, a spay/neuter outreach organization that I support, had a giant garage sale in town and we all went to that together. The Spay Station, an RV converted to a mobile surgical clinic, was on display and my friend Patricia, one of the directors of the organization, was giving tours. We piled into the RV and I almost immediately suffered a full panic attack. The RV felt so much like the ambulance I had been in. One minute I was admiring the small surgical bay where Dr. Mueller worked, the next, the walls were closing in on me and I couldn't breathe. I think the smell of antiseptic set me off and all the other associations came flooding back. Sara half-carried me outside. My dad sat with me out on a nearby bus bench while Sara completed the tour. As a vet student, she was interested in meeting Dr. Meuller and seeing the work she did.

I also took Sara to the Humane Society shelter and arranged for her to talk with our director, Laura Clark. Laura spent quite a bit of time with Sara and I could see that Sara had been encouraged by their meeting. I gave Sara a tour of our ratty old shelter building and told her how I hoped to help them move into a new building one day soon.

Mostly, though, Sara and I treated the week like a giant slumber party. We ordered a crazy number of Netflix DVDs, trekking to the mailbox with Nimby every morning to replenish our stash. We did a marathon of The Big Bang Theory, and of Heartland, the Canadian series about a ranch that helps emotionally damaged horses, and watched a mind-numbing number of movies.

Sara braided my hair every day before therapy and I felt presentable in a way that I hadn't before. I started trying to dress a little better and not look so much like a patient when we went out. Most of all, Sara reminded me what life is about—enjoying it. For the first time since I'd been hit, I had fun.

License to Drive

At some point I had to start driving again. I would have been content to wait months and use the para-transit system, but my mom said one of them was going to stay with me until I could drive. So drive I would. My dad took me to the mall overflow parking lot, empty in early November, to try in a safe area. The brace had just come off my right hand and I had almost no power in it, but I was determined to try.

Guiding the car around the turns felt like I was physically hauling it behind me with a rope. It took all the strength I had to turn the wheel and I could feel the screws in my arm plate straining not to pop out. I was taking 50 mg of oxycodone a day and wearing a 100-mcg Fentanyl patch. I would never have been allowed to drive under that much influence; my dad didn't think of it and I didn't remind him.

After my first day at the lot, I was exhausted, but it felt good to have done it. Freedom wasn't too far out of reach.

Kenn drove my dad down to the Seattle airport early one morning and I had a blissful day to myself before my mom was due in at the Bellingham airport. My friend Josh from the condo board offered to pick my mom up. I was so tired of being taken care of, I didn't give her a very warm reception. I knew I was being petulant and I just couldn't get over myself. On the way home, we saw a deer running with a broken leg. Josh called my friend Emily at the Humane Society. I hadn't realized they knew each other. Emily sent Animal Control out to try to find the deer, and Josh and I talked about our unexpected connection.

My niece, Jenny, was going to college at Humboldt State University in California. She decided to drive up here to spend Thanksgiving with us. I hadn't seen

Jenny in over a year. The day she was due to arrive, there was a terrible ice storm and we were sick with worry. Jenny arrived just as it was getting dark and shrugged off our tears and hugs, put off by the fact that we didn't give her more credit for resourcefulness. She had stopped at her cousin's house in Tacoma (her dad is from a big family and she has cousins just about everywhere) and he put chains on her tires, then drove her car up to Everett, an hour south of here, and took the commuter train back home. Jenny made Brussells sprouts to go with dinner; they were the best I'd ever had. This new, competent adult Jenny was delightful!

Nimby's little girlfriend Kali took to Jenny and sat in her lap for hours. This was completely unprecedented; we always joked about Kali's "autism." After Jenny's visit, Kali started venturing into my lap. Before long, I couldn't get her out of my lap so Nimby could have his turn! Poor Nimby took a long time to commit to jumping up, and Kali would see him lining up his jump and leap ahead of him.

In the evening there were just enough chairs for everyone—Jenny was a good sport and sat on the low, uncomfortable futon sofa. My mom and I had the new recliners. Nimby decided to take over mine. My mom tried to pick him up and plop him on the floor but he hissed mightily and she backed off. He's a big cat and he can be scary. Then she tried tipping him out and he hissed and growled and hung on for dear life. I knew this was about much more than giving up his place in my chair and I told my mom to stop. She couldn't believe I was giving in to such unreasonable behavior. Nimby has a unique temperament and he meant something by this; I refused to have him upset like that. I said I would sit in my office chair. My mom wouldn't let me do that so she sat in the office chair. It was a tense evening; my mom thought I was totally wrong to let Nimby have his way. The chair battle recurred several nights in a row and I insisted that Nimby be left alone. After Jenny left, he stopped claiming the chair space. Kali decided to move in and claim it as hers, but she was easy to pick up and plop on the floor. Even I could manage that.

OT Continues

My occupational therapy sessions were getting really challenging. I arrived an hour early for every appointment and did ten miles on the stationary bike. Most healthy people have a hard time doing ten miles on a stationary bike. Then I would pop two 5-mg oxycodone tablets and go in to Ken's therapy "cave," a room behind the open gym area. The first ten minutes of deep tissue massage to break up scar tissue were great. It hurt, but I didn't have to do anything and we had the funnest conversations. Then I would roll over on my back and begin the stretching exercises.

Every day I had to stretch my arm a little farther; Ken measured the angles to confirm progress. I remember watching the artificial skylights, which were plastic covers over the fluorescent light fixtures that looked like blue sky with clouds. Usually it was dark and rainy outside, so the fake skylights gave me cabin fever in the worst way. At the end of each run of exercises, Ken would ask, "Can you do one more?" again and again until I really couldn't do one more, or he decided we needed to move on to something else.

While I rode the exercise bike in the joint gym, I interacted with the other patients, and most of the exchanges were friendly. There was a fifteen-minute limit on the equipment and it took me about forty-five minutes to ride ten miles. There were two stationary bikes and they were rarely both in use, but I always gave mine up if anyone was waiting and I reached my time limit. One woman seemed to be heckling me; every time we were there at the same time, she reminded me of the time limit. I told her no one was waiting to use the bike, so there wasn't a problem. Finally she made a formal complaint to the gym supervisor.

I asked her why she cared about my use of the bike,

and she said I consistently went over my time limit.

I said, "But no one is waiting to use it, why do you care?" She snapped, "*I'm* waiting to use it!" I was incredulous. The woman wore street clothes—an expensive wool pant suit with dress shoes, and while she walked with a conspicuous limp, she didn't do any exercises, she just sat in a chair.

I said, "But you're not dressed as a patient, how was I supposed to know if you didn't tell me you wanted to use it? I thought you were just complaining." I had never once seen her actually use the bike. All the other patients wore appropriate clothing for working out in a gym. This woman did not use any other equipment or make any indication that she was there to do anything. I thought she was a family member waiting for a patient; many patients had a disabled spouse as caregiver. That was my only negative interaction with another patient. She never contested my use of the bike after that; I think I called her bluff. I never did see her get on that bike.

The wound on my wrist finally closed all the way and I was cleared for hydrotherapy. I was so happy. I always watched the small blue pool longingly through the glass while I was on the exercise bike. Llano often trotted in to the pool area with Krista the therapist and laid on the edge with his paws dangling in the water. As a Labrador retriever who was bred to fetch birds from the water, it had to take all his strict training to keep him from diving in. I was not much easier to restrain. Finally, I could get in the pool.

I've always been crazy about the water, I even bought a season pass to a nearby water park as an adult and often went alone to spend the whole day on the water slides. I used the local health club with the swimming pool, even though it cost twice what any other gym in town did. Hydrotherapy was a step back to reality for me.

My therapist was Kappy, Ken's pretty rival who often came in to give him a hard time during my sessions. Part of my massage time with Ken was spent conspiring for pranks to play on Kappy, and she pranked him back with a vengeance. In the pool, she was pure drill sergeant. I was so happy to be in the warm water, I willingly did as many underwater jumping jacks as she prescribed. Kappy interpreted my enjoyment as not being tired enough and she laid on the exercise, trying in vain to get me to complain. I was used to Ken "Can You Do One More?" Eastham; Kappy had no idea who she was dealing with.

At the end, I was allowed to paddle about while straddling a water noodle, those long Styrofoam tubes that kids play on. The noodle gave me enough buoyancy to paddle about without making any effort to stay afloat. In the water, my stiff, ungainly body felt graceful and Kappy almost had to drain the pool to get me out. I was exhausted but I'd had so much fun!

I was dismayed that I only got to go to one session per week. I had four sessions, then I got placed on a waiting list for independent pool time, one 45-minute session per week. I waited two months before I got the call saying I could come back. Until then, I worked out at the regular gym pool and did my exercises there. I had never noticed the bar on the wall there; I hadn't ever needed it before. It was cold in the regular pool and there were often children splashing around while I did my exercises. They always noticed my scars and asked questions. Mostly they wanted to know if it hurt. I always said yes, but I told them I had pills to take if it hurt too much. I talked honestly with them about what happened and their parents watched me cautiously to make sure I didn't say anything traumatizing to them. I told them that wearing a helmet isn't just something their parents make them do, it's something they really need to do. Without getting too graphic about what would have happened if I hadn't been wearing one, I told them my helmet saved my life and it had a big dent in the side that would have been in my head if I hadn't been wearing it.

Return to the Humane Society

I had two major milestone goals in therapy; one was to French braid my own hair again. The other was to get ready to go back to my volunteer duties at the Whatcom Humane Society. In order to do this, I had to successfully pick up a fifteen-pound weight from a shelf five feet off the floor, to represent a cat on the third tier of kennels. I was only slightly joking when I suggested that if the weight could be poorly balanced and covered in sharp points, it would be a better representation of my job.

They did use a bag filled with two-and three-pound objects to make the weight shift around in my hands. I didn't even try that for three months. My first days were spent lying on a table, trying to pull a wooden closet bar up over my head. Sometimes I used a black ring that looked like a steering wheel. Ken stood behind me, pulling on straps attached to the ring to force my arm to stretch. It reminded me of a medieval torture chamber. Ken said, with his typical dry humor, "This is for your own good," and "This hurts me more than it hurts you," which made me lunge backward at him with my arm, and he held the stretch and grinned while I gritted my teeth. I had a device to hang over my door frame at home that allowed me to stretch my shoulder painfully on my off days.

One day I came to therapy with a French braid and Ken asked, "Didn't your niece go home weeks ago?" Sara had been the one who braided my hair. I said, "Yes, she did," and grinned. At my next session, there was a sheet cake that said "Congratulations, Kristin" and the name of another patient, a young man who also had reached his rehab goal of returning to middle school. It felt great to be recognized for our accomplishments. There were often treats to celebrate our small victories, it kept everyone motivated and upbeat.

The annual Humane Society Volunteer Appreciation Dinner happened on my mom's shift. I never miss that. I knew there was no chance of being chosen Volunteer of the Year after being out of service from August on, but I wanted to cheer for the person who did get chosen, and spend the evening surrounded by all those amazing people. We are supposed to bring a dish, and I brought a giant pan of wild rice that I special order from the White Earth reservation in Minnesota, to accompany all the vegetarian dishes. It was easy to make and my mom carried the heavy glass dish. We sat with Trudy and her daughter Tracy, who has Down syndrome. The previous year I'd been shuffled away from the table as it filled up with other adults with Down syndrome who work there as cleaning staff. I was told they all wanted to sit together. But what about Trudy, Tracy's mom, who might want some connection outside the world of Down syndrome? I liked Trudy and wanted to sit with her, and I knew my mom would like her too.

We enjoyed catching up and Trudy's stories of her recent trip to Australia to visit her other daughter. I was sick of talking about my crash and welcomed someone else's stories. Then the awards began. There are about a dozen specialty awards given before the Volunteer of the Year is announced. The Volunteer of the Year is usually someone who doesn't have a full-time job; you have to put in a lot of time to earn the honor, whatever your mix of duties.

Trudy and Tracy won the Feline Friend award, for their faithful volunteering at both shelters. Tracy is so profoundly disabled that she can't speak, but she can work magic with some of our most troubled cats. The award was well-deserved and I cheered because I couldn't clap my hands. Rookie of the Year went to my new friend Judy, who I had trained to work with the cats. Judy quickly gravitated to the dogs and earned the "black shirt" status of being qualified to work with our most mercurial-tempered dogs. I was so proud of Judy! Then came the Most Inspirational Volunteer award. I cheered as a woman I didn't know was lauded for her work with the cats, and for adopting three black cats to save them from euthanasia. (Black cats are harder to adopt out than others.) Then Emily got up and said they were giving two Most Inspirational awards that year.

Emily started to describe a cat volunteer with such a great attitude, it couldn't possibly be me. I started tuning out. Then she said this volunteer also worked at Paws Awhile, our fundraiser gift store, and at all the events. I tuned back in. Then she told the story of my crash and how she came to see me in the hospital. She broke down in tears as she said, "Kristin was broken. She was just—broken." She described how I lit up with joy to see her and I ended up comforting her instead of the other way around (let her think that, her visit was an enormous comfort). She said I was all about getting back to my volunteer work and presented the award. I had to be helped up to the podium. I hadn't expected to win an award but spoke briefly off the cuff.

I said Emily often says that as nonprofit workers, our wallets are empty but our hearts are full. Looking around the room at the people in my life, my heart was full. I was so honored to be considered one of them. Then I started to cry, it got hard to keep standing, and I had to be helped back down.

Unfortunately for Sarah Fedecky, the Volunteer of the Year announcement was almost an anticlimax after that. But as they listed all the things Sarah did, I was humbled anew. I knew Sarah was best friends with Janet Hoffman, the tiny dynamo of a woman we nicknamed "The Hummingbird," (and the last year's honoree) but I had no idea she was such an active volunteer on her own. She was always there, walking dogs and not attracting a lot of attention. It was good to see her honored outside Janet's disproportionately large shadow.

Silver Comes Home

Kenn announced he was coming up for the weekend. This was both a good and bad thing; it was good to see him, but my place is small and with my mom there, it was even smaller. He had to sleep in my recliner in the living room. Kenn did not tell me he was bringing someone with him. As he rolled the gleaming Silver to the door, I ran to her, threw my arms around her frame, and cried. She looked fantastic; she had weathered the crash much better than I had. She had new, lighter weight wheels that Dean assured me were still up to the job of loaded touring, but now I didn't have to special-order my wheel rims from Germany every time I wore out a set, which I do about every six to seven years. When you ride three to four thousand miles a year, you wear out a lot of parts.

Most of her parts had been replaced—the drivetrain, wheels, handlebars, everything but the frame, seat post and luggage rack. The total bill was $1,200 but it was paid by the other guy's insurance. I could have soaked him for my new Rivendell as a comparable replacement for $2,000 or more, but I wanted my Silver back. She's my horse.

I rolled Silver into the house and parked her in the living room behind my puzzle table. The living room was barely usable now, but the storage shed was still being used as a junk drawer by my family, so she stayed in the living room. I don't think I could have locked her out there anyway. Most of the time people thought I was watching TV, I was just staring at my bike.

With Silver's return, I felt a kind of closure, that it was all over and everyone survived. I was still simmering at the guy who hit me, who got away with a small-time ticket, but I needed everyone safe at home before I could turn my energy outward.

Free At Last

Things were a little strained with my mom because I really needed my independence back. She didn't want to let me do chores like laundry and emptying the dishwasher, when that gentle bending and stretching was the best therapy I could have. Ken the therapist threatened to talk to her if I didn't; he wanted me doing those things at home. My mom's attitude was a generational difference, I was learning from my friends at the rehab center. In the old-school way a good caregiver took over the patient's space and personal affairs, leading to offensive terms like "invalid" to describe the patient. The home was arranged for the caregiver's convenience. The patient was supposed to rest as much as possible. The new caregiving philosophy leaves the patient in charge, and caregivers are only supposed to help when asked to. The home is left the way the patient set it up, unless the patient wants or needs it adapted, and the patient remains in charge of her personal business. The patient is expected to get up and try to do as much as possible; it's recognized now that too much rest leads to muscle atrophy and blood clots, and it limits long-term recovery prospects. Our bodies were built to move, and they decline fast when they're not allowed to.

My need to control the way things were done in my house was a source of constant conflict. My mom wanted to fold and put away the laundry, but I had my routines. For example, I have stacks of identically-sized flannel wipes that serve as handkerchiefs and napkins. Some patterns are hankies and they get folded in quarters to stack in their basket in the bathroom. Some patterns are napkins and they get folded a specific way to fit in their basket in the kitchen. My family expected me to let those routines go and just use tissues and paper napkins until I was fully recovered. I had so little control over my world; some days, properly sorting my flannel wipes was a thin thread of sanity to cling to.

We did some fun things, like one rare sunny day I took my mom on a drive through the country roads so she could look at the mountains. The Cascade Range of the Rockies stretches from British Columbia down through Washington and Oregon. I pointed out Blackcomb Mountain where the 2010 Winter Olympic outdoor sport venues were. We could even see some of the Olympic Mountains out on the Olympic Peninsula, across the Sound.

My friend Sylvia from Paws Awhile was a retired ICU nurse and she was familiar with long-term care issues. One thing she did to help was to take my mom out to lunch often, to give us a break from each other. I was a little jealous of them spending that time together, because I wanted to hang out with Sylvia too, but she knew we needed that break.

My mom and I set up my puzzle table in the living room and did jigsaw puzzles, on the advice of my occupational therapist, who thought it would help both my brain and my hand. I was supposed to sort pieces using only my right hand. I did this faithfully, and it was a challenge, but I love puzzles and I learned something as I continued doing puzzles long after the need for the benefit went away—it's okay to do silly things for their own sake. An activity doesn't have to be productive or even especially meaningful—it's okay sometimes to just do a thing because it's *fun*. That fleeting feeling of happiness is one of the great things about being alive. If you like to do something, don't worry too much about whether it's useful, just enjoy it!

I had tried not to subject my mom to my favorite DVDs, but we ran out of stuff she liked to watch and I really missed Buffy. My mom sat through many episodes, trying with all her might not to imply that she thought less of me for liking it. After one episode, I remarked that I had missed a piece of action in the climax that was key to understanding the episode the first time I saw it. My mom's jaw dropped in horror—"You've *already seen these* and you're watching them *again?*" I couldn't wait to e-mail my sister Beth, who is also a Buffy fan, and tell her that. I really did feel bad about subjecting my mom to my shows, but she liked even fewer shows than I did, and that's saying something.

My dad got sick with the flu for several days, and one morning my mom tried to call him and no one answered. She called the neighbor, who has a key, and asked her to go check on him. Gerry called back and said no one was home. My dad, of course, did not use a cell phone. My mom cried and prayed off and on for a few hours until my dad called. He was fine, he had woken up feeling better and gone out for groceries.

After this, my mom realized that my dad really did need her there more than I did. I urged her to go to him; I'd be fine. She called the airline and arranged to fly back the next day. This time I drove her to the airport. It was a hard good-bye, but I was so glad to finally be on my own again. I'm a social sort out in the world (to a point), but at home I'm a strict introvert and cats are the only creatures I can share my space with. The fact that I wanted to be home alone again did not mean, as my mom had to think on some level, that I was ungrateful and pushing her away, it just meant I was getting better.

My mom left a few days before Christmas and Kenn thought it would be fun to go to the buffet at the Skagit Valley Casino. I generally avoid such places, especially on holidays, because of the crowds and noise, but I wasn't about to try to host Christmas dinner either. I agreed to go. On our way to the dinner table, a short

Asian man bumped into me hard, his shoulder knocking against the plate in my arm. I almost sank to my knees with the pain. The man stopped and apologized profusely in broken English. I was in too much pain to be gracious and hurried away. I popped two Oxycodone as soon as we sat down but was still miserable all through dinner. After dinner, Kenn wanted to play the slot machines. I just wanted to go home. The noise and visual chaos were overwhelming and I felt assaulted.

My first adventure out of the house on my own happened the next week, a trip to Village Books. During my rehab, I read stacks and stacks of books. I have a rule about never turning on the TV before dark, and I held to it, even while watching a record number of DVDs in the evening. The Village Books "Chuckanut Reader" circular features book reviews and it's how I compile my reading list. In the October issue, a book caught my eye, "Riding With Reindeer," by Robert Goldstein. Mr. Goldstein is an unassuming man from Portland, Oregon, who bought a Bike Friday folding bike and rode it across Finland. His book was such an escape from the hospital world, it took me back to myself and fueled my resolve to ride to Free Spirit Spheres. He wrote in an engaging style and included all those everyday moments from tour like putting on underwear that hadn't quite dried on the line overnight, encounters with the local insect life, and random connections with people on the road.

Imagine my delight when I found out Mr. Goldstein was speaking and signing books at Village Books in December. The talk was at 7:00 and I drove there on my own, thankful for my temporary handicap parking placard. Fairhaven was packed and I got the only open parking space for blocks.

During Mr. Goldstein's talk, I had to get up and stretch frequently. Sitting in a folding chair was still a bit beyond my tolerance. I sat in the back row so I wouldn't bother so many people if I needed to get up and stretch. After the talk, I got into line quickly so I wouldn't have to stand too long. I introduced myself and apologized for getting up so often during his talk. I explained what had happened to me and how his book had been such a welcome escape for me. As I was talking, a woman behind me shrieked, "Oh my God, are you Kristin?" A little creeped out, I turned and reluctantly said "yes," and she said her husband was a therapist at the rehab center and they talked about me at the dinner table every night. I didn't even know her husband; I asked how he knew me. She said, "Oh, honey, cases like yours are what keeps those people alive. They see patients every day who aren't going to get much better, and when someone like you comes along and fights so hard and makes progress every day, they all use your story to survive."

The questions started coming from the other people in line, and I said, "We all came to hear Mr. Goldstein's story, not mine. Why not ask *him* something?"

Mr. Goldstein grinned and said, "I'm done, I've said everything I was going to. These people are interested, why not do a Q & A?" So I stood there at the front of the room and responded to questions until my legs felt like spent rubber bands, which felt like an hour but probably was less than twenty minutes. My new fan, the therapist's wife, walked me to my car and gave me a hug. I think this book was born that night; it was my first inkling that my story was interesting and inspiring to other people. I thought about future patients at the rehab center and decided a message of hope might be just the thing.

Around this time, Alice asked me to talk to a group she met with regularly to discuss spiritual matters from multiple points of view. They were meeting to discuss near-death experiences and they all wanted to hear about mine. Something about the hunger of the "White Light people" for my story put me off. I wasn't able to give them the message they craved, that death is warm and wondrous and not to be feared. I was afraid they'd take my story and make it theirs, twisting my words to confirm their own beliefs. I still wasn't certain how it had affected mine.

I didn't want to let Alice down, but she did understand. Sharing the experience in a book was different; it was part of a larger story and I deliberately did not address the body of near-death-experience stories out there, nor did I feel any need to learn the stories of others. I knew what had happened to me and that was enough. I don't want to waste my time in this life obsessing about what happens, or doesn't, when it's over.

Back to Work for Real

The day came when I couldn't do all my work from home; I had to go down to Seattle to participate in a meeting for the Ferris wheel. The City of Seattle was making us work for it, finding fault with every set of drawings we submitted and asking for more information with every redo. They were understandably reluctant to issue the permit; it was a big permanent change to the city skyline and not everyone was going to be glad to see it. They had to make sure their decision was legally defensible in case the permit was appealed, as often happens.

I booked a train ticket to get to the meeting; driving that distance was still too much. I was on too many painkillers to concentrate for the four-hour round trip, and too afraid of the six-lane highway driving. That meant leaving my house at 8:00 and parking at the train station, then riding the train south for about two and a half hours, or an hour longer than it would take to drive in the absence of traffic (which rarely happens; the travel length is about the same). I would catch the train at 6:40 PM, arriving in Fairhaven at 9:05 and getting home around 9:30. For a healthy person, that's a long day.

The train ride down was pretty comfortable. I was happy to hear the conductor, "Legendary Larry," do his opening announcement that always started with "Ladies and gentlemen, boys and girls, welcome…" and ended with him playing the harmonica as the train pulled out of the station. I had ridden with Larry on most of my bike-and-train excursions. I liked to check on my bike in the baggage car now and then, and once when Larry was in the baggage car, he caught me looking through the window from the next car. He looked annoyed, so I pressed my lips to the glass and blew my face up so he'd laugh. After that, we always chatted on the train. This morning he stopped by to say hello and was horrified to hear why I hadn't ridden the train in months.

Simon kindly picked me up from the train station in his white Manson Construction truck and drove me to the pier, where I hitched a ride to the Municipal Tower with Kyle and Hal. Their high-end black Mercedes has a finish like volcanic glass. The first time I rode in it the last summer, I surreptitiously shot photos of it and texted them to my friends. That day, Kyle turned up the sound system as we rode around town in butter-soft leather seats, impervious to the heat that rose from the asphalt in visible waves, singing loudly with Billy Idol as we cruised for parking spaces. This time I was just grateful for the ride. It was the first time I'd seen Kyle in person since the crash and he hugged me very carefully.

We met on the twentieth floor in a windowless conference room. This was the first time I had met the two main permit reviewers in person. I had to take a pain pill before we started and I struggled to keep my head in the game. Taking notes with my ruined hand was difficult and I used a specially adapted Y-shaped pen that I held between my first two fingers. I got sore after about two lines of writing, and by the end of the meeting, the pain was excruciating and my notes weren't very legible. I didn't want to ask anyone else to take notes; it was a responsibility that came with my position and I took pride in doing a thorough job. Later, Kyle sent his notes to supplement my own. He had noticed how hard it was for me to take notes so he took his own just in case. This was just one of the many ways he proved to be thoughtful, despite his stressful position. It's why he's so successful in the hospitality industry, he's a natural host.

The reviewers had questions about our application

materials, and there was some confusion over what was needed to fix them. I kept trying to make a list of things we needed to do. The more questions we asked to clarify expectations, the more questions the City reviewers came up with.

Midway through the meeting, the fire alarm went off. The entire sixty-two-story building had to evacuate. Of course the elevators were turned off, so we had to run down the stairs from the twentieth floor. My legs were still a bit shaky, and carrying anything was going to be a problem. I grabbed my purse and left everything else on the table. Kyle, ever the gentleman, took my purse and offered an arm to steady me while my other hand gripped the rail. Mary, the City reviewer, actually brought her heavy copy of the Seattle Municipal Code with her in its four-inch binder, and Kyle took that from her to carry too. By the time we got close to the bottom, I was afraid I would fall the rest of the way. My legs shook and my head swam. I wobbled outside on Kyle's arm, where we stood outside in a crowd, a cold winter drizzle falling, and waited for the all-clear. When it came, the others headed back up the stairwell and I told Kyle I had to wait for the elevator. There was just no way I was walking up those twenty flights of stairs. Kyle told Mary he was going to wait with me for the elevator and we bought coffee and pastries at Starbucks while we waited for the elevators to be turned back on. Kyle had kept Mary's giant manual and carried it back up with us in the elevator.

The rest of the meeting went smoothly after the fire drill; everyone was just anxious to wind it up and go before anything else squirrelly happened. I walked to the train station and waited on the hard pew-like benches until I creaked upright for the 6:00 boarding call. I slept the entire way home and Legendary Larry woke me up at my stop. I was deeply, bone tired and thrilled to see Nimby bound out of the bushes to greet me when I got home. He jumped into the car when I opened the door, loudly telling me about his day, and I led him inside, where he jumped in my lap in the recliner and we fell asleep five minutes into the Buffy DVD.

Riding Again

Kenn came up one weekend in March and I decided it was time to try to get on a bike again. I chose Blue, my errand bike, because she was a mountain-style bike and I could ride in a more upright position. I thought that would be a little easier than getting on Silver straightaway.

I put on the loaner helmet Dean had sent with Silver and flat shoes without cleats—I didn't want to deal with the pedal cleats and I use double-sided pedals so I can ride without the cleats on gravel and in heavy traffic. I mounted the bike and pushed off. I was amazed at how unsteady I was—I had very little muscle memory of riding, thanks to the stroke. All those hours pedaling the stationary bike paid off, though, and I could mostly concentrate on balancing.

The thrill of being on my bike again! I took a few spins around the condo drive and got off and hugged Blue. Then I took a few loops around on Silver, feeling even less steady. Kenn snapped lots of photos.

A few days later I took Blue to the Co-op for groceries. Leaving the condo driveway was another issue altogether. Traffic is not heavy in my neighborhood, but it exists. On four-lane Cordata Boulevard, the speed limit is forty-five and there is no bike lane. I was terrified every time I heard a car come up behind me. I would wince and cower until it passed. But I made it to the Co-op and did my shopping, and rode back with a basket full of groceries.

For several weeks, the co-op was as far as I could go. I explored the immediate neighborhood on Silver, all slow residential streets, but didn't go near busy Bakerview Road or beyond. While it was great to be riding Silver, it didn't feel like it used to. I was unsteady and riding was a lot of work. Techniques I had taken for granted, like turning at high speed, navigating speed bumps, and dealing with pavement defects, were all new again. It took weeks before I dared to nudge Silver up to fifteen miles per hour. Then it finally felt right and wonderful; I felt the surge of joy as the road rushed under my wheels, and I started looking forward to the day's ride again.

Spring was slow to arrive and I took my time too. Then it got to be April and I knew I needed to start training in earnest for the summer season. I ventured downtown to the library. It was terrifying and exhilarating. I used my new eyeglass-mounted rear-view mirror and it helped me feel more secure when I heard an engine coming up behind me. I could tell how big the vehicle was and if the driver was going to give me room or not. Getting back up the big hill on Northwest Avenue left me breathless, but I did it without getting off and walking. Gradually I worked back into my old ride routes, with the exception of a few busier ones I avoid to this day.

On one of my first ventures outside my neighborhood, I rode down a residential street in an industrial area, one of those streets that was laid down quickly and looks like a strip of asphalt with no proper road bed or curbs. A deep ditch ran on both sides of the street. I saw something ahead in the ditch, and as I rode closer, my brain did not want to process what my eyes saw—an electric wheelchair overturned in the ditch, with a woman lying on her side, half dumped out. The woman looked to be my age. I pulled up to her, leapt off my bike, and asked if she was hurt. She said no, and I asked if any part of her was pinned by the chair. Again, no. She said her name was Jan and she had multiple sclerosis. I introduced myself and explained that my arms and back had been injured and I wouldn't be much use getting her out of the ditch, but I had a phone and could call for help. She asked me not to call 911, to go to her apartment instead and get her husband. She gave me the gate code to get into her complex a few blocks away, and told me which apartment to go to. It took me a moment to explain myself, then Jan's husband got in his truck to follow me to her. When we reached Jan, another cyclist and a police car were there, and Jan was out of the ditch and back in her chair. She and her husband thanked us all and I rode off to a park bench, where I sat and thought about how terrifying that must have been for her, trying to enjoy a nice day with a simple walk and ending up overturned in a ditch. I imagined having a physical condition that was only going to get worse, never better, and I felt like a tourist in her world. Then I realized how socially comfortable I had been with the whole thing, how I hadn't given a second thought to assessing the situation and helping Jan. It almost felt like I was the one who was meant to find her—someone who would relate to her as just another person and not make a huge scene.

Other parts of me toughened up with increased riding distance, but my reattached hand burned like it was sitting on a hot stove the whole time I rode. I stretched it often but it cramped and felt bruised. Some days it actually looked bruised. Gradually the pain got to a tolerable level but it was more than a year before I rode without significant hand pain. My hand is still the first thing to go on a long ride.

It was a great day when I found my replacement helmet. I'm probably the pickiest person in the world when it comes to helmets; I insist on only two things but they are hard to find. First, I want a bug net. I'm allergic to bee stings and if I had a dime for every time I've taken off my helmet and had a bee fly away that would have been in my hair without the net, I could buy another bike. The second thing is, it can't have an "aero wedge" in the back. I've long had the opinion that the wedges are dangerous and if you hit the ground with the back of your head (which happened to me once at low speed, luckily), your neck would snap like Million Dollar Baby. Recently the Canadian government outlawed aero wedges. I knew I was right! Aerodynamic features only show measurable results at speeds higher than 23 mph, and I rarely reach such speeds on tour. When I discovered my German-made helmet with a bug net and rounded back, I was ecstatic and cheerfully forked over $120 for it. Returning my loaner helmet felt like removing another cast.

Graduations

The milestones kept coming. I had monthly orthopedic checkups. At the first one, the Steri-Strips that covered my hand stitches were removed and then the stitches themselves. There were dozens of stitches and it felt like my hand was being gutted. With the rigid stitches gone, my hand felt rubbery and flaccid. I was grateful for the brace that the nurse laced around it.

At the next appointment, Dr. Hoekema said I didn't need to wear the brace any more. I had been leaving it off at home sometimes and I was ready to put it aside. I still wore it in public when I thought there was a significant risk of a bone-crushing handshake or I just might need a little support.

When I entered the office for that appointment, my file was lying open on a table and I briefly saw my hand flayed open, the mangled tissue spilling out on the operating table like raw ground beef. I closed my eyes and tersely ordered the nurse to close the file. She apologized profusely. Two years went by before I was willing to look at those photos again.

I had to go for a vascular scan at the main hospital to check the progress of my carotid artery. There was still the risk that I would need stent surgery, which had a high death rate at the time. I arrived at the hospital and waited in two waiting rooms before I was called in to the scan area. By this time my blood pressure had to be through the roof, I was so nervous. The technician, Jane, put me at ease immediately. She promised me that nothing she did would hurt; the worst would be mild discomfort from holding various positions. We chatted about my experience for a bit and Jane was very interested in the spiritual path I'd been on since the impact. She asked her questions in a noninvasive way that I didn't mind. Then she did the scan with the lights dimmed. It felt more like a massage room than a medical procedure room. I heard the rush of blood through various veins and arteries; it was kind of creepy. The scan took about an hour. I asked Jane what she found, and she said she wasn't allowed to give me the results; that was up to my doctor, but she asked if she could give me a hug and said, "I just think you're so amazing." I hoped that meant good news.

Dr. Sohn is a pretty Asian-American woman, with a penchant for delicate, sparkly jewelry. When I got to her office, she told me that my scan was the most remarkable thing she'd ever seen. Blood flow in my carotid artery was completely normal! She said that spontaneous recovery of a collapsed lining like that was so unprecedented, they didn't even have a treatment plan for it. She asked me to continue the Warfarin and weekly blood tests for three more weeks so she could confer with her colleagues and decide what long-term maintenance and monitoring was appropriate. I asked if that meant they would consider keeping me on blood thinners indefinitely, and she said now the choice was between aspirin and some milder blood thinners designed for long-term stroke prevention. I asked her to please consider the fact that I was back riding and I ran a substantial risk of bumps and bruises, and I didn't want such a strong blood thinner that mild bumps would turn into major injuries. She seemed taken aback and said that after all they had done to save my life, it bothered her that I would run right back out and risk it again. I was taken aback too and asked if, after working so hard to save my life, she really wanted me not to go back to living it. With tears in her eyes, she thanked me for giving her that perspective. Then she told me how in the trauma center, the surgical team agreed to try to save my hand as long as my heart didn't stop on the table. Dr. Sohn had never had to go to the bathroom so badly in her life, but she was afraid if she took a break, I might code and lose my hand. It struck me anew how the people who saved my life were vulnerable human beings just like me, and I was so grateful that they all managed to get on top of their game that day.

Three weeks later I got the good news—aspirin only. I was nervous about taking aspirin because I'd had a cross-reaction with it years ago when I took it shortly after a strong steroid shot for allergies. I'd had uterine bleeding that lasted a month before it became a full gush and had to be stopped with a high estrogen dose. (I was furious when I woke up to find out I still had a uterus and this could happen to me again.) I had to detox from the Warfarin for three days, then begin the aspirin. It went fine, I had no issues with it. I bruise easily and bleed a lot when I get cat scratches at the shelter, but not so much that it's ever alarming.

By January I was progressing well in my therapy and using the weight machines to lift thirty pounds by pulling down on a bar above my head. After every two or three pulls, I held the bar over my head with the weight suspended to stretch out my stiff shoulder joint. I still had a long way to go before I felt like I was in my own body, and I had assumed that the therapy would last until that happened. One day when Ken came out to get me while I was warming up on the weights, he remarked, "Aren't you about ready to graduate?" I felt so threatened; they would cut me loose with that far to go? During the daily banter with Kappy, she echoed Ken, "Aren't you about ready to graduate from OT?" I felt like I was being booted out of the nest. At the end of the session it was time to get my slip to schedule more visits at the front desk. I said, "I guess we could go down to twice a week now, then?" to try to stall him from cutting me off altogether. I kept going for another month when Ken brought it up again, that he thought he'd taken me about as far as he could. I felt the stiff knot of scar tissue in my shoulder and felt betrayed. I explained that I still felt I had a long way to go, and he said, yes, I did, but I could take it the rest of the way on my own now. He would be there by phone or e-mail if I needed help, but it was time for me to finish my recovery at home and out in the world.

Just before my last session, I got the call from the hydrotherapy department that a place had opened up for me in a weekly independent exercise session. At least I would be able to come use the beautiful warm blue pool.

As my last session approached, I felt like I had to give Ken some kind of gift to show him how grateful I was for his help. I found a good photo of myself with Silver at my friend Jill's house in Portland, taken on my Bellingham-to-Eugene ride two years ago. I bought a triple picture frame and placed the photo in the left side and labeled it "BEFORE." I found some clip art graphics with bright red and yellow stars that said "POW!," "WHAP!," and whatnot, and placed a cluster of them in the middle section. On the right, I repeated the "BEFORE" photo and labeled it "AFTER." At the bottom, on a strip of paper, I wrote, "Ken, recovering from my crash was painful, scary, hard, and oddly fun," and signed it. My graduation day was just another session, but people kept coming by to congratulate me. At the end of the session, I gave Ken the picture. He grinned, his eyes filled with tears, and he hugged the daylights out of me.

I left the rehab center feeling cut adrift. There was nothing to do but focus on the future. I picked up the phone and called Free Spirit Spheres. They usually book out early in the season, but I told them my story and they loved it, and they were able to work me in for two weeknights in mid-June. That only gave me three months to get ready. I had a purpose once again.

Return to Volunteer Duty

Meanwhile, I was resuming my old life bit by bit. I returned to work at Paws Awhile in April and the shelter in May. I loved being back at the store and seeing my favorite customers, but working at Paws Awhile proved too hard on my back and I took another two months off before resuming my shift. Surprisingly, the shelter was easier, even though it involved a lot more bending and stretching. I received a hero's welcome back from the staff. They offered to help me with the difficult kennel latches, and with any cat I had trouble lifting. For the most part, I could manage them on my own, but my arms weren't strong and some of the cats took advantage of my lack of confidence. They're cats, after all. I had to get staff to help me retrieve many cats from under the kennel rows.

It made such a difference to me, though, to be able to provide some real comfort to those cats. I brought the pile of cat blankets I had made while recovering and once again every cat had a blanket I made. I like to save the new blankets that haven't been washed and still smell like my hands, and give them to terrified newcomers after we've made friends. That way the new cat smells his new friend all night and has a much less stressful time alone in the dark.

I learned the value of my cat blankets with Xander, a big black-and-white male who wouldn't come out of his plush hideout. I coaxed Xander out for just a few minutes of hugs and then he scuttled back inside when an airplane roared low overhead (the shelter was at the end of the airport runway). I spread a new blanket on the kennel floor outside his hideout and turned to see who I would visit next. A rustling sound made me turn around and I saw the corner of my blanket disappearing into Xander's hideout. A moment later, he popped his head out and gave me a slow-blink of gratitude. I've never gotten a response like that from a human I crocheted for; from then on I just made cat blankets.

One day Joni, the vet tech, asked me to sit with a cat named Raina, a beautiful dilute tortoiseshell (mottled gray and peach). Raina was hit by a car in a rain storm and had a broken hip, a head injury, and a mangled paw. Raina needed a TLC volunteer in the worst way, but she was too fragile for most of the volunteers. Joni thought I might be able to handle Raina with the empathy she needed.

I sat in a chair in front of Raina's kennel and let her step into my lap on her own. She curled up right away and purred. I told her I know what it's like to get hit by a car and that my paw was mangled too, and I showed her my hand. She seemed to understand. I held Raina for a long time, weeping in sympathy. When Joni came to check on us, she cried too. Raina was adopted very soon after that, but I made a few special trips to see her again before she went home.

Then there was Jude, the Nimby-sized ginger-and-white male who hated his kennel so much, he threw a true "hissy fit" when it was time to go back in. My first visit, he clawed the hell out of my back. I was terrified that Jude would not get a home because of his temperament. Nimby had a temperament that was often misunderstood. I had to make sure Jude got a chance. I started spending an hour or more with Jude on every visit, wearing him out with toys until he accepted the ride in my arms back to his kennel with passive resignation. Finally Jude was placed in foster care at Maplewood Animal Hospital. I went to visit him there and brought him a new blanket, a lovely white one with blue edging. The staff was full of stories about him already, how he was so smart, they left him in an exam room with the door locked every night, and he opened that door and another to greet them at the front door every morning. They gave up and let him have the run of the place. A staff member adopted Jude and he finally went home.

In May I got the opportunity to honor Llano, my therapy dog, at the Humane Society Woof & Whiskers Awards. This was an event where people and businesses in the community were recognized for their contributions to our work. A service animal was always honored too. I got up and told the story of what Llano did for me and especially for Joan. When I told how he nestled his head in her hand and helped her pet him, there wasn't a dry eye in the room. Llano's handler, Diana, accepted the plaque and let me hand Llano his giant nylon chew bone. Llano eagerly showed it to his "date," a golden retriever who works with him at the hospital. Diana gave a great talk about how Llano's job is to give and receive affection, and in the hospital environment, that is often the most authentic interaction a patient has in a day. Honoring Llano helped me to connect my "hospital world" to my real world.

Hydrotherapy Group

I loved my weekly hydrotherapy session. It wasn't just good, soothing exercise, it was group therapy. I made friends with other people who were living with disabilities, temporary and permanent. Vince, the therapist in charge of the pool, set the tone for a fun and healing atmosphere.

Discussing our aches and pains helped us to realize we were not alone, or even so special. We learned to celebrate the positive and never to indulge in self-pity, because someone else always had it harder. Gallows humor was not only okay, it was appreciated. I looked forward to seeing my favorite pool friends, exuberant Collette, my fellow volunteer Jill, and wise, kind-hearted Catherine, grandmother of twelve, who wore an enormous silver rosary everywhere, even in the water.

One man who came regularly was familiar to me, and we realized that we had both played in the same trivia league. Patrick used an electric wheelchair and had very little use of his arms and legs. I never did find out what caused this, only that he lives a full and active life. His wife, Ann, is a local attorney, and they were a great comedy team. One day Ann was telling us about a Russian pierogi shop that had opened downtown. Ann said, "They're wonderful bombs of gluten-filled goodness, forever denied to me." I said to Patrick, "You eat them in front of Ann?" Patrick sputtered, "She *walks* in front of me!"

Patrick came to visit me at Paws Awhile several times, always with his dog, Sadie. He took her to the nearby dog park and let her go swimming. A young volunteer asked me one day, "You know that guy?" I said yes, and she looked curious, like how would I know someone like that? Like I would have before the crash, she assumed he would be isolated and not have occasion to make friends in the community. She certainly wouldn't have expected him to be out playing with his dog on a sunny Sunday afternoon like anyone else.

Andre is a young man I will never forget. You will probably know Andre one day; with his sharp mind and social adeptness, it's entirely possible he'll be President. The one thing I know is that his personality will overcome any limitations his physical disability might present. Andre will go places you and I only dream of.

Andre was fourteen when I met him and he could talk books like a grown man. We shared a love of the Hunger Games series, and he put me on to some other book series as well. Everyone loved Andre, and every one of us knew a slightly different young man. With Paul, the grandfatherly type, he was a goofy boy. With Ann, he was an aspiring attorney. With me, he was the book and movie guy. Ann invited Andre to observe her in court and his mom, Sheryl, promised to get him a suit for the big day.

Andre used an electric wheelchair and had limited use of his body. We all joked that his mouth more than made up for it. One week the pool was closed for Veterans Day. The following week, Andre told us how he had organized an ice cream social to raise money for homeless veterans. A hush fell over the pool as we all realized that this young man who was so disabled was concerned about people he perceived as less fortunate than himself. If ever there was a poster child for getting over yourself, it was Andre.

At Christmas I surprised Andre with a backpack tag I had made, of the Hunger Games symbol. I used Shrinky-Dinks plastic for inkjet printers to make a professional-looking novelty before the first licensed merchandise came out. Andre was stunned that I gave him a Christmas present. Those are my favorite gifts, the ones the people don't expect. Just a simple way to say "You're special to me."

Bill was in his 80s and had survived a stroke. His body was bent in painful-looking ways and he had a large growth on one side of his neck. Even with all that, he was a handsome man and his dark eyes snapped with intelligence. Bill told the most interesting stories about his career as a professor of marine biology, his history of bicycle racing, and just about every other subject you can imagine. Bill and his wife, Karen, were both ordained ministers, and Karen or one of their adult daughters often accompanied Bill. Bill circled the pool five times each session, grasping the bar on the edge with each laborious step. We often joked that we were going to make him a foam dorsal fin because of the way he circled, and one day I pretended to be sucked into a whirlpool created by his circling. It was easy to dismiss Bill because of his age and infirmity, but I learned not to—he had the hearing of a bat and didn't miss anything that was said. Bill's keen observation of interactions in the pool led to him teaching me an important lesson after the Pam Incident.

Pam was in her eighties and hard of hearing. Pam couldn't hear much that was said to her, so she kept up a constant bellowed monologue, usually an inventory of self-pity. It was tedious to listen to, but I felt bad for her, everyone who might have listened to her had abandoned her. Pam came alone and she needed an attendant to help her in and out of the pool. She wouldn't ask for help, and the therapist on duty would usually notice her just before she got into trouble. I learned to get the therapist's attention while Pam was just reaching the steps.

One night Pam's dial-a-ride transit bus didn't come. It was late and the rehab center was closed. The receptionist wasn't able to go home until the last patient was picked up. Pam said she would sit outside under the awning, out of the rain, and wait for the bus so the receptionist could go home. I asked where she lived and it was close to my house, so I offered to take her home. The receptionist mouthed "Thank you!"

It didn't take me long to remember that the road to hell is paved with good intentions. Pam didn't know how to fold her own walker. It was a deluxe model and I couldn't figure it out myself. By this time, all the bags of dreck she carried with her were loaded into my car and it was too late to change my mind about driving her home. I had to take the walker around to the inpatient facility (in the pouring rain) and ask a nurse to show me how to fold it. Back at the car, the walker was so heavy that I twisted my back hefting it into my car, undoing the benefit of my hydrotherapy.

Pam kept up her shouted monologue all the way to Eliza Avenue, then she directed me to turn right. We went past the nice townhouse complex where I thought she lived and into the run-down trailer park behind the mall, known only to police and Animal Control officers. The road was so potholed that it felt like I was driving up a flight of stairs. I stopped in front of Pam's trailer, a metal single-wide with a rickety wheelchair ramp built on. I got out and stepped into ankle-deep water. I sloshed around to the passenger side and assembled Pam's walker on dry ground, then rehung all her bags from the handles.

As I opened the door to help her out, her adult son came out from inside the trailer. Pam hadn't told me he was home (and why he couldn't pick up his mother was beyond me). He ignored my greeting and lit a cigarette. He made no move to help me with his mother. I made sure Pam got inside and got out of there as fast as my car could hop the potholes.

The next week, Pam wasn't there, but I told Bill

what had happened. He shook his head and said sternly, "You need to remember that you're a patient too. It's nice to want to help her, but you should never hurt yourself in the process of helping someone else." He was right, of course.

The week after that, Pam was there and she told everyone how I was her ride now. I said, "Pam, I'm sorry, but I have plans tonight and I'm going the opposite direction from here. Can you get a ride from Whatcom Transit?" I returned to the shallow end where Bill was resting between laps and he said, "I'm proud of you." I asked, "What for? I didn't offer her a ride." Bill grinned and said, "Exactly! You have boundaries!"

After a year of attending hydrotherapy, I started to feel like I was wearing out my welcome. Kappy made a few cracks about the waiting list and I felt they applied to me, even if she didn't mean to direct them at me. I talked to Vince about giving up my spot, and he told me that not only did I work the whole time I was there, unlike most of the people who just basked in the warm water, I was good for the patients, and I would be welcome there for as long as I wanted to come. I kept going for another six months. Vince decided to go back to school and we had a party to send him off. I was overcome with emotion; I looked around at these people I swam with every week and realized I would have considered them a ragtag bunch two years ago, but now I knew them to be heroes, every one.

Vince's replacement, Laurie, was great, and I still enjoyed the support group aspect of therapy, but I felt it was time to move on. On my last day, I brought doughnuts for everyone. As Kappy munched hers down and thanked me, I told her it was my last day. She saw the card I had put on the counter next to the doughnuts; it said, "It's very popular to talk about heroes these days. You all taught me how to be one." Her eyes filled with tears and she wolfed her doughnut.

Laurie urged me to come back if I had a setback or felt I needed a session, and offered me a punch card option. I haven't gone back yet, but it's good to know I could if I wanted to.

Alternative Medicine

My body was still so compromised, I hadn't had a period since the one that started right after my crash. It was still too busy reconstructing itself to bother with notions of reproducing. My hair had fallen out at the normal rate without growing any new hair, and it was thin in spots. My nails had grown out with a deep groove marking the weeks they hadn't grown. In February, six months after the crash, my period started up again. I had hoped that it just wouldn't bother and I'd be spared all that menopause nonsense. Just like always, I had disabling menstrual cramps. This brought up a new complication; I couldn't take ibuprofen for my cramps because I was on daily aspirin and you can't mix the two. Tylenol was marginally better than eating Pez. The high dose of narcotics I was on helped a lot, but as I eased back on the dosage, it became more and more of a problem.

Dr. Sohn suggested replacing the aspirin with one of the new anticoagulants designed for long-term stroke prevention. I'm not comfortable with a lot of these new medications and I decided to tough it out.

Then a friend suggested I try marijuana. I had used it before to ease cramps and found it highly effective. One puff at the onset and I was good for my two heavy days. I couldn't smoke anything anymore, not with lungs that had been so badly damaged. In the hospital, they couldn't even use ammonia or chlorine-based cleaning products in my room because my lungs were so scarred. I got online and learned how to steep the ground buds in butter to make magic brownies.

I have a friend who is an herbal healer and he suggested, based on our interview, that I try the less psychoactive indica varieties for pain relief without total loss of mental capacity. (When I brought a 63-year-old friend with MS to him, he suggested the same, and she said, "Oh, dear, I think I'd like something a little more all-purpose.") I found I still got hammered with a relaxed, indifferent feeling, but if I didn't mind sacrificing the evening to Netflix, it was quality pain relief. One variety I tried made me paranoid and I was afraid I'd harm Nimby. I tossed that batch of brownies and crossed that variety off my "OK" list.

I found in talking with my friends at the therapy pool that many of them used marijuana in addition to our other medications and found value in it. Many didn't get the relief they sought and gave it up, but the attitude overall was that it was another tool on the pegboard, it should be picked up and used where it would help. The hospital was a safe place to talk openly about our marijuana use.

Recently Washington law legalized possession of up to a quarter ounce of marijuana for recreational use. It was still illegal to buy or sell it; you just couldn't get busted for having a little for your own consumption. It was common for people to say, "It's legal now," but the law was a Catch-22. It kept the jails from being stuffed with petty criminals, but the "War on Drugs" still raged against the growers and sellers.

Getting a medical use prescription was not easy. My doctor couldn't write one because her practice had an agreement not to be a prescribing facility. I would have had to take her recommendation for a prescription down to a clinic in Seattle, where I could be issued a medical user card. My doctor said that clinic wasn't a comfortable place for a lone woman, and even if I could use a dispensary (our local one had been raided at least three times by the Feds), I wouldn't know who I was getting it from and the strength and effect were not predictable. I decided to not bother with getting a medical user card. The laws relaxed further a year later, and retail sale for recreational use was legalized.

The Visit That Should Have Happened Last August

About the end of May, my parents came to visit again. This time it was a real visit, the one we should have had last summer. We planned to go up to Canada like we had intended to.

I worked furiously on the house, trying to present the place I had wanted to present last summer. It was hard, though, with all my cycling and arm exercises, plus regular work, I didn't have much energy left over for housework.

They did notice I'd been working on the place, though. I'd gotten friends to help cart away all the stuff I'd gathered back up for donation and disposal, and just the reduction of the volume of stuff in the place made it look better. We spent a few days revisiting friends my parents had made while they were out here the first time, and we went to a trivia match, where we placed honorably. James was thrilled to see my parents again. I was thrilled to be able to use the bar bathroom without my Bottom Buddy.

For the trip to Vancouver, my parents wanted to stay in the hostel at Jericho Beach where I normally stay. A converted Canadian military barracks, it's a charming old building that didn't have to be altered too much to serve as a hostel. It is a lot more rustic than a hotel, and I knew my stories had romanticized it a bit for them and they might not do as well in the dorms as they might think, so I booked a private room for them and my usual dorm bed for me. It was weird driving the car there; I had never driven in Vancouver before and the highways were chaotic and bewildering. I'm sure the amount of oxycodone I was on didn't help. I was still weaning off the smallest size Fentanyl patch, 12.5 mcg/hour, and in mild withdrawal, as I was every time I backed down a level from the original 100s I left the hospital with. Even under the influence, I was better able to get around Vancouver in the car than my parents would have been. At least I knew the city. My plan was to drive only to the hostel, then leave the car behind and use public transit like the locals do.

On the way in, we stopped at the Vancouver Aquarium in Stanley Park. It was too early in the day to check in at the hostel and it was the perfect way to spend a rainy afternoon. When we got out of the car, the rain turned to a solid curtain. I glanced around for a pay kiosk for the parking, and saw nothing, so I figured we were in a free lot. I should have known better; I doubt there is a free parking space within the city limits. With the rain coming down as hard as it was, I was more concerned with getting my parents inside and not slipping and falling myself.

We spent three fun hours in the aquarium. I had to sit and rest often, but it was fun to show my parents the ecosystem exhibits that reflect conditions along the various coastal zones in the region. My job involves a lot of marine biology and I was able to show them all kinds of stuff they'd never seen in the midwest.

My favorite exhibit is the giant columnar tank that starts on the bottom floor and ends about four feet above the mezzanine, so adults can lean over the edge and observe the life in the tidepools formed by depressions in rocks near the top, and kids can see through without risk of falling. The water level rises and falls, synchronized with the natural tides. Down below there are rockfish, sturgeon, flatfish, and the usual array of sea stars, anemones, urchins, and more. You can observe all levels of the tank from the spiral staircase that curves around it.

When we left the aquarium, there was a sodden $40 parking ticket on my car. I carefully removed it and laid it out to dry on the dashboard. We went on to the hostel and checked in. The hostel was allegedly remodeled for use as an Olympic dormitory, but only the basement looked different to me. The dining room had been spruced up with nicer tables and chairs, and there was an actual order counter and menu now. Before, there was a nightly special and if you wanted something off-menu, Hans the chef would make it if he had the ingredients. I missed the old format and especially Hans and his golden retriever. The menu didn't appeal to my parents so we asked at the desk where the nearest good restaurant was. The concierge suggested The Naam, a place with a great reputation that I'd been wanting to try. We ventured out there and discovered that it was a vegetarian restaurant. Great for me, okay for my dad, disaster for my mom, whose Midwestern tastes are anti-adventurous. She ordered a grilled cheese sandwich and was served a monster of a sandwich on nine-grain bread, oozing with five kinds of cheese and lightly sprinkled with herbs. She had to admit it was delicious. My dad and I exchanged relieved glances—disaster averted.

On the way back to the car, I saw some hats in a store window and realized I was looking at the object of a two-year quest. When I lost my job two years before, my uncle Hank had sent me $200 in cash, with one request; that I find a hat just like one he had seen in a photo I sent from the Olympic torch procession. He thought the hat represented a white bear, and he lives in White Bear Lake, Minnesota. When I blew it up to get a better look, I saw that it was a white-faced Mickey Mouse, but I never had the heart to tell him. I just determined to find him a white bear hat if it meant I had to learn to knit and make it myself. Unbelievably, the white bear hat stared benignly from the store window, bathed in the red glow of the CLOSED sign. We planned to go back and get it in the morning.

My bunk mate in the dorm, Katerina, was from Austria and she was delightful. Her English was perfect and she invited me down to the game room to play foosball. Normally I would have loved to go, but I was in so much pain from the day already, I was in bed for the night by 8:00. The next morning I invited Katerina to have breakfast with us. My parents were a little surprised to have a guest at breakfast, but they liked Katerina as much as I did. She had plans for the day so we set off on our mission. First we stopped to retrieve the white bear hat. I bought the matching mittens for a total of $45, a small portion of Hank's original gift.

Then there was a bike shop I liked in the Kitsilano neighborhood where I'd had an emergency repair done on my bike once. I'm always nervous about taking Silver to bike shops because so many shops don't "get" my bike. I had a good feeling about this place going in; it was called "Different Bikes." As I rolled Silver in, the guy at the counter said, "Well, you're in the right place. This bike is gorgeous!" He exclaimed over every little detail and he recognized that the wheel I needed fixed was hand-built, and built well. He undercharged me for the repair and made me a respectable offer to buy my bike. Of course I declined and I put a large tip in the employee pizza fund jar. I rewarded their excellent service by coming back the next year for bike luggage.

I'd been touring with panniers that were meant for grocery store runs. They did the job, but not very well. I even rode from Bellingham to Eugene with those flimsy bags and a few stuff sacks tied to the luggage rack with a bungee net. It was time to get proper touring bags. Almost immediately, I homed in on a pair of giant Axiom bags with all the right pockets, and rain covers that stowed in their own zippered compartments. They even had net pockets to hold a wet swimsuit or "camp laundry" that hadn't dried all the way.

They were the Louis Vuitton of bicycle luggage and I just about swooned with joy, thinking of traveling with them. They cost $210. I brought them to the counter and paid without blinking. When we got back to the car, my dad handed me a check for $100 to help with the cost.

We took the car back to the hostel and boarded a bus downtown, where we got on a "hop on, hop off" tour. These popular bus tours follow a fixed route and you spend as long as you like at each attraction before getting back on. If you don't want to get off, you just keep riding and listen to the tour guide until you reach a place you want to see. It was a great way to see the city with non-cyclist parents. Late in the afternoon, I was tiring out and the bus was due to come get us at our stop at Granville Island. We waited over an hour; I still don't know what went wrong, but by the time the bus finally came, there were so many people waiting that they had to send more buses to get everyone. We got on the second bus and I was nearly wilting with pain and fatigue. If I had been thinking more clearly, we could have just walked a few blocks south and picked up a regular bus route to get to the next stop on the tour bus line.

That night we dined at the Boathouse Café, an upscale restaurant on Kitsilano Beach. Many movies and TV shows have scenes filmed there, including Psych. We had a maniacally expensive dinner and I ordered a glass of white wine, grateful that no one connected the dots with my pain pills. Once again, I sent a disappointed Katerina down to the game room alone at 8:00.

Our last day in Canada we planned to spend at Whistler. I woke up feeling like my spine might snap in a thousand places. My back was very done with the hostel bed. I had taken six oxycodone to get through the night and I was loopy at breakfast. I agreed to let my dad drive that day. On our way out, I found a parking ticket stuck to our windshield. I had paid the parking and gotten up early to feed the meter. The meter company had it set so you could only pay in advance until six the following morning, then if you didn't plug the meter again by six, you would be ticketed. My current parking payment showed clearly on the dashboard. I brought it inside and showed it to the concierge, who said the parking enforcers often came through and ticketed everyone, in the hope that the less proficient English speakers would simply pay the ticket rather than go to the trouble of contesting it. This native English speaker was having none of that. I even talked a man from Yemen through the process of contesting his ticket on his iPhone. I waited until I got home to deal with mine, but I got my ticket cancelled and the one from the Aquarium reduced to half.

The drive to and from Whistler was spectacular. I take gorgeous mountains almost for granted, but my parents were slack-jawed with awe. I had to take over driving for a while to keep my dad from driving over a cliff as one dazzling peak after another presented itself. Whistler Village was crazy-expensive; we could barely afford to park there to look in the shops at things we couldn't afford. It was fun to see, but we were happy enough to head home.

I stopped for gas at a station along the highway and I paid for $40 worth of gas at the pump before heading in to the washroom. I asked my dad to pump the gas; I thought he heard me. He had gone inside to pay cash for another $40 worth of gas that he thought I was pumping. I took the wheel and we got about ten miles down the road when my fuel light went on. I asked my dad if he had pumped the gas and he said no, he thought I had. It turned out we had paid $80 and driven away without any gas. We were so embarrassed, we didn't even go back to straighten it out. We just stopped at the next station and filled up for real. I made sure to laugh a lot at the situation, because I could tell my dad was already upset with himself. No point in me getting upset too.

When we hit Vancouver, the afternoon peak traffic was in full swing. We literally stopped on Highway 1 for many minutes at a time. It took an hour to go three miles. The sun blazed into the car like a laser and my air conditioner couldn't keep up. Finally we reached the bridge I needed to cross. I missed the exit! For two more hours, I tried to get back to that bridge and kept getting cut off by one-ways or other problems. When we finally did get across the bridge, I got lost again. I wanted to pull over and cry from frustration but I've learned that one doesn't melt down first in my family; you just start a spiral and end up wishing you'd stayed stoic. We drove around for three hours with several bathroom and direction stops before I recognized that we were headed the right way on the King George Highway. We stopped at a safe-looking café and had a good dinner before taking it the rest of the way home. My dad remarked that I was "tough as nails." I said when you've taken a chest tube without anesthesia, there isn't much that can really get to you any more.

We were so glad to get home! The next day we did nothing, we just let Nimby and Kali entertain us.

Overdoing It

While convalescing over the winter, I applied for a Nexus pass. The Nexus program allows people who frequently cross the border to be pre-screened and marked as "trusted travelers." The pass costs $50 and it's good for five years. I decided to get the pass because as a cyclist, I was required to wait in a line at the border behind people getting their vehicles inspected. I often had to stand more than an hour. There was no place to sit, and it had been hard enough to get back on the bike and ride twenty-four miles home before I fractured my spine. The Nexus pass would allow me to bypass the car inspection line and get priority processing.

In April I received notification that I had passed my background check and I had an appointment for my interview at the border station. The May day dawned sunny, so I decided to ride the twenty-two miles to the border.

As often happens in the Northwest, the morning clouded over quickly and by the time I left, thinking I was plenty early, a stiff, cold headwind was blowing. I rode as fast as I could against the gale and still arrived a few minutes late. More panic ensued when I realized I wasn't in the right place; there was a separate Nexus office over a mile away. I rode hard for it and hitched up on a standpipe close to the door, knowing that might earn me a ticket. I ran in breathlessly and apologized for being late. The woman at the counter was about to give me a bracing lecture when I picked up a credit card lying on the counter and said, "Whose is this?" She got flustered and I took a seat while she tracked down the card's owner. I had to wait about twenty minutes as they slotted me in after people who had arrived early or on time.

First they took my photo. I smoothed my wild hair back into its braid the best I could. The woman at the camera asked if me if I would usually be in cycling clothes when crossing the border. I said yes, I would be, and I had a passport with a photo of me in regular clothes that I would be carrying as well. She sighed and took my disheveled photo.

Next I waited for the interview. I was called into another room where I stood at a counter and a Canadian border guard asked me questions about the purpose of my travel in Canada, what I relied on for protection on the road (my phone and my wits; in short, I was unarmed), and why I felt I needed expedited border service. I explained that getting into Canada by bike was a snap; the officers came out and processed me curbside most days, but getting back into the US was a monumental hassle and often took an hour or two. Then the US guard came out, introduced himself, and said, "I'm the guy you were just complaining about." I sputtered until he laughed and said he was just giving me a hard time. I said, "I'm sorry, harassment is usually my thing. I don't know how to be on the other end of it." He laughed again and that was pretty much it; he asked some standard questions and I was free to go.

I went outside, unhitched my bike, and realized I could barely lift my leg over the seat to mount. I had used all my energy to get there and didn't have any reserves to get home. With legs of soggy concrete, I pedaled a mile to El Paso Del Norte, a Mexican restaurant known more for its variety of strong margaritas than its food. Predictably, my lunch was three times the size of my appetite. I ate too much food, paid my bill, and struggled back aboard the bike with a full stomach. By this time the wind had shifted so it was blowing in my face again going home (again, a common phenomenon in this part of the country). I got to Smith Road, knowing I was five miles from home, and actually cried because that five miles felt so long. My right hand burned and I could barely put any weight on the handlebar. I limped in to home, noted my total mileage—52, went inside, vomited, and slept in my recliner in my sweaty cycling clothes until dinner time.

That was my record long ride since the crash (my "before" record was 132) and it was too much. I had to rest a few days before trying to ride again. (Two years later, my upper limit hasn't risen significantly.) My upcoming trip had 48-mile days in hilly country. I knew I had to train harder if I was going to make it without making myself sick.

I started doing weekly trips up Samish Way to Lake Padden Park and the Mount Galbraith trailhead, the highest point in Bellingham accessible by road. It was an 800-foot climb over six miles, and to get there and back was a 32- or 48-mile loop, depending on whether I went around Lake Samish. Every time I chose the cutoff road and skipped the lake, but it was still a significant training ride. I got to the point where I could make it to the top of the hill without too much effort. There were two gigantic hills on the way home as well; by the time I topped the second one, I was ready to be done, with nine miles left to get home.

Drunk-Dial

I was home one spring evening, watching a DVD with Nimby in my lap, when my phone rang. The call display showed that it was my former boss, Darcy. My relationship with her was probably the most complex and destructive one of my life. Darcy hired me to be her editor and report writer, yet she provided zero training. Instead of telling me what she wanted, she berated me when I did it wrong, and I learned from her complaints how to do it next time. Yet when we went out after work, she would get a drink down and suddenly start showering me with praise. She was incredibly charismatic; everyone around her admired her and wanted to win her favor.

Over time, Darcy descended into alcoholism. The transition from heavy drinker to hard-core alcoholic happened slowly and others saw it before I did. I had worked so closely with her that I'd taken on the role of enabler without realizing it. Her charisma had morphed into a manipulative stranglehold. I regularly found myself walking to meetings at clients' offices and getting a phone call five minutes before the meeting started, with her saying she was sick and I was in charge. There was never any preparation; she didn't let me know what she expected of me in these meetings but was quite ready to tell me how I'd let her down after the fact. I did talk to her about how unfair this was, but we never mentioned the elephant in the room—her drinking that caused it all.

I often got the same report back from her, reviewed twice. First while she was drunk, full of red ink and semicoherent criticism. Then the next day, she wouldn't remember having done it and she'd print and review the report again sober. The comments were rarely similar.

Darcy traveled a lot and often had me sit for her animals. I had to stay over; the dogs were very high-maintenance. This was fine when I was married and welcomed the chance to play house on my own, but after I moved into my own house, I had my own cat and home to take care of and staying at her house was an inconvenience. She started paying me more. Depending on her blood alcohol level, a five-day stay could rack up as much as $200 or as little as $30. It was completely random. I discovered that some of her ex-boyfriends that she met online still had keys to her house. That was when I told her that staying over wasn't an option anymore; it wasn't safe. I called her on the fact that she only even acknowledged me at work anymore when she needed me to house sit. She didn't take that very well.

I went to see one of the other partners and told him I thought my job was in danger if I said no to Darcy's personal requests, and I wanted that on record in case she did anything impulsive. Sasha, my friend and coworker who also worked for Darcy, was talking regularly with the partners about Darcy's drinking. She was frustrated by how little they were willing to do about it. I told the partner that what Sasha was saying was true and I wished they'd listen. That's the only time I spoke up for Sasha and I've always regretted not doing more to help her. I was even more stuck in the enabler role than Sasha was; at least she worked in another office most of the time and wasn't on a short leash like me.

Darcy was let go in 2004. It happened one morning and my world was turned upside down in an instant. I had been distancing myself from Darcy for some time, but this was jarring and unexpected. The managing partner asked me if I had any feelings I'd like to share. I said "Not today. I need to process my feelings first. I think what you need to hear right now is that I'm not going to do or say anything damaging to the company, and I can promise you that. Can I go now?" I never did "share." I don't think I ever fully processed what I felt. I went to visit Darcy at her home a week later. She'd had surgery and I was concerned; she'd said it was for a breast issue and I was afraid she might have been diagnosed with cancer just before losing her insurance. Her boyfriend answered the door and I saw Darcy slide a large glass of wine behind the door as I walked in (clearly visible through the window in the door). It only took one look to tell the real story; Darcy had gotten breast implants. I decided I was done.

Darcy continued to call me regularly, always after 10:00 at night and always slurring drunk. I would be nice but gently hustle her off the phone as fast as I could. In her condition, this often took more than an hour. Sometimes if she was really drunk, I would just hang up and turn off my phone. She wouldn't remember it the next morning anyway.

By the time I moved to Bellingham, we were estranged. She moved back to the east coast shortly after I moved north and she came by with another friend once. I had hoped she would come to my house to meet Nimby. Instead, Darcy wanted to meet at the swanky Cliff House restaurant and started giving me directions. I reminded her tersely that I live here and I know the way. We ended up sitting and drinking, of course, without ordering any food, until she was potted and her friend took the keys. I hugged her good-bye and left, feeling used again. I decided it was the last time I would let her make me feel that way.

When her call popped up that night almost a year later, I felt defensive, but I told her what I had been through and my amazing recovery. She said in a very patronizing way that I had always healed slowly from injuries and acted as if I'd just been bumped and exaggerated the whole thing. I ended the call quickly because I was too angry to go on talking. Her speech was slurring and I suddenly felt the entire twelve years we'd known each other was a monumental waste of time.

I fumed for days over that call. I remembered the time I'd been seriously hurt falling down my back steps in the rain as I walked out to stake my daffodils that were bending in the wind. I had hit my right buttock hard on the edge of a wooden step and crushed my piriformis muscle. After the massive and dangerous hematoma healed, I would be walking along and suddenly my leg would just buckle underneath me because the piriformis wasn't firing in the right order with the other muscles that move the leg forward. I went into physical therapy for a few months to retrain the scarred muscle. It's one of the largest and most important muscles in the body, yet Darcy and some other coworkers acted as if I were doing something frivolous or shameful by getting physical therapy on my butt. All that resentment boiled up and I was furious about every slight I'd ever taken from her with the enabler's good-natured forgiveness. I decided I was really done with her this time and I deleted her contacts from my phone and e-mail.

You're hearing "this time I was really done" over and over again. This is the sad reality of loving an alcoholic. You keep saying you're done, but they pull you back in again and again. Just like the alcoholic, the enabler has to hit bottom too and find out where to finally draw the line.

I Finally Meet Eve

It was finally almost time to go. My bags were packed, the cat sitter was booked and I was leaving in the morning. It is a challenge to leave on a bike with a cat who knows he's being locked in, so I put my packed bags in the car and put my bike on the car rack, securely locked, overnight. That made me nervous, but it made for a quick getaway in the morning without having to open the front door wide enough for Nimby to slip out.

I was so keyed up the night before, I barely slept. I got up and did the morning hugdown with Nimby, then when I didn't unlock the kitty door after I fed him breakfast, he was On To Me. I gulped a protein drink and cut up my morning apple and put it in a Ziploc bag to eat it at the train station, grateful that Kali hadn't come by yet to spend her day in "kitty day care." Turning her away might break my heart. I was plenty early as I retrieved the bike from the car rack, mounted the bags, and shoved off with Nimby watching me from the bedroom window, his worried gray face almost pulling me back. Leaving him is always the hardest part of the journey.

The eight-mile ride to the station was cool and pleasant. For once, no drama at the train station. I've had many trips aborted because of train cancellations; the tour bus they send is no good because it doesn't have a bike rack. I've created a Plan B for these occasions in which I ride to the border (30 miles from Fairhaven), ride another few miles to the bus stop in White Rock, and bus into Vancouver. That day the train was on schedule and I spent a pleasant half hour chatting with Mary, the station agent. Like many people in service jobs, Mary has been doing it long enough to develop a certain weariness of humankind, which, like all true professionals, she hides well. Having spent years in retail myself, I offered my sympathy one day when a passenger tested Mary's patience, and I earned my passage into her world. Mary likes me because I'm always on time, I follow the rules, and I invite her to dish on the passengers who don't. Mary got my bike loaded with plenty of time for me to struggle with my bags down to the passenger car.

My new bags had a shoulder strap that was designed for carrying both bags together. I could only handle one at a time slung over my right shoulder, and carried the other bag with the regular handle in my left hand, leaving one hand free to cope with doors and whatnot. It was much better than the old days when I had the small panniers and a bunch of large stuff sacks hanging off them with carabiner hooks. Still, I had a small hitch in my mid-back from the shoulder bag, and a definite pain in my left arm where the bag's weight pulled at the plate.

The train ride was pleasant and I bought a coffee to go with my apple and energy bar. I saw so many bald eagles out the train window as we passed through White Rock and the Delta area, I lost track of the number sometime after a hundred.

Before I knew it, the train was stopped in Vancouver. My bike was unloaded from the baggage car and rested against a fence, close to the station. I was at the back of a long line waiting to go through customs. My shiny new Nexus card didn't buy me a thing in this line. Two women in cycling gear were ahead of me and I started to chat with them about where they were going. A man behind me chimed in and I turned to see that he was in gear too. He said, "I'm sorry, just tell me if it's none of my business, but the scars on your arms look fresh. I'm an occupational therapist and I'm interested in how you're able to ride with those." Ugh, I hadn't even made it past customs without having to tell the crash story. But he was polite and asked good questions. The line didn't move very far in the time it took me to tell it. This man surprised me, though. He said, "Thank you, you didn't owe me that." He asked me to follow him and he led me up to the front of the line. I grabbed Silver on the way and hooked on her bags. The man summoned a Canada Rail employee, flashed his hospital ID, and said, "Excuse me, but I'm this woman's doctor. We didn't call ahead for special accommodations but she really can't wait in this long line. She's only a few months off a spinal fracture. Can you please send her ahead?" Stunned, I allowed myself to be led to the next customs agent and waved into the busy station. The man was right behind me. I said, "I don't know how to thank you!" He squeezed my good shoulder, grinned, and said, "Just have the time of your life out there." I never even got the guy's name.

I rode through town, not at all confident of my directions. Vancouver is a busy city and the riding can be a little intense downtown. I got turned around and ended up in Chinatown just as it started to rain. I pulled over at a bank and ran into the lobby with my map. The Asian-Canadian security guard looked at me and I said, "I didn't want to pull out my map on the street and look like a total tourist." He said, deadpan, "No, because a white lady on a pricey bike in Chinatown blends right in, as long as she's not looking at a map."

I decided not to put on my bright yellow rain covers yet, since I was already conspicuous enough, and it would just be more to pack up when I got to my bus stop. This time I knew my directions and rode straight to the bus stop, where I caught my bus with one minute to spare. It was my first time using a bus bike rack since the crash and I had a devil of a time folding the rack down and then getting my bike up on it. After the 40-minute ride to the Horseshoe Bay ferry terminal, I couldn't get the rack back up in the stowed position.

The driver had to come out and help me. Fortunately, Canadian drivers actually do that. I explained my predicament and he let me practice a few times to make sure I could do it next time.

The BC Ferries are nicer than ours in Washington State, reflecting Canada's greater investment in infrastructure. Instead of a rope to tie your bike to a rail, there are proper bike racks on the auto deck. The vessel was smaller than the seven-story monster I took last time I crossed to Victoria from Tsawwassen to the south. This was still a giant beast of a boat, though, with three auto deck levels, and a restaurant, gift shop, and concierge for continuing travel on the passenger level. I cruised the gift shop's book rack for my vacation read; it's a tradition to treat myself to a book from the all-Canadian-author selection on the ferry. The book I wanted, Ape House by Sara Gruen, was $21. I balked at the price and decided to hit a book store in Nanaimo. I had two magazines in my bike bag. I subscribe to Mental Floss, a magazine for trivia buffs, and I save the issues all year to read on my bike tours and recycle along the way, lightening the load. The ride took an hour and a half and I decided to have my dinner on the ferry. I ordered a plate of poutine, a traditional French-Canadian breakfast food consisting of thickly sliced potatoes (French fries in lower-class restaurants), brown gravy and tender melted cheese curds. I'd never had it before and was delighted to find it on the menu. The guy at the counter said if I didn't like it, he'd bring me something else. He came to my table 20 minutes later and asked if I'd like something else. I held up my empty plate and said, "Yes, I'd like seconds, please."

The announcement came that we were heading into port, and I went down the flights of stairs back to the auto deck, where I unlocked Silver and waited with the other cyclists and pedestrians to get off first. The

big ferry doors rolled open onto the Nanaimo terminal
and suddenly it hit me what I was doing. This was *it*,
this was my trip to Free Spirit Spheres. This was my
declaration to the universe that I will not be stopped.
All the fear and pain, all the labor it took to get here
rose in my heart and I stood there and bawled while
the other cyclists mounted up and rode off. I realized
that I had to clear the ramp or I'd be made to wait and
get off last, so I pulled it together and hurried up the
ramp. It took a few attempts to find the right road to
town, and it was a busy road. I only had three miles
to ride to get to the hostel, though, including one really steep hill. Before I knew it I was at the Painted
Turtle Guest House. It looked unexpectedly funky and
European. I hitched Silver to an antique-looking lamp
post and went to check in.

Sara, the lady at the desk, looked a little too much
like my niece Sara for comfort. Seeing her gave me
that wavy head-injured feeling again that made me
doubt reality. She sent me up to the second floor, where
I opened the dorm door with my key and located my
bed, which was occupied. The occupant wasn't there.
She had taken the lower bunk even though she was
assigned the top; this happens often in hostels. I went
back downstairs to explain to Sara that I couldn't possibly manage the top bunk, not with my damaged
arms. I had taken my jacket off and my scars were laid
out in all their angry glory. I had to explain my story
again, and I asked if she would mind explaining to the
other guest that I had to have that bed. Sara did the
Canadian thing and put me in a private room at no
additional charge, so no one had to be made uncomfortable. She carried my bags upstairs and told me to
ask for her every time I book from now on; I was a VIP
guest for life as far as she was concerned.

That night in the common room, I watched a remarkable interaction between a Chinese man and

a Ugandan man who didn't speak a word of any language in common. After a few frustrated attempts in French and English, the Chinese man gestured to the foosball table. The Ugandan man grinned and pulled a Loonie (dollar coin) out of his pocket to start the game. Those men played foosball for hours that night and it didn't matter that they couldn't talk to each other; by the end of the night they were firm friends.

My bed was wonderful, a great improvement on the standard hostel bed that is little more than a cot mattress. Still, I barely slept until I gave in to exhaustion at 3:00. There was a bar right across the street and another attached to the hostel, and live bands played in both, long into the night. The bar across the street sold deep-fried Nanaimo bars and advertised that they would deep-fry any food item you brought in for $5, so there was the occasional tourist vomiting on the sidewalk after discovering that sugar, grease and alcohol are a bad combination. In the morning a guy was out there hosing down the front walk to start a new day.

I got up early despite the short night to get started on the 42-mile ride to Free Spirit Spheres. I wanted to give myself all day to do what would have taken me three to four hours a year ago. As the road through town gave way to a busy highway, I started to panic. The cars whizzed by so fast! I had to breathe deeply and will myself not to give up. I was still on the outskirts of Nanaimo when my left shoulder gave a strong electric twinge, indicating that I was fatigued and should stop. I was only one sixth of the way there. I realized then that this trip was very premature and I wasn't ready to ride this far alone on new roads, but it was too late to turn back. I noticed a Chapters bookstore (Canadian for Barnes & Noble) on my left and pulled over for a break. Normally I boycott all chain stores in favor of local independents, but I needed to sit down with a scone right now and Chapters offered a guarantee of a good break. Best of all, they had Sara Gruen's Ape House on sale for $16. I bought it and happily crammed it into the last inch of headspace in my saddlebag.

Returning to the highway, I found a bike path running parallel that offered a break from the speeding traffic. I decided to follow the path as long as I could still see the highway to find my way back to it if they diverged. At one point I had to cross another intersecting highway. There was a tunnel under the road a few hundred feet down the path, but there was graffiti around the entry and it looked sketchy, so I chose to use the crosswalk at the light instead. As I rode carefully across, a woman in a car stopped in my path and said, "You're supposed to use the tunnel. You can't cross here." I asked if she was married and she said yes, what did that have to do with anything? I said, "Only a woman who takes a male presence for granted would suggest to another woman that she enter that tunnel by herself." As I rode on, a man on a bicycle who had been behind me at the intersection cheered me as he passed and shouted, "I wouldn't use that tunnel either!"

The path took me halfway to Parksville, the midpoint of my journey. Riding on the highway was more tiring than the path because of the constant tension caused by the speeding traffic so close by. I was only slightly aware of the panoramic beauty around me, I was too worried about surviving to take much of a look. Occasionally the shoulder narrowed for a stream crossing and I had to snug up too close to the guard rail to navigate the six inches between the shoulder line and the edge of the bridge. I pulled over at a safe-looking diner called Smitty's for a lunch break. I tend to favor mom-and-pop diner type places on the road because while you usually won't get anything exciting there, you can count on a solidly adequate grilled cheese sandwich if nothing else is appealing. The wind had calmed and the dark clouds were spreading out and changing from defined masses to a uniform gray overhead, which meant the rain was about to start. I covered my bags with my rain covers before I went inside for a surprisingly delicious meal of a trendy Mediterranean chicken wrap. I made it another half hour down the road before it started coming down hard. At least I'd turned onto Highway 19A, the calmer two-lane coastal highway, from 19, the main highway across the midrib of the island.

The rain was so intense that I pulled over at a bus shelter to let the worst of it pass. I was soaked to the skin; even my new rain jacket stuck to my fleece sweater in dark sodden patches. It was cold and I was glad I had put on my wool tights in the diner washroom. By the time I reached Qualicum Beach, ten miles south of my destination, the sun was struggling out from behind the clouds and my socks were almost dry. I stopped at a grocery store to get provisions for my stay at the Spheres. The store was one of those delightful Canadian urban markets set in a small town to cater to tourists—lots of local specialties and gourmet food available in small portions.

There was no more room in my bags, so I used a bungee net to tie the plastic grocery bags to the top of my luggage rack. The apples listed dangerously to one side but the load seemed stable enough. The first few miles out of Qualicum Beach were pleasant, along a gently winding coastline with a wide shoulder. I felt safe, warm and dry, and my good mood returned. Then the road turned slightly inland and started getting hilly. By the time I reached the turn for Horne Lake Road, I was so exhausted I wasn't enjoying the ride any more. I walked up the steep hill from the highway and could barely swing my leg back over to start riding again at the top. I followed the directions from the resort's web site and soon I was standing at the end of the dirt driveway. Only a large house number sign marked the driveway. A few steps in, another sign said "By appointment only." They were expecting me; I kept walking. The wooded drive opened out into a clearing with a charming big wood-shingled house on the left, with a decorative stained-glass window by the door. A small parking lot held two cars, and a sphere under construction hung from a grove of mature trees, surrounded by scaffolding. I didn't see anyone so I took out my phone and checked for a signal. Two bars; I tried calling. I got voice mail and said I had arrived and I'd be walking around exploring the grounds until I saw someone to check me in. A moment later Tom came running down the front walk, waving a clipboard. He greeted me by name and said he was so happy I'd made it. He said I could leave my car in the lot and take the bike back with me if I wanted. I said there was no car, just me and the bike. His eyes got very wide as he realized I had in fact cycled from Nanaimo.

Tom led me along a gravel path lined by decorative solar lights. Metal and glass sculptures popped out of the grass in random places. It was like stepping into a fantasy world. We stopped so Tom could show me the shower trailer, a mobile home featuring two bathrooms with showers and an indoor kitchen area. The trailer also housed a sauna. The translucent-roofed deck out front had a propane grill and picnic tables, and lounge chairs to provide a place to sit outdoors in the rain. I hadn't even seen my treehouse yet and already I was enchanted.

We turned into a small grotto with a picnic table and a mushroom-shaped shingled outhouse with the composting toilet I shared with Eryn, the neighboring sphere. My eyes were drawn upward by the mass in the trees above, and there was Eve, my sphere for the next two nights. A spiral staircase wound around the tree to the door that looked like a space ship hatch. Eve hung there like a giant wooden Christmas ornament, shining with a foil banner that said "Congratulations!" What a welcome. I rested Silver against the picnic table and Tom asked me to lead the way up the steps; he planned to replace the staircase over the following winter and he wanted to be sure I was steady enough to handle the elderly steps. I only carried one pannier up the narrow steps because I would probably flounder about with two, and then I'd be judged unsteady and wouldn't be allowed to stay. I was still full of the rehab center mentality of earning permission to be independent. On the landing, I let Tom show me how to open the hatch door.

I said "Hello, Eve," on my way in and Tom smiled. I said it only seemed respectful to acknowledge her and ask permission to enter. I told him that's what I liked best about the place when I visited the web site, that he talked about the spheres by name as if they had souls, the way I talk about (and to) Silver. I thought I caught a faint whiff of incense as I stepped inside, the cedar-and-sage blend I favor for spiritual purification of a space. Maybe it was just my imagination. She was made of cedar, after all.

Eve's interior was very much like that of a camper. The floor was flat and Tom showed me all kinds of cabinets that held all kinds of amenities like electric tea and coffee pots, window shades, extra pillows and the like. A cabinet under the bed, covered by a dust ruffle that doubled as a cabinet door, would hold my bike bags nicely. A shelf ran around the top at just above eye level, stocked with games and books. Recessed lighting shone from above the shelf. Stereo speakers offered surround sound and Tom showed me where to plug in my iPod. Best of all, Eve's ribs were visible inside the structure. Strong, whole cedar ribs that would surround me as I breathed inside, healing my own ravaged ribs. I had chosen my goal perfectly.

As we sat inside Eve dealing with the paperwork, Tom noticed creaking sounds that didn't bother me a bit. He fussed around outside on a ladder while I unpacked, until he was satisfied that Eve's gentle bobbing motion was generally silent. Then he came upstairs again to take his leave and asked, "Would you mind if I gave you a hug? It really means a lot to us both that you're here." I gladly reciprocated.

After Tom left, I looked around the sphere and only one thing was missing—Nimby! He would adore this place! I felt a physical ache of missing him, then pulled myself together and put his song, "Follow the Day" by Polyphonic Spree, on the sound system. It was his song because he followed me everywhere. Often when I was tired on the road, I imagined Nimby plodding along behind me, following dutifully, and it helped me press on.

I had bought myself a custard fruit tart at the market in Qualicum Beach and I laid it out on the flowered placemat and brewed a whole pot of rooibos tea. I sat and savored my fruit tart and stowed the dirty plate on the back shelf, then there was a knock at the door. Rosey was there with the traditional treat basket. My eyes just about popped at the assortment of cookies, muffins, fruit, yogurt, juice—even a bottle of hard cider. It was enough carbohydrate matter so I didn't need to leave the compound before checkout time. (Even then, I left with my bags stuffed with road treats). I invited Rosey in for a cup of tea, grateful that I had brewed so much of it. She sat on the other side of the camper table and we chatted for a few minutes. Then Rosey said, "I wanted to wait until I met you to decide if I was going to tell you this, but I came here last night and meditated to make this a healing space for you." I grinned and said, "I can totally tell. I smelled the cedar and sage when I walked in and the energy in here is just incredible. I love that you did that, thank you." She went on to tell me how she had used Eve as a healing space during her own recovery from illness and she knew there was something special about healing here. I told her how I felt embraced by Eve's strong ribs and how, since I had fractured nine of mine, I looked forward to breathing within the great ribs.

I told Rosey about the trip up and how many times I'd had to explain my story, and that I felt ambivalent about that. I would like to be more free to share or not share, but my scars were so visible, they begged to be explained. Rosey assured me that they'd fade in time and I'd be able to decide whether or not to share. She offered her own experience, that because she survived an often fatal disease, others expected her to be a "poster child" and spearhead all the local fundraising events. Rosey had worked hard to reclaim her life and had to decide how much she was going to allow herself to be defined by her survival of this disease, and how much energy she needed for moving forward and living the life she'd worked so hard to save.

I thought of my decision not to talk to Alice's spiritual group about my near-death experience and felt the discomfort about that fall away. As we talked, I had the sense that this conversation was the reason I had been drawn to this place. I was Meant to be here, in this moment with Rosey, and everything else that happened on this trip would be a happy extra.

When Rosey excused herself to resume her typical crazy-busy day, we hugged and I sat down to write the postcards I had bought in Nanaimo. The peace of the place seeped into my being and I was happy to spend the evening listening to music and reading my new book.

The next day was cold and cloudy, and I had to wear my long tights and fleece again. I was inclined to stay inside and read. In the afternoon I rode out to explore the First Nation Reserve just north on the highway. I stopped at a Chinese restaurant and truly struggled to park my bike. There was just no place to lock up. Finally I looped the lock cable awkwardly through the wood lattice on the fence around the porch. A man came out and laughed at me for bothering to lock up. I said, "If you were alone in a foreign country and this was your only way to get home, you'd lock it up too." I went inside and checked the menu. The food looked about like what you'd expect in a rural Chinese restaurant anywhere, but the "War Won Ton Soup" looked promising. I took a chance and was presented with a bowl as big as both my buttocks. It was amazing soup, loaded with vegetables and won tons and prawns, and the won ton meat didn't taste like ground-up hot dogs the way it does in many low-end Chinese restaurants. I ate until I was stuffed.

I rode back to the Spheres on an uncomfortably full stomach, and the skies opened just as I got in. I pulled Silver up on the deck of the trailer and waited for it to let up enough to go back to Eve. My laundry that I'd washed in the sink and hung out on the rope rail of the spiral staircase was soaked. I wrung it out and hung it back up inside, close to the heater.

The rain started up again and with it came a heavy wind. I went down to secure Silver under the eaves of the composting toilet. I didn't even think to lock her on the roofed deck of the trailer, or ask Tom to put her in their garage. I went back up into Eve and read while she swayed gently, and occasionally lurched, in the wind. Around 9:00 there was a knock at my door. Tom asked if I was okay up there or if I'd prefer to come down and stay in the house. I laughed and said I was having the time of my life, and I couldn't bear to come down. Tom grinned and said if I changed my mind, the house would be unlocked, the downstairs light on, and I wouldn't have any trouble finding the guest room.

The storm raged until around 3:00 and I laid in the luxurious bed, being tossed about. I kept my glasses on and watched the trees whipping in the wind until it was too dark to see anything. Then, of course, I had to go to the bathroom. I made a mental note to bring a large yogurt container to use as an emergency night pot next time and put my jacket on over my night shirt. I got wet and cold, but I turned up the heat and fell deeply asleep until morning dawned with tenuous sunshine. I couldn't believe I had to go back already. I just got there! But I'd finished my book around midnight and I missed Nimby.

Silver was half buried in leaves and she made various creaking and groaning sounds as I rolled her up the path to check out. Tom insisted on taking her to his workshop to clean her up, give her a mechanical check, and spray some fresh lube on her chain. Then he gave me directions back to the highway that would save me from having to climb the huge hill I had coasted down to get there.

Rosey and Tom both hugged me good-bye and I left in happy tears. Tom's directions got me back to the highway and the ride was pleasant and uneventful back to Nanaimo. I found a Subway for lunch in a strip mall outside Parksville and then it was time for the exchange back onto Highway 19. I had to ride a cloverleaf on-ramp, that wasn't very pleasant, nor was going over the overpass, but the shoulder was wide and the weather was good.

Back at the hostel, there was a long line for the front desk. Sara saw me come in and she parted the crowd and said, "Sorry folks, but this lady gets priority processing." I told her that wasn't necessary, but she insisted and then called for Hilde, the other concierge, to carry my bags up to my room. I thanked Hilde and found to my relief that the bottom bunk had not been taken. My roommate was sound asleep, so I put my things away as quietly as I could and went and sorted my laundry out in the bathroom. I got my wash started, then went to Gina's Mexican restaurant nearby for dinner. I treated myself to a margarita and wobbled the half mile back to the hostel on Silver.

The next morning, I finally met Christa, my roommate from Alberta. A young family was in the common room, a father, mother, 3-year-old boy, and one well on the way. The mother offered me an omelette, which I politely declined because of my egg allergy. In true Canadian fashion, she took six of her son's Fig Newtons and arranged them on a plate with a sprig of grapes and served it with a flourish. I offered them some of my Starbucks instant coffee packets and we had a companionable breakfast together. Then it was time to head for the ferry.

I stopped at the grocery store first for more of the wonderful yogurt that Rosey had served at Free Spirit. I went to Bastion Park to eat it while a man played bagpipes. On the bluff top, surrounded by open space, the bagpipes weren't loud and overwhelming like they are indoors and I enjoyed the music. I tipped him with a Toonie (two-dollar) coin I had in my pocket and rode on into town, where I browsed in a used bookstore until it was time to head for the ferry terminal. At the tollbooth, I suffered a complete and sinking panic as I realized my wallet was missing.

I rode the three miles back in to town so fast my heart raced and sweat trickled down my back. My wallet wasn't at the bookstore and I looked in the park, knowing that if I had dropped it there, I wouldn't see it again. How was I going to get back into the US without my Nexus card? My last hope was the grocery store, the last place I had seen it for sure. As I walked in to the store, the cashier smiled and said, "Hi, Kristin" and held up my familiar sky-blue wallet. She laughed and said she was supposed to ask me questions to make me ID the wallet, but I was clearly suffering and she couldn't bear to watch. She had checked the photo beforehand and knew it was really me (good thing I had my Nexus photo taken in cycling gear after all!).

I thanked her profusely and rode back to the ferry terminal just as fast, knowing I had to catch the next vessel or I might miss my train connection in Vancouver. I rode onto the boat just as they were about to raise the ramp.

Back in Vancouver, the bus was easy, bike rack and all. I had a few hours before I had to be at the train station, so I rode the nine-mile seawall trail around Stanley Park, enjoying a slow pace in the sun. The park was crowded with locals enjoying the beautiful summer day. I started toward the station and realized I didn't know my way back as well as I thought I did. I ended up on the Cambie Street Bridge and had to edge by many homeless people to make my way across. On the other side, things started looking familiar and I found the station with no trouble. I didn't realize I had to be there an hour in advance for an international train trip. I just made it on the train.

Back in Bellingham at 7:40 PM, I still had eight miles to ride home. I savored the light traffic and the beauty of the view of the bay along State Street. The sun was getting low and the sky glowed brilliant orange, the few clouds outlined in silver. Nimby predictably shot out the front door when I opened it, but that was fine, it was plenty light out and we played our stair games and I let him help me put the bike in the shed. I didn't make him come back in until it got dark at ten. I had only been gone four nights, but I felt like I'd climbed Mount Everest. We had done it—Silver and I had made our pilgrimage to Free Spirit Spheres. I still had a long way to go, but now I knew I had what it took to get there.

Indecent Proposal

In July I was feeling pretty good about things. I had made it to Free Spirit Spheres and life was just going to get better from there. Then I stopped at the mailbox one day and there was a thick envelope from a government agency. I wondered if it was related to a civilian military support job I had applied for two years ago that I hadn't really wanted to get, but needed an application on my unemployment log in order to get my benefits. I pedaled back up to the house and opened it. There was a letter on top, saying that Darcy, my former boss, had given them my name for a job reference for a high-level security clearance position with the government. The reference form was a bubble sheet. I started to fill it out with a ball-point pen as directed. Then I came to the question, "Do you know of any drug or alcohol abuse?" I stopped. I couldn't send this in; I couldn't answer that question truthfully and the letter said that filling out the form constituted agreement to be under oath. I put the packet aside for a few days to mull it over.

During that time, I told just about everyone I knew, including my parents, Sasha, and I even called my former therapist who helped me through my divorce to talk it over, because she knew my relationship with Darcy very well. It was Esther's question that settled it for me. She asked why I had told so many people about the reference request. I didn't have an answer for her, but a few days later it came to me. I had not only told a lot of people, I had told the very people who wouldn't respect me if I lied for Darcy. In telling all those people, I had armored myself against backing down from what I knew I had to do. The only choice left was how I was going to do it.

Should I send in the form filled out truthfully? Or

should I tell Darcy I wasn't able to lie for her and just not send it in? A long time ago I had told Darcy I would provide a job reference, but that means talking to someone on the phone about her strengths and glossing over her weaknesses, you don't ever volunteer information about a substance abuse problem. This was a direct question under oath. I never agreed to that. She didn't ask me about this ahead of time because she knew I'd say no. Her only hope was to put me on the spot. She was using me again, and it made me angry. I didn't agree to be used any more.

My phone rang one evening while I was out with friends. I saw it was Darcy and let it go to voice mail. Later, when I listened to her message, two things were clear; one, that she was drinking, and two, that she was stressed. Her message was uncharacteristically subdued and she asked me to please send in the form and call her if I had any questions.

The next day I sent her an e-mail that said I couldn't answer the form untruthfully and gave her a choice; I could send it in with the truth or I could not send it in and she could explain to them why not. The woman can charm the skin off a snake, I had no doubt she could think of a story. For three days we e-mailed back and forth. She said she had been sober for a year and a half, which I knew was a lie because I had spoken with her two months earlier and she was drunk then. At various times she claimed to have gone cold turkey on her own, to have used a private counselor, and to have gone to AA meetings (that'll be the day). The lies were worse than before because she wasn't even trying to stay consistent with her own story. She begged me to call her on the phone and I refused, and she never tried to call me. Finally she said to shred the form and she'd figure something out.

My neighbor, Jackie, used to work for the same agency in Human Resources and she said if I didn't send the form back, a lawyer would visit me at home to find out why not. I waited, but none ever came. Later I found out she got that job. I wondered briefly what story she told them, but didn't really care. I could live with my choice and that's all that mattered. And this time I was really free of Darcy. I felt a bit of a loss, but the friend I had loved wasn't in there any more, or if she was, she was buried too deep to retrieve.

I also realized that this moral crisis had been about who I am, now that this thing has happened to me. I understood from the beginning that my response to this situation would determine whether I had learned anything and changed as a result. I wasn't a person who could be sucked into the enabler role any more, not even temporarily to get rid of an unpleasant reminder of the past.

It struck me that I had been able to rely on my parents for moral guidance in this situation, and that had been the case all my life—my parents did what parents are supposed to do. Darcy hadn't had any sort of guide; her role models were alcoholics and she only saw chaos. The only principle they seemed to have passed down was the notion that they were better than other people because of their money. The secrets she kept because of her alcoholism prevented Darcy from having any meaningful friendships. I felt grateful for the solid support network I had, and a bit of compassion for Darcy.

The best part of having done the right thing was the note I got from Sasha telling me she was proud of me. Hearing that from her made it all worth it.

Victoria

The trip to Free Spirit had only been a few days long, but I'd had enough experiences to fill one of my old ten-day treks. I was addicted to bike touring anew. And it was a new style of touring now, I was beginning to understand. Instead of trying to pound out 80-mile days, I needed to schedule 30-40-mile days and learn to view the hostels as more than an inexpensive night stop. I had to do what didn't come naturally; turn more of my attention to being sociable. The hostels were a rich opportunity to meet people from all over. It was time to stop resisting those connections and embrace them.

I had learned about the Galloping Goose bike trail while in Victoria last summer. The connecting Lochside Trail, which many people mistakenly think *is* the Galloping Goose, runs from the ferry terminal in Sidney on the Saanich Peninsula to Victoria, where it transitions to the Galloping Goose and goes on to Sooke. I loved the Lochside and wanted to see the whole trail system. And something in me was obsessed with repeating everything I normally did every summer. Victoria was a new piece in the routine, but I wanted to go back. It was the last hostel I stayed in before I got hit, and going back was somehow reclaiming my life.

I decided to make it easy on myself and drive to the ferry terminal in Tsawwassen and pay for four days of parking. The alternative was to take another day to get there, and yet another to get back. I was busy at work and wanted to schedule a break without inconveniencing my clients. I actually worked two hours in the morning before rounding up the cats and leaving. I picked Kali up off my bed and plopped her outside on the patio, then locked the kitty door. Her indignant face conveyed perfectly, *"Dude, what the hell?"* I hated to separate the friends, but Kali belonged at home while I was gone, and Karen came to care for Nimby.

The ride on the ferry was great fun. I decided to hold off on getting my official vacation read until I found the mystery book store in Victoria, Chronicles of Crime. That was one local independent store I wanted to help stay in business. I had discovered it last year when I saw a black cat on the condo balcony above the store pacing back and forth over the sign as if to make sure I saw it. I asked inside, but the cat wasn't affiliated with the store, she just lived upstairs and advertised for free.

The Lochside Trail was such a pleasant ride! As I had only ridden it once before, I remembered everything but it still came as a happy surprise. I was actually disappointed by how fast I made it to Victoria. I checked in and claimed my lower bunk, then went to the market to stock up on food. Back at the hostel, I discovered I still couldn't open a lot of packages with my damaged hand. I went to the front desk and asked to borrow a scissor. I explained to the young man at the desk that I had stayed there last year just before getting hit. He said he thought he remembered me, wasn't I there with another lady? I said yes, but we hadn't known each other until we met there and made friends. He grinned and said that was what hostelling was all about. Then he got kind of choked up and said, "I'm really glad you came back. You know, that you *could* come back."

Several times while I was there, that young man walked into the kitchen commons and shouted at everyone to switch off their devices and talk to each other. "This is a hostel, man, not an internet café. You're here to meet people from all over the world, so *meet* someone." The use of electronic devices has become so isolating that some hostels have no-device policies in their common areas.

The hostel bed was brutal; it took five oxycodone to make it through the night. (My normal ration at this point would have been three; I was still taking five milligrams every three hours.) I woke up in a narcotic fog, still in so much pain that I woke an hour before my alarm was set to vibrate under my pillow. I needed that extra hour to get ready; I was moving very slowly. By the time I retrieved Silver from the bike room, though, I had psyched myself up for the day. The sun was brilliant at 7:30 and there was a fresh, cool polish on the morning. I stopped at the harbor to take a photo of a yacht with a helicopter mounted on the back and texted it to Kyle at Pier 57, whose family's lesser yacht had just been featured in Sunset Magazine. I captioned the photo, "It's okay, I still think you're a man."

The bus stop was actually a row of buses parked along one street. I had been prepared for this by a very helpful transit company employee on the phone. She had told me which bus to board, and to ask to make sure it turned into a different route when it reached the next town over. I wasn't sure exactly where to get off; the bus went down a rural highway and stops were few and far between. I saw a sign where the trail crossed the highway and pulled the cord to get off. It turns out I got off too early and missed the first 10 kilometers of the trail. By the end of the day I wasn't sorry. I pushed myself plenty hard as it was, and I had given myself an excuse to come back and do the trail again.

The trail went through an astonishing variety of landscapes. First it felt like I was back on the Swedish coast, with magnificent fjords and idyllic farms out on the delta lands. The trail surface was packed dirt with gravel, and the gravel made me feel a little off-balance and afraid of falling. I rode using the flat side of the pedals so my feet weren't cleated in. A few times the trail pitched steeply downhill and uphill again to cross short bridges over ravines. I walked those stretches. I wasn't willing to risk hurting myself again.

The trail was full of people that day, and in Canadian fashion, they all smiled and said hello. I wished I had a bike bell and I resolved to buy one as soon as I could. Later I found out it's the law, you have to have one in Canada. As a tourist I would never be ticketed, but as a "Wanadian" (their slang for wannabes), I wanted to conform.

The trail passed through an arid stretch where the bare dirt was yellow and fragrant juniper trees lined the trail. Later, I saw a painting by a Bellingham artist that so perfectly depicted the place, I asked him when he had seen it. He said the painting was of a hillside trail in Greece.

Silver and I wound through farms and residential areas as we got closer to town. Finally there was some development and I stopped at an A&W for lunch. The cold root beer never tasted so good.

That night after my shower, I put on my new convertible North Face pants and bright red taffeta blouse over a tan t-shirt. I even had matching short socks to wear with my cycling sandals. I felt coordinated in a way I'd never felt on the road before. I had never splurged on proper travel clothes before, but I'd used the rest of the money Uncle Hank sent me for the white bear hat to buy the outfit on sale. I hadn't allowed myself to spend that money until the quest was fulfilled. When I looked in the mirror, I was startled by how good my hair looked. It was the first good hair day I could remember since long before the crash. I almost asked someone to take my picture before I went to sleep on it and ruined it. A large amount of my hair had fallen out while I was in the hospital and it had looked thin and limp. The new growth was finally long enough to give it some volume. I looked vibrant, healthy, and perfectly normal. I felt pretty good too; the pain was giving me a break. The hostel bed broke that streak decisively, with another five-pill night.

The next day I went exploring. I rode into the Beacon Hill neighborhood, Victoria's answer to Seattle's Discovery Park area. I saw a young buck deer with fuzzy antlers happily munching on someone's front hedge. I tried to stop for a picture, but he leapt over the rock wall and bounded away with a spring in his step that I envied.

I got lost on my way back to town but wasn't even nervous; I was on the tip of an island, how far could I stray? When I started to get tired, I pulled over and consulted a map. It directed me back to town and I stopped at a Chinatown bubble tea shop where I had an "Evil Orchid" drink. While I sipped the bubble tea in the sun, Karen called and put Nimby on the phone to say hi to Mama.

I went back to the hostel and ate Vietnamese leftovers for lunch, then rode to the mystery book store, where I had a fun chat with the owner, and found the book I had left behind the year before, still waiting for me. Then I stopped at the bike shop and dropped Silver off to have her brakes tightened up—Chad had put in new cables and they had stretched out to the point where I wasn't stopping well. While they worked on my bike, I went to the bead shop and chatted with the owner there. Bead shops are a great way to learn about the culture and the native minerals of any region. I asked the shop owner what was unique to the area and she showed me some large pink-and-gray-mottled rhodonite beads. I planned to use them in a wedding present for Lauren, who is as big a Canadophile as I am.

There was a busker festival on the town square; street performers of all types were out doing their thing for tips. I went through all my Loonies very quickly. That evening I set out at 9:00 on a ride around town to see the twinkling all-white harbor lights. The streets were so crowded with happy revelers that I had to walk the bike most of the way.

The only disconcerting thing about the trip was my bunkmate. She appeared to be from China and spoke no English. She stayed in her bunk, disconsolately staring at a tablet computer, the entire time I was there. I never saw her get up. I couldn't tell if she was jet-lagged or depressed, and I couldn't talk to her to find out. Her suitcase was the size of a PT Cruiser and I had to stumble around it to get to my things.

On the way back to the ferry, I stopped at a senior art festival at a community center. I found a large boulder painted to look like a seal, but it looked a lot like Nimby, who with his mottled brown fur and his enormous size, looks like a sea lion when he's lying down. I took a photo of it and named it "Nimby Rock." I bought a black cat wall hanging for Vicki, our Humane Society board president. Vicki is an advocate for the black cats, who don't get adopted as readily as "more interesting" cats.

After I got home, I noted in my travel journal when you come home from a good resort, your own stuff seems like crap. When you come home from hostels, your own stuff seems luxurious. Even though I still had to sleep on my back and it was horrifically uncomfortable, I was really glad to be back in my own bed.

Singer 60

The next "reclaiming my life, returning to routine" event was the annual Singer 60 bike ride. Five years before, I had been at my friend Julie's house on the Hood Canal when we went next door to her cousin Nancy's for lunch. An older man was there, a neighbor named Harry Singer. Harry had seen my bike parked out in front of Julie and Nancy's shared driveway and was full of questions about it. He loved the story of Silver and invited me to join him on his annual "Singer 60" ride from the Southworth ferry terminal to his house, just down the road from Julie's and a mile north of my Aunt Bobbie's. Harry invited a group of friends every year and he decided, based on Silver, that I was Singer 60 material. After talking privately with Julie to make sure Harry was a safe person, I accepted. I don't like riding in groups or forced social situations, but this seemed like something I might not want to miss.

I had to get up awfully early to catch the ferry for the 9:00 start of the ride, but it was worth it. The course was gorgeous, the people were fun, and the ride ended with a barbeque on Harry's back deck and a camp-out in his huge beachfront back yard. The second year, since I was coming from Bellingham rather than Seattle, I decided to drive to his house the night before. I took a wrong turn and accidentally followed a pedestrian path down to the beach that I thought was his driveway. I had a hell of a time turning around in the sand, and as I drove back up the steep slope, the path dissolved beneath my wheels and the car slid over the edge. All that stood between me and a 60-foot plunge down a ravine was a blackberry thicket.

Carefully I removed Silver from the rack on the back, my feet sliding on the newly exposed sand. If the car was going down, it wasn't taking Silver with it.

I called Hyundai Roadside Assistance for help and no one could come until the next morning. Miraculously, the blackberry vines held the car overnight. I spent a restless night in Harry's guest room, listening to the neighbors' party get louder and drunker, sure that at some point they would tip the car down the ravine just to amuse themselves. In the morning, after the riders left, the tow truck driver was able to winch the car up to solid ground without a scratch. A neighbor drove me out to the town of Union so I could join the riders for lunch and the last stage of the ride.

After that I was a permanent fixture in the Singer 60 storytelling circle. The ride was a big summer event for me. I didn't quite fit into the group; they were racer-influenced and rode impractical racing-style bikes. They considered themselves bike tourists because they had ridden all over Canada and Europe supported by SUVs. That's not touring, that's sport riding. People whose bikes don't have luggage racks can't legitimately call themselves tourists. This bunch seemed to disdain my bike because it was slightly heavier than theirs. My bike turns like a bus because it's designed to handle stably with a load, and the lower center of gravity sacrifices a bit of agility. I couldn't do what I do on their bikes; the wheels would buckle and the frames would fatigue and break.

I sensed that I wasn't the perfect fit for the group, but Harry shared some of my attitudes and I think he invited me to join it in the hope of getting some old-school representation. Harry is an amazing athlete; at 77, he toured across Europe (with bags) after a hip replacement. Midway through Italy he came down with a severe infection and had to be airlifted back home, where they removed the offending replacement joint and left him with no hip for six weeks while the infection healed. He repeated the surgery, went through rehab, and was back on his bike the next summer! Not only that, he laid a hardwood floor in his beach house, something I wouldn't have tried *before* I got hit. Harry had been a role model for me during my recovery.

Last year I had taken the train to Kenn's place in Edmonds and had him drive me to the ferry the next morning, using the ride as the starting point for my 235-mile loop tour through Victoria. It had rained hard on last year's ride, but we still had fun. Well, most of us did. One of the riders, Lori, had five flat tires. I found her by the side of the road in tears on her fourth flat and offered her one of my puncture-resistant tubes. She recoiled as if I had offered her a cyanide capsule and said, "that thing weighs six ounces more than it needs to." I shrugged and said, "Well, I rode from Bellingham to Eugene without a flat using these. And I've spent zero time fixing flats by the road today, so from where I sit, *on my bike seat*, it doesn't look like I'm the chump." That was the point where I realized I might be done riding the Singer 60. It was a logistical nightmare to get there from Bellingham and I was feeling the love a little less every year.

This year, though, I had *something to prove*, and I was determined to ride the 60 (which was actually 64 miles, but who's counting?). I knew I couldn't make the full distance, so I offered to drive the support truck for half the shifts. Normally each rider takes a turn, but most would prefer not to, so I was popular again. I had to bring a staggering amount of stuff with me and I had to manage all of it on the ferry with my bike. I had driven to Kenn's and he drove me to the ferry, and I barely made it on the boat without piling my gear all over the ramp. My left shoulder ached with the strain of holding the load upright.

I had to stay on the auto deck for the whole ride because I didn't want to leave all that stuff unattended. On the other side, I only had to flounder a short distance to Harry's truck, where I unloaded the inflatable bed (a simple air mattress wouldn't do with my ravaged spine) with electric pump, and all my gear.

This year there were about a dozen riders, most of them "regulars." I rode the first portion of the ride, the pleasant jaunt along the shoreline to the public market in Manchester. It was good to see everyone again. Some of them had heard what had happened, others had no idea. I kept pace with Mary Ann, a long-time rider, and we chatted between spurts of fast riding to catch up to everyone else. I drove the truck past some construction in the second portion and Lynn, Fred's wife, rode in the truck with me. The construction was a little more than she wanted to deal with. We had a fun conversation and I realized I'd never really gotten to know Lynn before. On the third portion, Mary Ann asked if I'd ever considered buying a lighter bike. Well, that didn't take long. It struck me that Mary Ann had not lifted my bike and had no idea whether it was heavy or not. The fact is, a good lugged steel frame only weighs about a pound more than an aluminum frame, and it's birdlike and graceful and holds up in a crash, unlike aluminum, which crumples and shears apart like a soda can. I was tired of educating the crowd to the real world of touring bikes every summer.

Back at the house, we had the usual cookout with lots and lots of beer and wine, and everything cooked on the grill. Fred and Lynn had brought zucchini that they sliced down the middle and grilled. I wished I'd thought of that. I had brought nitrate-free sausages and had to keep mine carefully segregated from the identical ones that were cured; the nitrates give me blurred vision, lethargy and disorientation. I had to hover over the grill to make sure no one mixed up the meats.

We spent the cool summer evening playing horseshoes and sitting around a beach fire. I tossed rocks into the water to startle the bioluminescent plankton. A soft glow bloomed around each splash. Harry drew me back into the group and taught me to play horseshoes. I was terrible at it but it was fun. People kept trying to correct my technique and I dropped out of the game. Technique wasn't an option yet; I was still learning to use my reattached hand. All I wanted to do was lose the game laughing.

The conversation around the fire turned political and I was amazed to find out I was in a bunch of Republicans. The region is generally very liberal and I've always enjoyed being able to express my majority opinions in safety, especially after spending four repressive years in Missouri. Conservatives exist in Washington, definitely, and especially in the rural areas like the Canal where we were (but most of these people came from the city).

Cyclists tend to be nature lovers and conservationists, so I had expected this group to lean toward the left. Jim told a story about "having the honor to meet Newt Gingrich," who I consider to be a downright evil man. I politely kept my mouth shut until someone noticed and remarked upon my silence. I said, "I'm sorry, I'm a tree-hugging, gay-marriage-supporting, pro-choice, separation of church and state defending, ACLU card carrying pinko." At least this explained their comfort with using SUVs to support their bike travels. Drill, baby, drill.

At bedtime I hooked up the electric pump for my inflatable bed and claimed a spot on the living-room floor. It was a cool night and a lot of people didn't want to bother pitching their tents. They dragged their sleeping bags inside and the floor was covered with bodies. People looked at my large air bed and I felt like they were judging me for taking up too much space. The bed was noisy, too, every time I moved it made vinyl farting sounds. As I pulled on my night wrist braces and put on my elastic head gear to keep my mouth closed while sleeping on my back, people looked away in embarrassment. I wished they would all just go sleep outside and let me be.

Mornings were always good on the Singer 60. The group banded together and made a big breakfast, and everyone pitched in to clean up. I was brutally sore and sleep-deprived after the night on the air bed, but I popped a pain pill and got ready to do my share.

I stepped out to the beach first to call Kenn and ask him to come get me in his van. I didn't want to have to struggle back across on the ferry with all this gear. I'd reached the end of my pain tolerance, and keeping a smiling face through breakfast was going to be as much as I could do. It would take Kenn two hours to get there and it was a lot to ask, but I needed a bailout.

I offered up the rest of my nitrate-free sausage to share, and Gertie, Harry's girlfriend, enthusiastically took them to cook up. I wasn't paying attention and found that every last bite of sausage had been cut up and mixed into scrambled eggs. With my egg allergy, I wasn't getting any protein that morning. I took a couple pancakes—only enough egg in those to produce a light case of the sniffles and a rash on my chest.

After breakfast I took my place at the sink and washed dishes until my hands pruned up. My back was screaming but I wanted to do my part, and standing at the sink offered me a bit of social escape. Finally Kenn arrived and sat and chatted with everyone for a few minutes until I prodded him to help me load up. I hugged everyone and we were on our way.

As we climbed the steep driveway, I was glad I had participated, but even more glad to be going home. On the long ride back, I reflected that I'd proven what I needed to, but another lesson I had learned from the crash is that life is short, we don't have enough time, and we mustn't spend it in ways that don't fulfill us. With only a light pang of regret, I let my heart say good-bye to the Singer 60.

You Are Here, Again

My last bike trip of the summer was planned for September, when it can be one of two ways here; Indian summer or monsoon season, with nothing in between. My friend Jamie, the promoter for the Wailin' Jennys, had e-mailed to say the Jennys were playing in Vancouver on Friday night, at a small theater on East Broadway. Jamie offered to pick me up and give me a ride, but it was the perfect excuse to take one last weekend of summer on the bike. I could wear my convertible pants with a nice top to the show. Finally, I would have the chance to tell Ruth Moody about how her song, "You Are Here," affected me. The Jennys have throngs of fans who all want face time after the show—their after-show reception tends to be as long as the performance, so I wrote Ruth a letter in advance in case I didn't get any one-on-one time with her. I hated having to type it, but my hand went numb after three lines of writing and I would never make it to the end without a mistake.

The trip was hastily planned and poorly timed, as I needed to be in Seattle for work the following Monday. The final permits had been approved, after various delays that had made for an anxious summer, work-wise, and I had to be there for the first day of construction. I decided to take the train to Vancouver, to make sure I got home on time and to save my energy for enjoying the weekend, rather than getting there and back.

After I arrived on the train, I rode straight to the theater where the Jennys were performing so I could scope out the bike parking situation. There was a rack right out front, but there was also a large encampment of homeless people across the street at the Skytrain station. There was no way I was leaving Silver locked out in front of the theater from seven o'clock until after eleven. I decided to take the bus from the hostel. That meant a four-block walk alone in the dark when I got back, but it was preferable to risking Silver. The guy at the hostel desk assured me it was a safe walk and many people took the bus back to the hostel late at night after an evening at the bars downtown.

I had made my hostel reservation over the phone and asked for a bottom bunk. When I got there, I saw that they had given me the disability accommodation area, a single set of bunks in a room by itself at the end of the dorm. It was a long way to the bathroom, but it was ever so private and I loved it. There was lots of extra storage space and even a set of five hooks on the wall. I had my own light and switch and could close the door between my area and the rest of the dorm.

I arrived on Thursday and the show wasn't until Friday night, so I went to Banyen Books, my favorite bookstore (the one where I discovered the Wailin' Jennys' music), and bought the book *Sarah's Key*. That book kept me up late reading, I could barely put it down. I'd had no idea that the infamous roundup of Parisian Jews in World War II had taken place in a velodrome, a bike racing stadium.

In the morning I explored the campus at the University of British Columbia. I found the Chan Center, where I had seen the Jennys last, and where an episode of Psych had recently been filmed, using the center as the venue for a sci-fi "con." I poked around the student bookstore a bit. The weather was cloudy and I was really just killing time before the show. I went back to the hostel for a nap, knowing I'd be out late that night. I still wasn't making it through most days without a nap.

At 3:00 I walked up the hill to the bus stop and caught a bus downtown. I got off at the wrong place, on the wrong side of the Burrard Street Bridge. It didn't matter, I stood there orienting myself for a minute, then walked to the nearest Skytrain station. I zipped to the Commercial Drive station and there I was, on the restaurant strip known as "The Drive." I was to meet Jamie at an Ethiopian restaurant there. He was waiting out front and stepped out and waved. We hugged and he introduced me to his friend Joe, his niece, Maureen, and her friend from France, Valerie.

The Ethiopian menu was overstimulating—everything sounded good, and I wasn't allergic to a thing on it. We ordered a large sampler plate with a bit of everything. It was a double-dipper-phobe's nightmare; we all scooped from one dish using the spongy Ethiopian bread that forms the base of the cuisine. The one woman who appeared to do everything—wait, cook and serve—scuttled over to admonish me to eat with my right hand. I showed her my ravaged right wrist and said I understood the custom (based on the cultural assumption of the left hand being the one that does bathroom duty), but my left hand was clean and I truly couldn't manage the food with my right. She apologized profusely and said, "Eat how you like, and may God grant you fast healing." I thought that was just perfectly gracious and left a huge tip.

After dinner the girls wanted to go to a pub. The drinking age in BC is nineteen and it's twenty-one in Washington. The girls were twenty and it was a thrill for them to be able to get a legal beer. I had a hard cider—I had recently discovered at trivia that hard cider is lower in alcohol than beer or wine and it looks like I'm drinking a beer (which I am allergic to because of the barley). It was important to me to blend in and not look "special." We had a delightful time at the pub until Jamie and I got nervous about getting good seats and we agreed to run ahead and get in line while the girls had another round.

While Jamie and I stood against the wall in line, a young man came up and introduced himself to Jamie;

he was another one of Jamie's "adoptees." Jamie had met Paul via the blog on the Wailin' Jennys web site and had agreed to meet him in person at the show. As one of Jamie's web site adoptees myself, I could hardly begrudge Paul. The nerdy young Asian-Canadian man seemed a little needy and unsure of himself, and Jamie picked up on that vibe quickly and tried to disengage himself a little. I decided it wouldn't cost me anything to be nice to the guy and took up some of Jamie's social slack.

When the doors opened, Jamie rushed for the front row and claimed the center seats. Paul sat between Jamie and me, and after an initial flash of annoyance, I decided to be okay with that. The show was amazing, as always, and we were so close that the Jennys recognized us and grinned. When they sang "You Are Here," I wept openly. Paul looked at me in alarm; Jamie reached across him to squeeze my hand.

After the show, Paul got in line with us to meet the Wailin' Jennys. I could see it was a huge moment for him, just as it had been for me, so I introduced him to the ladies, Nicky Mehta, Heather Massey, and Ruth Moody. Each of them is my favorite Jenny for a different reason. Nicky for her poetic lyrics, Heather for her versatile voice and style, and Ruth for the unabashed emotional intimacy of her songs. As I reached Ruth in the line, I handed her the envelope with my note and said it was for her to read later, but please do read it, it was about her song, "You Are Here," and it was important to me that she know what it meant to me. Ruth gave me a slightly nervous but gracious smile and slipped the note in the pocket of her dress. After the line dispersed and we were alone with the ladies, I chatted a bit with Nicky about the lyrics in her songs. Then it was time to go. I could see that Paul had hoped for a longer-lasting connection, a more earth-shattering experience, so I took him aside and said, "Now you follow them on their web site, you keep posting on their blog, but only real stuff that's worth reading, not just to take up space, and you follow the musicians that they talk about too, get in on the whole scene. They have their lives and their families and friends; you need to make your friends on the fan side." As someone with an "in," he didn't really want to hear that from me, but I felt for him and wanted to leave him with a path toward the connections he craved.

I was exhausted from staying up late and from the intensely emotional evening. I said good-night to everyone and Jamie asked how I was getting back to the hostel. I eyed the homeless encampment on the sidewalk, rowdy on this mild fall evening, and asked if he would mind walking me to the Skytrain station. He said don't be ridiculous, he could give me a ride back to the hostel.

Like most tech-savvy men, Jamie preferred to listen to his GPS rather than believe I knew the way, so I saw a new part of the city on the way back. At the hostel he got out to say good night and two men who were staying at the hostel came up and talked to us. Jamie enjoyed chatting with them and I stayed outside with everyone until Jamie was ready to go, then hugged him good night.

The next morning was rainy and I rode to the Museum of Vancouver to spend part of the day looking at three big exhibits: Vancouver Through the Decades (there was a '50s exhibit called Dorothy's Dream House and I spent a long time waiting for the video on the big black-and-white television to flash the title so I could show it to my mom), an exhibit on gay and lesbian families of choice, and an exhibit on the east Indian Bhangra music that is so popular in Vancouver. Vancouver has the second largest population of Indian people outside India in the world—London has the largest. The Bhangra exhibit had musical instruments commonly found in Bhangra bands set out on tables, with short videos showing people how to play them. I had to take frequent breaks to sit down because my back was so sore from the big night out before. The steely grip on my fracture site that I called "the Clamp" slid out of my control on any long diversion from my routine.

The sun came out and I got to ride on the shore-line trail for a while, then it was time to take the train home.

Three months later, I attended Ruth's solo show in Mt. Vernon with Jamie and some more of his friends. After the show, we were invited to the Green Room party in the basement, where Jamie served his home-made maple ice cream, which was pure heaven. Ruth said a warm hello, then I said, "back in Vancouver in September, I gave you a letter—"

"Oh my God, Kristin!" Ruth pulled me into a hug and when we pulled away, both our eyes were wet. Ruth had been at her parents' house in Victoria when she found the letter in her dress pocket while sorting laundry. She read it, then brought it downstairs to show her parents. Ruth loved that her music connected us in that way. I was glad I shared that with her, I just had a feeling it would mean something to her. Ruth wears her heart on her sleeve, and it's a good heart.

Construction Day

Finally, the Ferris wheel construction was back on again. I had to be in Seattle to do marine mammal monitoring, watching for whales while the crew pulled piles with a vibratory hammer. I dearly hoped not to see anything out there. Our schedule was way too tight to accommodate a shutdown!

Already I had to apply for an extension of our environmental permits. We had to be able to finish the in-water work in order to install the wheel above the deck on time. In salmon country, there are "approved work windows," set by the Army Corps of Engineers and state wildlife agencies, for the protection of juvenile migrating salmon. Our work window slammed shut on February 15, when the first fry were expected to emerge from the mouth of the Green/Duwamish River system. It would take a miracle to finish the work by then. It would take at least three months to process the extension request, in which I had to demonstrate how the work we'd be doing during the extension period would not harm the juvenile fish. I was suddenly very busy.

Around 11:00, Kyle came out to my perch on the third-floor balcony with his girlfriend, Jenny, and a gift-wrapped box. He bounded up to me like a golden retriever and hugged me hard, and said, "This—(and gestured to the workers on the pier) is all you. This would never have happened without you." He handed me the box and I opened what I knew to be two dozen of the most expensive caramels available in the city, wrapped with a silk ribbon that Nimby claimed immediately upon my arrival home a week later.

The construction crew invited me to have a drink with them in the bar after work. I drank my chardonnay and held off on my much-needed pain pill until I got to Kenn's house, where I was staying for the week. I would be working in Seattle every other week until construction was completed. I could have worked down there every week, but I couldn't physically handle more than four days at a stretch, and I couldn't leave Nimby with his sitter for five months. We hired extra people to pick up the monitoring work.

After the small-pile work, which only required one monitor, they started driving the "big cans" and three of us were required. Brad took the pier point as lead monitor, my friend and coworker Paul took Alki Point, and I took Magnolia Bluff. Work started at sunrise and we had to be out watching the water twenty minutes before the vibratory hammer started. It took a good thirty minutes to set the pile in place for vibing, so they lifted the pile off the barge in the dark and set it in the water just as the first gray of dawn made it possible to see. We couldn't see anything on the water until the red glow just before sunrise, so that's when the twenty-minute clock started.

Getting up at a specified time was hard for me; I still slept fitfully and I was much healthier when I could wake up naturally in the morning. On this job, I usually hit my deep sleep phase right around the time I had to get up.

The mornings were freezing and I came dressed in my winter gear plus a fleece-lined stadium blanket poncho. Despite my bundling up, I was chilled to the bone and my pain level was intense. By noon the sun, if it made an appearance, warmed me up to the point where I felt drowsy and fought to stay awake. Once I must have dozed for a minute, because I woke up when my head fell forward to find that someone had left $2 on the bench beside me. People thought I was homeless! With my expensive scope hidden under the blanket when I wasn't using it, I guess they would.

One day I thought I spotted two very small orcas

swimming into the harbor. I ran alongside them on the hillside as far as I could, oblivious to anything but keeping the critters in my sight. They disappeared, but they were too close to shore and too small to be orcas; they were probably Dall's porpoises, the small black-and-white dolphins that were often mistaken for orcas. Two baby orcas would not be swimming together without an adult orca watching, but I took my responsibility seriously and had to make sure of what I saw. After the run, I stopped to catch my breath and the Clamp set in with a vengeance.

This cycle of freezing mornings and warmish afternoons went on for two four-day shifts. Then I had a bitterly cold windy day. I sat in the car with my spotting scope as much as I dared. The view wasn't as good as it was out on the park bench, but it was too cold out there. The plate in my arm throbbed; the metal couldn't retain warmth like bone and it chilled my arm from the inside out. It rained off and on.

When I checked in with Brad that night, I said I couldn't do it anymore, it was too much. We agreed to trade places. I got the pier loft and balcony and he got Magnolia Park. I found I could see the entire bay from indoors with my spotting scope if I sat on the upper tier of the abandoned food court. There were dusty old glass-cased diorama exhibits from the gold rush era up there. I thought of Kyle and his brother growing up in this place, with their own merry-go-round and all this unused space upstairs with so much to explore. It must have been magic.

The magic wore thin for me very quickly as I discovered that the circus music that blared from the carousel was on a five-song loop that ran from open to close. My iPod could not drown it out. The industrial ear plugs I wore during pile driving, plus the numbing noise of the pile driving, *almost* drowned it out, but still I could hear *"Take me out to the ballgame..."* One day when I knew Brad was home, I took a video clip of the carousel roof from the mezzanine, with audio, and sent it to him. He cursed me, saying he'd actually gone a few hours without hearing circus music in his head and I ruined it.

The End of an Era

In October I received word that the hostel in Port Townsend was closing. This was a crushing loss to the cycling community. Hostels in the US are few and far between, and this was a special asset in the hostel network. Because most of its patrons were older than typical hostel users, it was known as The Grayhair Hostel. Having gone gray at 40 and refused to color up, I was an exuberant representative of that demographic. Port Townsend was the first hostel I ever stayed in and I had a strong attachment to the place.

A final party was scheduled for the weekend after Thanksgiving. I decided to go, and since Kenn had never been to a hostel before, and it would make the logistics much easier, I invited him. Kenn travels with a truly incredible amount of stuff and I knew he'd have to have a private room. I wanted to be in the dorm because I'd stayed there so many times before and I wanted to meet the other women who would be there.

We left on the sunny morning after Thanksgiving and got all the way to the ferry terminal on Whidbey Island, about 60 miles, when I realized I didn't have my pain pills. How was that even possible? I couldn't make it without my pain pills. We had reserved ferry tickets because the ferry has a small vehicle capacity, but we had to turn back for the tedious return drive. We got the pills and headed back, arriving at the ferry around 4:00 in the afternoon. There was room to get us on so they honored our expired tickets. Later I discovered I'd had a back-up bottle of pills in the pocket of my bike bag all along; it was buried under my lock.

The hostel was packed and people camped in vans in the parking lot. Lots of people dropped by but didn't stay, just to say good-bye. All the furniture was gone from the common room except the big old dining-room

table with postcards and foreign currency contribut-
ed by guests under a clear acrylic top, so people stood
to talk. I could only make it a few minutes at a time
before I had to ask someone to let me sit down in one
of the two remaining straight-back chairs, or take a
break in my room.

A roommate from my first stay at that hostel was
there for the party. We caught up (my story was a little
too interesting) and fondly re-read our entries in the
guest book from all those years ago.

We had brought an extra pumpkin pie from
Thanksgiving and a young tour group from Scan-
dinavia attacked it like piranhas. I spoke a little
Swedish with one of the girls, Monika. The boys in
that group carried on loudly all night—we did not
sleep much. They had some of the worst beds in the
system and I wouldn't have slept much anyway. They
were conventional twin beds with mattresses so worn
out, you could have rolled them up like sleeping bags.

In the morning when I came up for breakfast, Kenn
was already eating with his new friend, a 93-year-old
man named Worth. Like Kenn, Worth was a ham radio
operator and they set up a radio in the common room
and played with it for a bit while I got to know Worth's
daughter, Heather. Worth and I took turns using one of
the scarce chairs while most people stood. It felt odd to
accept a chair from a 93-year-old man, and I probably
imagined the people looking at me when I did.

After breakfast, I showed Kenn the concrete bunkers from World War II in the park nearby. It was too
cold to stay out long; a scouring wind ensured that I
would get no pain relief before lunch. Still, the bunkers
were so fascinating that we had to explore. I imagined
making a hostel out of the old bunkers, with their gun-
sight windows and a dining area modeled after a military mess hall. I would stay in a hostel like that.

Leaving the hostel was almost too sad to bear. So

many memories, and such a necessary place. A group is trying to restore it, and I hope they do. The US needs a hostel system on par with Canada's. Hostelling is good for Americans; it pulls us out of our own little world and forces us to join the real one.

This is Not America

I began to get an inkling that my attorney wasn't a winner when I received a form that he had filled out on my behalf, for my signature. The form was filled out in pencil and looked like a third-grader had printed it in sloppy block letters. I sent Keith Beckstrom an e-mail saying that the form concerned me, that I expected a certain minimum standard of quality and I would never send anything like this to one of my clients. I asked him to resend the form properly typed. He was offended, but so was I! I showed the form to my mom and she said, "You got a dud, didn't you?" I was afraid she was right.

The other thing that bothered me was that Keith never got angry or even slightly passionate on my behalf, and he seemed to think I shouldn't want anything, that being alive should be enough. I was plenty grateful to be alive, but living was proving to be expensive. My total medical bills were approaching $1 million, my ability to generate income was reduced, and I needed a real advocate. I sent all my copies from the case file to another attorney, one who specialized in cycling law. I had no idea this man existed before then or he'd have been the first one I called. He reviewed the case and said he couldn't do any better for me, but he sympathized with my feelings about my attorney's attitude.

The issue had nothing to do with what I should be entitled to, and everything to do with who paid. The insurance companies' liabilities were limited to those spelled out by the policies we had purchased. The driver who hit me would normally be personally liable for anything over and above that amount, but my insurance company performed an asset review on him and found him to be more or less penniless, with low future earning potential. They did not want to get involved in pursuing additional damages. There is no other source for the money in cases like this, at least in Washington state. Other states have funds to compensate victims in cases like mine. In Washington there has to be a crime committed, and apparently causing damages you can't pay for isn't a crime a here. I went by his home and saw a shiny new white Dodge Ram pickup out front. I took issue with the fact that he received a new vehicle; they should have given his compensation to the victim in this case where he couldn't meet the total damages, but insurance law doesn't work that way.

Things were wrapping up with the attorney and it had slowly, over a period of months, dawned on me that I wasn't getting any settlement. Here, in the country where you get $8 million for spilling hot coffee in your own crotch, I was going to walk away broke with a permanently maimed hand. I was entitled to $50,000 from each insurance policy, the hitter's and my own. Anything I still owed the hospital would be taken from this amount, and my attorney got a third of it as his fee. When I signed the contract, I thought anything he got me *that I wouldn't have been entitled to without his help* was the amount I paid a third of. He didn't get me a dime over and above what I was already entitled to. Perhaps he protected some of it from claims by others, and perhaps he advocated a bit with the insurance companies to cover my medical bills, but honestly, what he did could have been done by a paralegal. Like me. If I hadn't been distracted by the business of learning to walk and use my hand again. What I had to pay him amounted to a year's salary for me, and he did maybe two week's work for it.

I felt used and shafted. I couldn't sue the guy who hit me because he didn't have anything to sue for. I was prepared to sue for his family business, where he lived in a trailer behind the shop, but the attorney wouldn't have anything to do with that. I wanted to garnish the guy's wages for life. I wanted him to feel a lifetime of the pain he inflicted on me so carelessly. It was hard to keep my sunny outlook with the knowledge that he wasn't going to have to do anything for me. Lying in the ICU, I had been sustained by the thought that at least working would be optional for the rest of my life. As an American, I had every right to think that. Why should it make any difference that I was hit by someone who had no assets? Does that mean that all poor people are free to commit negligent near-manslaughter with no consequences? I firmly believe that if the tables were turned and I hit someone else, I would not get away without consequences. Why could he?

A billboard sprang up near my house that said "Buy liquor for a minor and face a $5,000 fine." I wanted to spray paint below it, "Hit a cyclist and it's only $150."

After the President of the Cascade Bicycle Club contacted me, I wrote an affidavit in support of the Vulnerable Road Users' Bill, which is now law, thanks in part to my testimony. Anyone who hits a cyclist or pedestrian now faces an automatic 90-day license suspension and minimum $5,000 fine. During the suspension, the driver's record is reviewed and if the record is bad enough, the license is permanently revoked.

I wrote an appeal of my own case to Washington's Attorney General, Rob McKenna, and received the most patronizing response—it made me cry, it was so bad. Basically, they said I had no recourse, but they were glad that such a good and productive citizen survived—I read between the lines "to pay more taxes." Rob McKenna ran for Governor that year and I told everyone I could about his letter in the hope that it might sway them from voting for him.

Amid all this, I had to argue with my health insurance company to pay for the regular chiropractic care and massage therapy I needed in order to keep going. The company argued that I wasn't experiencing any long-term improvement as a result of the treatment. My doctors and I argued back that I would eventually reach a plateau in my physical healing, but I needed the maintenance care to keep from backsliding.

The day finally came when I went to Keith Beckstrom's office to sign the settlement forms. It took everything I had to lift the pen with my mangled hand and sign my rights away in order to collect the paltry amount now.

And I didn't even walk away with a check that day. The money was released into an escrow account, where the attorney would take his fee off the top and then send me what was left. By my accounting, he took too much. I still owed the hospital $9,000 and that should have been subtracted from the total before figuring in his fee. I felt too beaten down to fight it. I just wanted to end our association and get out of there. To this day, I tear up his holiday cards before pitching them in the recycling bin.

To help me work through my feelings, I sent a letter to my insurance agent's manager. I told her how I had stated explicitly to my agent that I was more interested in good coverage than low premiums. The agent never showed me any tables comparing coverage levels and rates; I did not know such tables existed before my new agent showed them to me. A policy that offered $1.3 million per accident only cost $25 per month more than I was already paying! My old agent had not even told me about that policy. I would have jumped at the chance to buy it back then.

Sending that letter helped, even though I heard nothing back and never expected to. My insurance agency's web site, with the smug banner, "We have your back!" angered me and I had to let them know they hadn't had my back at all.

I began working on a letter to the guy who hit me. This one would take months to write.

And a Wheel Takes Shape

Monitoring continued in Seattle through the winter. The harsh January and February weather kicked in and I was very grateful to be working indoors. We had hired some extra help to do the outdoor monitoring, young college students who were better able to withstand long hours in the cold than we were. One week I sent my friend Chris down to work in my place, because I had the flu. I was incapacitated twice as much as an average person with the flu, because of the increased body aches and the strain on my spine and ribs every time I threw up.

A snowstorm hit while Chris was in Seattle and he was stranded down there an extra week. He stayed in a motel and was an extraordinarily good sport about it, considering he has a wife and two young children at home, and he was responsible for child care after school.

Even after I recovered, I just wasn't able to brave the weather and come down to take his place. The Amtrak wasn't running because of the winter landslides over the track, and I wasn't able to drive in the snow—not because I lacked the skill, Lord knows I learned to drive on solid ice, but because the post-traumatic stress kicked in and I panicked over the lack of control. I could just barely make the drive in good weather.

It turned out I was needed back in the office anyway; our extension was not being readily approved and it looked like work might stop on February 15. That would spell financial disaster for Hal and Kyle, and I lived in terror of failing them and derailing this huge project. I spent my days writing supporting arguments for an extension and discussing them with the regulatory agencies.

Finally, on February 14, I received the extension. It couldn't possibly have been cut any closer. I was back down in Seattle by this time, trying to negotiate the extension while keeping both eyes on the water, returning calls when the hammer was idle and I could actually hear the phone. When I got the e-mail with the extension attached, I called Simon immediately, then Kyle. Kyle and Hal were out of town but Kyle whooped with joy. Later, after work, we all went to the Fisherman bar to celebrate. The workers whose jobs I had saved all came by to thank me, and more glasses of wine were put in front of me than I could possibly drink. (Two glasses would put me down for the count those days.) Lucky for me, Kenn took the bus to work. I asked him to work late and walk down to the pier and pick me up with my car on the way home.

Kyle called from his Crab Pot restaurant in California and asked to be put on speaker. He announced the good news about the extension that we'd already heard, and he said in honor of Simon's and my achievements, drinks were on the house tonight. A deafening cheer went up from the work crew. Simon and I hugged each other with tears in our eyes. Never mind that I could barely stagger downstairs when Kenn arrived, as much from pain as from drink, it was a Very Good Day.

Full Circle:
On the Other Side of the Scrubs

Between work shifts in Seattle, my friend Kathleen who served with me on the board asked me to come over one afternoon. Kathleen was about to have knee replacement surgery. Her late husband's family had offered to stay with her and coach her through her recovery, but she wanted to find out if I would be her coach. I had told her about how my mom wasn't able to hurt me enough to effectively coach my therapy exercises, and her worry wasn't so much that her own relatives wouldn't be able to hurt her, but that they wouldn't recognize the importance of follow-through and they'd let her get away with not trying. She knew I understood and would push her as hard as I had pushed myself.

I was honored to be asked and didn't hesitate to say yes. It was a huge time commitment, but we were almost done with the monitoring work and I would have the time. I attended a six-hour class for patients and their coaches to prepare for the surgery and recovery. The class was given in a room on the third-floor surgical ward where I had spent two weeks. As I made my way to the classroom, I ran into all kinds of familiar nurses. One big man named Curtis stopped and we stared at each other a second before we remembered each other—Curtis had been an ICU nurse when I was there. He couldn't believe I remembered him. I said of course I remembered him, he was one of my favorites. He stopped, genuinely surprised, and asked why. I said, "Because when I picked on you, you slung it back hard. You treated me like a real person and not a fragile thing. You can hardly imagine what that means when you feel like you're not a real person any more." Curtis blinked back tears and said, "I was having the worst day of my life before you came along and made it the best," and hugged me hard.

I asked if Agnes was there, the nurse who had fed me so well, but she was off that day.

The class was mostly repetitive information, since I had used the therapy gym alongside joint replacement patients for months already, but I listened carefully anyway, determined to be a good coach for Kathleen. I think my comfort in the hospital environment was reassuring to her, even if I did tend to steal the show.

Kathleen's surgery was on a morning in April. I went to see her around dinner time, giving her plenty of time to recover and nap before bothering her. When I got there, she looked shockingly white and fragile, and I found out why—her surgery had complications and she had to go back again the following morning. She was already on her limited food and water to prepare. My heart went out to her. Her classmates would have their first therapy session the next day while she went back under the knife. The change in her therapy schedule threw a wrench in my plans and I went home to rearrange my week.

The next day Kathleen looked much better. Her second surgery had gone well and she was rallying for the recovery phase. I couldn't believe she wasn't taking the time out she must have needed so badly. She was excited for her first therapy session and ready to make up for the extra day of not eating. She sent me to the cafeteria to get her a gluten-free chocolate-dipped cookie.

At her first therapy session, I could see she was determined to catch up to the rest of the group. She was a day behind and the therapist made sure she didn't overdo it, but she was so determined to try. I decided I had a worthy patient who hadn't really needed me to push her, she was pushing herself plenty hard.

We did therapy at the hospital for two days, then Kathleen got sent home. Her late husband's brother and his wife were staying with her so I didn't have to do anything for a few days, but I came by to check on her and make sure she was getting both her therapy sessions each day. One day she had skipped a session and I was appropriately disapproving. The in-laws slapped me away like a mosquito. Oh well, I thought, they're leaving soon and I'll be coaching, and we'll see who misses therapy then!

There was one day when Kathleen just wasn't getting started and it got to be 1:00 in the afternoon. I gave up and got ready to leave for a ride. At 1:15 she called and said she was ready. I said I'd see her at 3:00 and pushed off for my ride. As much as I felt for her, she needed to respect my time too and I explained that as kindly as I could. She took it surprisingly well.

After a week of in-home therapy, Kathleen was ready to go to the rehab center, the same one where I went. I drove; Kathleen wouldn't be able to drive again for several weeks. I folded her lightweight walker into the back seat and tried to be as attentive to the getting-in-and-out process as I could. I remembered being left behind when I couldn't unbuckle myself and didn't want to inflict that feeling on her. It was weird going back into the rehab center and actually checking in for an appointment. I'd had the run of the place for so long. I remembered to respect Kathleen's autonomy and let her check herself in.

In the gym area, the therapists all knew me and came to see how I was doing. I introduced Kathleen and made sure everyone knew we were there for her, not me. The therapists loved having me on the other side of the scrub suit and most of them called me "Rock Star." I told them Kathleen was their new rock star. It didn't take long for her to deserve the praise. Her range-of-motion measurements were off the chart.

Kathleen's surgical complications and her less-than-perfect home therapy regimen hadn't held her back at all, she was at the top of the class. My respect for her grew and I made sure she got her share of the attention.

There was an East Indian woman there, Ravinder, who had terrible pain and the therapy was especially difficult for her. A young man came with her as her coach one day, and I recognized him as one of my nurses from the inpatient center upstairs. I reminded him who I was and he beamed with recognition. Ravinder spoke very little English, so I asked him to tell her I thought her name was beautiful, and that he had been my nurse upstairs. When Ravinder understood, I looked at her and said slowly, "Your son is a very good man. You should be proud of him." She and her son both beamed, and Ravinder seemed to have a better session that day. I realized how important it is to feel some connection to the other patients, and how hard it would be if you felt isolated. From that day on, Ravinder and I always smiled at each other, and she reached out to make friends with other patients. Her son reported that she was learning more English from being exposed to more people.

Kathleen recovered so quickly, the sessions were over before I knew it. It kind of made me realize how seriously I had been injured, that I was in therapy so much longer. Kathleen had her other knee done a year later and she coached her best friend through a knee replacement.

Mother's Day

It was looking like my parents wouldn't be able to make it out this summer. Kenn was going to meet his brother in Minneapolis and see a baseball game. He had a friend-fly-free ticket and offered to take me along so I could go to my parents' house while he hung out with his brother. I was nervous about flying; I was told that my lung damage could make the air pressure change painful. My niece, Leah, got married in Florida the weekend before and I chose not to go, partly because of the cost and partly because I was afraid to commit to a six-hour flight. My family understood my decision but they were disappointed. Going for Mother's Day might make up for a bit.

I bought a connecting flight from Bellingham so the travel wouldn't be so grueling. I don't understand people who fly in and out of Seattle; it's only $60 more for the round trip from Bellingham than taking a shuttle bus, and it saves four hours. My wage bracket made that a no-brainer. I also believe in paying for convenience; my time and sanity are worth a few dollars.

The small-plane flight to Seattle was easy. When we boarded the jet to Minneapolis, that's when the trouble started. Just like the Seinfeld episode where Jerry flies first class and Elaine flies coach, Kenn upgraded his ticket as his club status allowed, and boarded before I did. I flipped him off on my way back to coach. The jostling of the cattle-car boarding system was intolerable. I took several direct hits in the arm plate. When I sat in my aisle seat, it wasn't over—I had to get back up to let my seat mates in and they jostled me too.

Using the bathroom was miserable; it was so hard to maneuver in that tiny closet without hurting myself. The flight was a "redeye" and we were scheduled to arrive in Minneapolis at 5:00 AM, 3:00 AM by our time. I got no sleep on the plane, I was too sore and uncomfortable. I tried pacing up and down the aisle but the other passengers resented the disturbance. By the time we landed, I was exhausted and cranky as hell. My dad remembered what to do, he took me straight to Starbucks and I ordered a fruit smoothie to reconstitute a bit. I slept for six hours when we got to their house.

When I woke up, I met Missy, their new rescue cat. She was a sweet brown tabby with white paws, from a situation where too many animals were in too small a space and not well cared for. Missy was so used to competing for food, she would go straight to her dish at mealtime and wolf everything down so no one else could take her food. My parents had lost their beloved Emma right after my mom went home for the last time. They brought her in for a routine procedure and she was brain-damaged under anesthesia and had to be put down. Emma had been a highly domesticated, affectionate cat. Missy was skittish and distrustful, but I knew my parents would persist until Missy tolerated some affection. My first night there, Missy slept on my bed. My mom was miffed! Shortly after I left, Missy started sleeping with them.

After I woke from my long nap, I needed to stretch my legs. My dad suggested we take a walk around the condo complex's walking path. As we walked, I worried about the way my dad lurched with every step. We settled into talking the way we did when he stayed with me, and I was fully aware of how close I came to missing this deeper relationship with my dad. He didn't use e-mail and his hearing trouble made him a secondary participant in phone calls. I would never have had all that one-on-one time if I hadn't woken up from that initial impact.

It was a short visit, and not long after I got back, my

dad had a mild heart attack. He had surgery to correct the blockage that caused it and he walked much more steadily after that. I sent him a Road ID bracelet for his birthday, with his family contact information on it in case he fell while running. I wear one myself, with an online link to my complicated medical files on it. On my dad's card, I wrote, "Because I'd rather have you than my inheritance."

The Big Comox Adventure

I went into summer determined to do even more trips than last year, and get close to my old level of activity. Not so much the total mileage, but the total time out on the road. It was a terrible spring—cold, windy and rainy. I didn't worry that I wasn't training hard enough; it was the best I could do, given the conditions. I went to the gym when I could. I still had to do arm exercises several times a week; I will probably always have to.

During the cold spring, I used the pool often. I have to wear a swim cap; my curly hair gets damaged too easily by the chlorine. I have to baby it with super-hydrating care products all the time. I had just put it up in a bun at the therapy pool where no one ducked underwater, but for proper lap swimming, a cap was a necessity. I bought a fashionable silicone swim cap and the first time I went to use it, I couldn't get it on my head to save my life. I worked at it for twenty minutes, until my right wrist swelled visibly. In tears of frustration, I gave up and swam bareheaded. Later, I got online and watched a video on how to put on a silicone swim cap. It was easy at home, I just spread my fingers to stretch the cap and drew it over my head, pulling my hands out from under it. At the gym, no such luck. Once again I worked at it until my wrist swelled and my left arm throbbed. A hole tore in the cap; in frustration I ripped it some more and threw it away.

I got online and researched swim caps for people with disabilities; the old 1940s-style bubble caps were popular because they were easy to put on. I looked at photos of smiling adults with Down syndrome and cerebral palsy wearing their bubble caps that they presumably put on themselves, sighed, and ordered one of my own. It was easy as can be to take on and off, it kept the pool water off my hair, and I looked like I was seventy years old in it. So be it, compared to the other irritants I dealt with, this fell squarely into the realm of first-world problems.

My big trip of the summer was scheduled for June, the same week as last year's venture to Free Spirit Spheres. I planned a return trip, with an extension to Comox, close to the northern edge of civilization on Vancouver Island, which is actually about the island's midpoint. The northern half of the island is mostly high mountain wilderness. I had always been curious about the northern island towns and wanted to visit. Now I had a great excuse.

Years ago I started ordering washable menstrual pads from a company called New Moon Pads. I stumbled upon the web site by accident while looking for the maker of some pads I had bought here in town. I wanted similar pads, but wondered if bigger ones were available. On the New Moon Pads site, I found exactly what I wanted and then some—she had handkerchiefs, "paperless towels," and all kinds of wonderful green personal care products. I placed a small order.

When the order arrived via Canada Post, I was blown away by the quality of the pads. They were so comfortable and easy to deal with, and the web site offered all kinds of tips on how to manage washable pads out in the world so you didn't have to switch to disposables at work. There was even an herbal teabag attached to the enclosed brochure. I felt pampered. The proprietor, Renee, had her photo on the web site and a note to her customers, and I sent her an e-mail to tell her how impressed I was (and to expect a really big order soon).

In the manner of people who were destined to be friends, Renee and I didn't stop talking to each other for three years. It started with lighthearted chatter about the Olympics in Vancouver. Preparations went on for years as roads were widened and stadiums were built. We were about equally distant from the venues and it was so exciting to look out our windows and be able to see the mountain where all the outdoor events were taking place.

I had actually spent more time in Vancouver than Renee while they were gearing up for the Olympics (Renee had the sense to stay home), and I was able to tell her how traffic had been all bollocksed up and the hostel where I usually stayed had been closed for renovations so it could be used as an Olympic dormitory. (The top athletes in the popular sports stayed in Whistler Village and the new Olympic Village in Vancouver; I'm guessing the Slovenian curling team bunked at Jericho Beach). There was much to discuss about the opening and closing ceremonies, and the heart-stopping moments of competition in between. I attended the torch parade as it passed through the Peace Arch from Canada into the US and back, and got close enough to feel the heat from the torch as it passed by.

We quieted for a few months, then as I planned more bike forays into Canada, I started sending messages to Renee again. After I got home from the rehab center and checked my e-mail for the first time, there were several messages from Renee asking if I was okay, she hadn't heard from me in a while. I laboriously replied with two fingers of my left hand and told her what happened. She responded with an outpouring of support and told me how her former brother-in-law had been killed on his bicycle, hit by a truck the same week I was hit! Working through my recovery with me helped her work through her grief, and our friendship was set in stone.

As I planned my return to Free Spirit Spheres, I e-mailed Renee and asked if she would like to meet when I passed through Comox. Of course she would!

Knowing what a private person Renee generally is, I wasn't sure she would respond so warmly to the prospect of me showing up in her space, but by then I wasn't just a customer any more. I planned to stay in a hostel about ten miles from her house. We would have one day to spend together before I rode back to Free Spirit. I didn't want to overwhelm either one of us with an extended visit.

As the day of departure drew near, the forecast degenerated rapidly. Temperatures were dropping into the 50s during the day, and rain was predicted every day. Free Spirit Spheres books out for the summer by March; changing my reservation was not an option. I revised my packing list to include an extra change of cold-weather gear. I was already riding heavy with the addition of a backpacker pad to make the hostel mattresses more bearable.

Departure day arrived with a bright sunny morning. I had to wait in the customs line this time, with no friendly occupational therapist to spirit me to the front of the line. The sky had clouded up during the train ride and a soft rain started to fall. The transition to the bus was awkward this time. I knocked the rear wheel quick release tab open when I loaded the bike on the bus and had to close it before I could board the bus or the wheel could have bounced off in transit. On the other end at the ferry terminal, I realigned it and rode around a bit to make sure it was straight. Apparently another young man had a similar problem; he was beating on the wheel of his mountain bike furiously. Every time it wobbled in the forks, he would beat it some more. Another tour cyclist and I exchanged glances. After about fifteen minutes of watching this kid abuse his bike, the other cyclist got up and gave his bike a hug. I laughed and patted Silver reassuringly.

I had poutine again on the ferry and found my way

out of the ferry terminal lot easily this time. I found the hostel with no trouble and smiled when the familiar façade came into view. The lady at the desk told me Sara was working at a fancy restaurant a few blocks away. That was kind of a letdown, but at least this time my bed hadn't been taken. My roommate, Christine, was an occupational therapist! She was traveling from Calgary and had just come from Tofino where she learned to surf.

The next morning I woke up at 8:30, very late for me on the road, with my eye swollen half shut. It was probably a reaction to the dusty hostel pillow. My eye looked terrible, but I took a Benadryl and doused it with antihistamine eye drops, and the swelling went down a bit. I still had a lingering headache and congestion. It was windy and cold, and my progress was very slow. The bike felt heavy and I felt sluggish. I found the same diner again for lunch and stopped at the wonderful grocery store in Qualicum Beach.

When I pulled in to Free Spirit Spheres, I didn't find anyone for a while. I greeted my old friend, Maggie the cat, and sat on the steps of the house until I heard whistling—that had to be Tom. He came bounding up to me and kissed me on the cheek. Later that evening, Rosey came by with the loaded snack basket and her sister, Mary. We chatted a bit and agreed to talk more when I came back from Comox. It felt odd to be there only one night, like I hadn't quite arrived yet. I wrote in my trip diary that night, "This isn't meant to be a night stop, it's a retreat." I drained my iPod down to a half charge that first night and I hadn't brought the charger because it usually lasts weeks between charges.

The first words in my trip diary for the ride to Cumberland are "Brutal ride!" I took Tom's advice and used Highway 19, the major highway across the midrib of the island to spread out the climb into Cumberland rather than do it all at once from sea level at Royston. The rolling hills would have been pleasant if I hadn't been riding an overloaded bike. My speedometer vacillated between 6 and 29 miles per hour, with the majority of time spent at the low end of that range. I needed a washroom in the worst way, but using the bushes was too uncomfortable. I knew how to squat in the woods from my years in Montana, but I had to leave Silver up on the shoulder and shinny down the embankment, and taking a leg out of my shorts just seemed too risky with the bike unattended. Finally I found a rest stop that I had to ride downhill to reach. I was reluctant to sacrifice the elevation, knowing I'd have to ride back up, but the pit stop was no longer optional.

In typical Canadian fashion, the rest stop featured composting toilets. I was getting used to a gentle breeze on my bum from the fans below. I sat outside on a bench and ate the Danish I'd taken with me from Rosey's snack basket and watched the Denman Island ferry work its way across the water in the distance before I climbed back up the entrance ramp to the highway, then huffed up a truly gigantic hill. Often when I'm on a long, hard hill, I start counting pedal strokes to pass the time, and usually by 200, I'm at the top. On this hill I counted 1,000 pedal strokes before I gave up counting.

The last few miles into Cumberland were all uphill as well; Cumberland is an old coal town in the mountains and the hostel is located at 2,089 feet. The Free Spirit Spheres are at 416 feet. That is a significant amount of climbing. The day's ride was only thirty-one miles, but I felt like I'd ridden a hundred. I could barely pop my bike lock closed as I locked up outside the hostel. It was only 2:30 and the hostel office didn't open until 4:00. There was a coffee shop just around the corner and I went there to have some soup and read. After a memorably good bowl of broccoli cheddar soup, I fell dead asleep at my table and didn't wake up until 4:15. Apparently my sleeping at the table didn't bother anyone.

The Ridin' Fool Hostel is an independent hostel, meaning it wasn't a member of Hostelling International until they joined the following year. "Indie" hostels are generally very good, but they don't undergo regular inspections to make sure they meet certain standards, and there are occasionally surprises.

My first surprise was my "mattress." It consisted of a 2-inch-thick layer of open-cell polyurethane foam on a slab of plywood. Thank God for my illicit backpacker pad. The woman at the desk had looked me in the eye and asked if I had any of my own bedding, and I looked her in the eye and lied. I felt justified when I saw that bed. The no-personal-bedding rule is to prevent the spread of bedbugs. My backpacker pad has a rubberized nylon shell, so my nightshirt is more likely to transmit bedbugs than the pad, and no one is telling me I can't wear the same nightshirt to bed in two places.

My second surprise was the lack of laundry facilities. The woman at the desk explained that a guest had damaged the washing machine a few years ago so they had stopped offering laundry services to guests. I told her that cyclists generally travel with one change of clothes, and as a hostel that caters to cyclists, she didn't really have the right not to offer laundry services, that was a basic thing that all cyclists need on the road. She said that they catered to mountain bikers who arrive in SUVs with their bikes on the back, and very few cyclists actually arrive on their bicycles. I felt more like a throwback to a bygone era than ever.

The building itself was gorgeous, polished wood floors and banisters, with an imposing dark wood staircase right up the middle. The common room was big and pleasant, with a large, fully equipped kitchen.

I had the entire dorm room to myself; the other guests all had private rooms. I realized while setting up my space that I had left my phone charger back at Free Spirit Spheres. My smartphone could hook into the wifi and I had, for all intents and purposes, a tiny computer. The only problem was, the battery indicator was flashing red. I put a note up on the fridge asking if anyone had a charger that was compatible with a BlackBerry. I offered $10 to borrow it for two hours.

A woman in the common room offered me her iPhone charger, which didn't help with my phone, but I recharged my iPod back to full so I could enjoy music in Eve when I got back to Free Spirit. Then a man came and knocked on my door and said, "I don't want your money, but if this helps, you're free to use it." It was a Samsung charger and it fit perfectly. I thrilled with relief as the little lightning bolt came on to indicate that my phone was charging.

After an hour on the charger, I had no excuse not to check in with Renee. Suddenly I was nervous. I had come all this way, what if this was just a giant bother for her? What if she was secretly creeped out by the visit but too nice to say so? When she answered the phone, it was the first time I had ever actually heard her voice. We laughed nervously for a minute, and then I said I had something embarrassing to ask of her, and she said, "Wait, before I forget, I want to tell you to bring your laundry with you and you can do it here." That was exactly what I had planned to ask! I told her how the hostel didn't offer laundry and she thought that was as odd as I did. We arranged for me to come over around 10:30 the next morning. I breathed a huge sigh of relief and set to enjoying the evening in Cumberland.

I had a view of a house across the street from my dorm window, and a colony of about a dozen feral cats was in full early-evening activity. I watched the cats come and go, interacting with each other and occasionally hunting mice or birds. When I went out to the common room to check on my devices, the woman with the iPhone charger was just pulling a big tray of potatoes roasted with garlic and onions out of the oven. She served a heaping bowl to everyone in the room, and we assembled all the various condiments from the kitchen on the table and everyone chowed down. We got to know one another and I told them about coming to meet Renee, but avoided the crash story. I just didn't want to suck all the attention in the room, the way I always did the minute I mentioned it. I remembered Rosey's advice about choosing when to share and when not to, and felt grateful again for meeting her.

The night on the thin "mattress" was painful, but I was tired enough from the long ride to get some sleep. The band played at the corner bar until well after midnight and ear plugs only turned down the volume and blurred the notes so I couldn't recognize the songs. I gave up and listened to the music until they quit for the night. I woke up hours before I needed to leave for Renee's and I watched the dawn routines of the feral cat colony while the sun came up.

There was the usual routine of declining the communal scrambled-egg breakfast (thanks to my egg allergy) while I ate my apple and breakfast bar. This hostel had a coffee maker and provided the coffee, so my packets of Starbucks instant didn't give me any social advantage. I took a shower and watched the cats some more, and then it was finally time to go.

The ride to Renee's was amazing, a 2,000-foot drop downhill to sea level along a wide road with bike lanes. I left most of my stuff behind at the hostel so my bike felt light, like I was riding on the back of a bird. There was a short ride along the waterfront, with pullouts where you could observe the rich marine life in the intertidal zone. I saw eagles and herons and lots of sea birds I didn't recognize. I was running a little early and I was nervous, so I pulled over and watched a heron strike at a fish in the shallows and devour it.

I turned left from the waterfront and climbed three hundred feet back uphill to get to Renee's, losing my time advantage while crawling along and sweating on my clean clothes. Her house came into view and my heart pounded as the craziness of the errand hit me full force. Then Renee stepped out from the carport and there was no time left to ponder the wisdom of taking such a social risk. We put my laundry in first, as the machines were right inside the door. Renee showed me her handmade wool dryer balls and that was that—our mutual interest in all things crafty kept our conversation fueled for the next nine hours. Renee showed me how she makes her pads, and she made me a new pad and a set of handkerchiefs with rainbow peace symbols on a black background while I watched. She let me run the serger for one of the hankies.

Renee's husband Ken came home and they invited me to stay for dinner. As we sat out on the back patio with wine, overlooking the huge and gorgeously gardened back yard, I gave Renee a necklace I had made and brought along for her, a pink-and-green stone tulip with a matching bead chain. Tulips are a major agricultural product of my region and I thought that made a good gift. Renee seemed floored that I had packed a gift along in my bike bag.

After a dinner of salmon Caesar salad and lots and lots of wine, Renee and Ken offered to drive me back uphill to the hostel. I gratefully accepted. Their large SUV made short work of the 2,000-foot climb. Renee enjoyed looking inside the hostel, as she had worked in that building years before when it housed a local craft market.

It was still light out at 9:00 PM and I was still a bit hungry as the wine started to wear off and leave me a little shaky. Renee's dinner was very healthy for a regular day; the demands of bike touring make me need lots more complex carbohydrates. A young man in the common room asked me where he could get something to eat at this hour and I offered to walk him to the convenience store a few blocks away. I found out he was a medical student from Vancouver and he was taking a break from his studies to do some mountain biking. When we got back to the hostel with our goodies, we realized we were alone in the building. The staff left at 10:00 and we were the only guests. The doors to the private rooms were all locked, but there was no one in them. We laughed with relief that we already knew each other and didn't have to spend the evening tiptoeing around a creepy stranger. We stayed up talking until about 11:00 and then went to the dorm rooms we had all to ourselves.

At 3:00, the other guests from the locked private rooms staggered in loudly. One of them even showered and blow-dried her hair at that hour with the bathroom door open! I stuffed my earplugs in tightly and waited for them to settle down. I didn't make any special effort to be quiet when I got up at 7:00 to ride back to Free Spirit.

I decided to head back along the coastal highway and take my time. Rosey had told me I should check out an art gallery in the town of Union Bay, so I pulled over there and was greeted by a lovely Siamese cat. I took a photo that remains one of the best shots I've ever taken—the brightly colored curtains behind the blue-eyed cat, with the dull stucco wall on a cloudy day providing contrast that made the colors pop out.

When I pulled over at the gallery, the strap on my shoe broke. I had noticed it was coming apart and had hoped it would hold together long enough to get me home. The shoe was a sport sandal designed for cycling, and it was the ankle strap that broke, leaving me with what amounted to a flip-flop. I passed by a home with a store built into the garage, advertising sewing services. It was within the stated business hours and the open sign hung in the window, but no one came when I knocked and the door was locked. I rode on to one of those rural convenience store-lunch counters, and while I waited for my lunch, I found a two-dollar made-in-China sewing kit, like the kind you get in hotels, and stitched the strap back together, covering the table with a napkin so I wouldn't offend the owner by having my shoe on the table.

Not long after I left Union Bay, it started to rain hard. I put the rain covers on my bags and zipped up my rain jacket. My wool tights kept my legs warm even while wet, but it was not pleasant riding. The low-quality cotton thread I had used on my shoe pulled apart when it got wet and the shoe strap broke again. I had to press my foot toward the front of the pedal to keep my foot in the shoe. I pulled in to Free Spirit soaked and shivering. Rosey was still cleaning the spheres and mine wasn't ready yet, but she shooed me into the sauna and took my clothes up to her house to dry them. I waited in the warm sauna, naked but comfortable, until she came back with my clothes still warm from the dryer. Then I moved back into Eve and napped for hours while the rain pelted the sphere.

Between storms, I moved Silver into Tom's workshop to keep her out of the rain. I hung my wet rain jacket inside to give it a chance to dry out. Then I went back to Eve and tried to repair my shoe again with the sewing kit. I could see that no repair I made was going to hold long enough to get me home. I needed good strong leather stitching, like... the stitching I was staring at on Eve's door handle. I was surrounded by the kind of craftsmanship I needed! And the craftsman was just down the path. I went back to Tom's workshop and showed him my broken shoe. Of course he had just the thing, and he didn't do the work *for* me. He showed me the correct tool, an awl that could lock-stitch a strong sinew thread, and demonstrated how to use it on a rag towel. I practiced for a bit, then took the tool and thread up to Eve and fixed the broken strap, and reinforced the other shoe where it was coming apart in the same place. My hand was numb from the effort but I was so pleased, I took a photo of the tool lying by the repaired shoe before I returned the tool to Tom. Bike touring is all about resourcefulness, and I felt like I'd hit the jackpot. Never mind that I hadn't checked my equipment before leaving; I should have seen the wear and replaced that shoe a month before the trip. Still, I handled the problem and made another memory out of it.

In the morning it was time to go, and I took my time packing up. I retrieved Silver from Tom's workshop and loaded her up, making sure I had all my chargers and whatnot. I left some Starbucks instant packets behind for other guests.

While I waited for Tom to come for checkout, I chatted with a guest who was there from New York with her husband. She asked me what it was like growing up there, and I asked, "You mean the Pacific Northwest?" She said, "No, I mean here. Aren't you, like, Rosey's sister or something?" I laughed and said no, Rosey had plenty of sisters, but I wasn't one of them. Why did she think that? She said, "Well, every time you need anything, they drop everything for you. I just assumed you were related." I explained our history and we got to talking about my visit north to Renee. The woman was a gynecologist and was very interested in spreading the word about Renee's pads to her patients. She believed firmly that washable cotton pads were much healthier than disposables.

Tom is not one for a fast checkout experience. He loves his spheres and he likes to know how other people experience them. We talked for quite a while. Rosey was off at a Special Olympics event in town; she had become very involved with developmentally disabled people. Like me, she had found her volunteer niche. Tom gave me a note she wrote me and I waited until my lunch stop in Parksville to read it. Her kind words warmed me and I folded the note carefully into my trip diary to keep.

The ride from Parksville to Nanaimo was not fun. There was a strong headwind and I even had to pedal downhill. My knees strained against the overloaded bike. The last ten miles on the highway were painful and I was exhausted. On the outskirts of town, I knew I was in trouble and needed to pull over for a snack break. A Taco Time sign beckoned and I worked my way across the highway to get to it. I found an abandoned storefront. I wanted to cry. There was a McDonald's across the street and I went there reluctantly. I won't be reluctant again; their menu had evolved a lot since my last visit. I got a Thai chicken wrap with fresh vegetables in it, and a real peach smoothie, and I sat in the nicely decorated restaurant and felt my spirit reconstitute. The separated bike trail into town was a delight after the refreshing meal.

Back at the hostel, my roommate Christine was still there. I didn't get assigned to her room, I got placed with Barbara, a woman in her fifties, and a seventeen-year-old girl from Vancouver whose mumbled name I never caught. I sat and talked with Christine in the common room until it got late. She asked me lots of personal questions about my recovery and offered almost nothing of her own story, though I gleaned that she had broken up with a man who was subsequently diagnosed with cancer, and she had gone back and been his caregiver for a long time. He was still back home in the final stages of the disease. I don't know what prompted her long walkabout at that point, but she was contemplating her own mortality and seemed to need something from me. I liked her and wanted to help her find whatever she was looking for.

Barbara and the young lady sat up talking until 2:00. I used my sleep mask and ear plugs and tried to be a good sport for as long as I could. Finally I sat up and asked them to please at least turn out the light and whisper. They went to bed.

In the morning I had my usual breakfast routine and got ready to leave. As I was hauling my bags downstairs with aching arms, Christine stopped me and said, "You shared so much of yourself with me and I didn't share anything back. I just want you to know that I needed something from you and I'm grateful to you for sharing like you did. Thank you." We hugged and I left with that magic feeling that I had been *supposed* to be there then. There were so many synchronicities on this trip. The difficulties are part of the adventure; meeting Renee had made it all worth it. It had been an awesome trip.

Floundering For Closure

The legal process of my case was still disturbing and felt unfinished. A stranger hit me and I knew his name and age, but nothing else about him. I had seen his face just before he hit the Dodge Durango, and I knew he had been driving inattentively. I had ridden my bike by the address on his driver's license and discovered that he lived in a room behind his parents' business, a run-down looking repair shop.

The whole idea that I was expected to conclude the case without ever meeting this guy was so artificial! I knew it had to be that way because of the legal system, and we were all hiding behind our lawyers and couldn't speak to each other directly. But the case was over and I just couldn't let the guy—let's call him Jack—get on with his life, completely unchanged by what happened, when I had to live with the consequences every moment of every day.

I asked my attorney if there were any restrictions on communication with Jack. The attorney thought it was odd that I would feel any need to speak to him, but he said I was allowed to contact him as long as I didn't threaten him or ask for anything. Apparently my attorney thought I was supposed to think of this as an accident and Jack was no more at fault than the moon and stars.

I began working on a letter to Jack that took months to complete. I thought about what I most wanted to say, and I found the answer in the most annoying question I was frequently asked: "So, are you back to one hundred percent now?" I'm sorry, that's a dumb question. Nobody who had any understanding at all of what happened to me would expect that I could ever be back to one hundred percent. I *severed my hand*, for God's sake. I don't have all my original parts. I'm not okay! That was what I needed him to know. That the "accident" he walked away from with a shiny new Dodge Ram truck was more than an interruption to my day. That truck made me angry; it was all chrome grill and it made me think, "What, so next time you hit a cyclist, you can make sure you finish the job?" That was an arrogant truck. A compact car would have made me feel like it was possible that he was ashamed of what happened. Even a modest pickup. That Ram was showy and screamed "I regret nothing."

I sent the letter to Esther, my former therapist, before mailing it, to get her feedback. She had taught me so much about social interaction and what point I wanted to make versus the expected outcome of what I did to make that point. Esther helped me reshape the letter and simplify it a bit; I tend to assume my audience is on my own level and this guy was a young man who hadn't gone to college, as far as I knew. Finally I felt I had it right. I printed it, signed it, and walked it to the mailbox. As I shoved it through the outgoing mail slot, I had the feeling that I had just set something in motion that I couldn't stop.

•

August 1, 2012

Dear Jack,

It's taken me two years to find the words I want to say to you. Yes, it's been almost two years since you hit me on Hannegan Road. My attorney says it's okay to write to you as long as I don't ask you for anything or threaten you in any way. I need you to know that I'm not okay.

I remember things that head trauma patients typically don't. I remember the impact, the bones breaking as I was flung down the hill and the certainty that no one could survive what was happening to me. I remember lying in the ditch with my lungs collapsed, struggling to breathe until the ambulance arrived. I remember my shattered body being lifted onto the backboard and feeling the jagged edge of every broken bone. I remember the chest tube being stabbed in between my ribs without anesthetic and I remember the life-giving air filling my lungs. I remember the intense burning from my right hand where it hung by a flap of skin at the back of my wrist. Most of all, I remember pain like nothing I ever imagined.

I spent six weeks in the hospital. One week in ICU on a respirator, two weeks in the surgical unit, and three weeks in inpatient rehab. My injuries:

- Shattered humerus (upper arm bone, so badly shattered it had to be replaced with metal)
- Fractured scapula (shoulder "wing" bone)
- Fractured skull
- 2 spinal fractures
- Every single rib fractured on the left side
- Torn liver and spleen
- Collapsed lungs
- My right hand was for all intents and purposes amputated; every nerve and blood vessel was severed
- My carotid artery collapsed from the impact. The carotid is in the neck and supplies blood to the brain. Blood clots hit my brain 23 minutes after impact, resulting in a stroke that affected my whole left side.

After I got out of the hospital, I had to have in-home care for three months and I was in outpatient rehab three times a week for six months.

I missed four months of work and I've only been able to work part time in my home since this happened. It will be at least two more years before I can work a full-time job outside my home. I get no unemployment compensation or disability pay.

My surgeons did not expect me to be able to live independently again, but I do that and I've even gotten back on my bike. I do the hostel touring I used to do before, but instead of 80-mile days, my limit is 40 and I'm better off with 25. Instead of multi-week adventures, I can go up to five days before my need for pain meds increases a lot and I have to get back to my own bed. (I am still on constant pain medicine.)

As for my own bed, I've had to sleep on my back for two years. I'm a side sleeper and sleeping on my back is terribly uncomfortable, but if I turn over on my right side, my spine and all my ribs light up. My left shoulder is so damaged, I can't even turn on that side. It takes drugs to get to sleep at night. I wake up in pain and get up and stretch out as fast as I can.

I have limited feeling in the last two fingers of my right hand. Both the ulnar and radial nerves were severed. The radial nerve was a clean cut and the reattachment was a complete success. The ulnar nerve, which serves the outer portion of the hand, was shredded and almost half an inch had to be cut away in order to provide a flat attachment site. I have to be careful not to burn my hand when cooking because I don't feel the burn before I smell it. Thanks to an incredible number of hours of therapy, I have full movement of the hand and I can still do the beadwork and other art I did before. Handwriting is hard, though; I can only write a few lines before I lose control of the pen. The scar tissue on my wrist is incredibly sensitive. I can't wear sleeves that brush against it. I have to apply lotion about once every hour or it dries out and I get an unbearable tickling sensation. Because the heel of my hand was torn away, resting my hand on a handlebar was unbearably painful for a while. It still hurts.

I have to see medical specialists every two to three months and my regular doctor once a month. I have to have expensive scans to make sure there's enough bloodflow to my brain. I will be on monitoring and medication for the rest of my life. Your insurance was the state minimum and your policy was exhausted before I got out of the hospital. My better insurance kicked in on top of that and my policy has been exhausted. Now I'm on my single-payer health plan, which costs a lot more and pays a lot less than a company's group plan would. The St. Joseph's Bridge Assistance Plan covered $20,000—that's a charity.

To date, I am out of pocket about $30,000 and the flow won't stop any time soon. This has been almost as devastating financially as it has been physically.

I refer to what happened as "the crash," not "the accident." An accident happens when everyone is doing everything right and something completely unforeseen happens. Nothing unforeseen happened that day, you were just going too fast and not paying attention. I remember riding along in the bike lane and feeling a squirrelly vibe and looking up. I remember the overwhelmingly creepy sensation as I realized you had no clue you were about to slam into that Durango.

I knew before you did that something was wrong. We all have our inattentive moments at the wheel, but this was way beyond common inattention. The fact that you hurt someone was not accidental; it was the natural consequence of your distracted driving. I wish I had fired my lazy lawyer and pursued prosecution for criminal negligence, but my energy was completely consumed with my own recovery process.

I understand that you got off with a ticket. I live with the real consequences of what happened every minute of every day, and I think you should live with them too. I would like to say that you ruined my life, but that's not exactly true; I am far too strong and I have too much of a purpose in this world to allow you to do that. But the woman you hit is not okay.

Sincerely,
Kristin Noreen

I never heard a word back from Jack. I never expected to. The letter was about me saying what I needed to say, and I knew he probably wouldn't even finish reading it once he saw what it was. I just needed to say all that in order to let go of the outrage I felt. I don't know that I really have let go of it; it's just lessened enough in intensity that it doesn't burn me alive. If I knew he felt terrible about what happened, I could forgive him, but until I know otherwise, I'm assuming he enjoys his sweet new truck.

Opening Day

My left knee was injured from my overloaded bike trip. Unable to ride Silver, I felt lost, like the rest of my summer was ruined. But ready or not, Opening Day came! The sunny June day couldn't be more perfect. I went down on the Airporter Shuttle bus, knowing I would drink champagne at the reception and I wasn't going to be able to drive ninety miles home. It was a Friday, so Kenn arranged to drive me home that evening and stay the weekend at my house.

I dressed in a new skirt and an elbow-length tee that covered my arm scar. I wanted people to see an environmental professional, not a poster child. I brought along a card for Kyle that said, "You're the star!" Kyle graciously shared full credit with his dad and brother, who did a lot, but it was Kyle's baby and I knew it, and I wanted him to know I knew it. Inside the card, I wrote how proud I was to know him.

I knew seating would be limited on the pier and that no one could defend a chair reserved for me in that big a crowd, so I brought along a cane that folds into a tripod seat. You straddle the seat and it's surprisingly comfortable. The cane would help me take the pressure off my injured knee. It did detract somewhat from my "not a poster child" image, but that couldn't be helped. I had to get through the day.

I still bring that cane anywhere I plan to use public transit. Because I look normal, able-bodied people aren't willing to give up a seat for me. The cane tends to bring out the best in other people.

On the bus, an older gentleman got on in Burlington and asked me what I was doing in Seattle that day. I said I was going to the Ferris wheel opening day ceremonies. He asked if I planned to ride the wheel and I said of course. He smirked and asked, "Do you think you'll actually get on today?" I smirked back and said, "I'm very sure I will." He sat there a minute and asked, "Are you related to the people who own it?"

I always enjoy that moment between the dismissal as an ordinary-looking woman and the moment the person realizes I'm a science and law professional. That never gets old. I explained my role on the project and the man's eyes grew round and big as Ferris wheels.

Getting off the bus in Seattle, I walked downhill from the Convention Center, leaning heavily on the cane as my injured knee objected to the slant of the sidewalk. After a few blocks of walking, I saw the top of the wheel peeking out over the building tops. That was the first time I had seen it finished, with the gondolas on and everything. I had to be careful to watch the sidewalk ahead of me and not walk right into people as I watched the wheel come into view a little more with every block I walked. It was sleek, gorgeous, magnificent. I was so proud to have helped change the city's skyline forever.

The pier was a zoo—thousands of people milled about and the line for first-time riders was already stretching for blocks down Alaskan Way. Kyle called to me, looking the part of proud owner in an elegant navy suit and lavender dress shirt. His fiancée, Jenny, was working the check-in table and issuing VIP bracelets to the wheel crew. I got my bracelet and tucked my card into Kyle's shirt pocket.

I went upstairs to the construction office to wait the hour before the opening ceremony. There I found Simon and we hugged and stared bug-eyed at each other, repeating variations of, "Oh my God, we pulled it off, didn't we?" I turned to sit down and found myself face to face with one of my idols, Seattle comedian Pat Cashman. Pat reminds me a lot of SNL's Phil Hartman. I had met Pat before at a company event he emceed, and he remembered me! It confirmed my impression of Pat as one of the most genuinely gracious people of all time. Pat rehearsed his opening speech, occasionally trying out material on Simon and me. It was almost an anticlimax when we headed downstairs, where the UW Marching Band was playing and the cheerleaders performed incredibly acrobatic dance routines. (Kyle comes from an old Husky family and the performance was probably to reward them for their alumni support.)

I found a place near the pier's outer rail where I could set my cane seat down and looked for Brad and his wife, Debbie. My phone vibrated in my skirt pocket and it was Brad, trying to find me. We finally located each other, too far apart through the throng of people. We stayed put as Pat Cashman opened the ceremony with a great comic routine in which he managed to snark the new mayor and his predecessor with the same joke.

The mayor gave a talk, then the Wells Fargo Bank representative who was responsible for financing the project. Next, Kyle got up and talked about the history of the project and how it finally came to reality. He said the project could not have been done without the outstanding contributions of two people. The first, of course, was Simon, who worked so many overtime hours that his wife pretended not to recognize him that night (in fact, many of the construction workers thought *I* was Simon's wife!). Simon made it happen on time and nearly sold his soul to do it. I cried a little as I applauded furiously. Then Kyle moved on to the second person and you could have knocked me into the water with a feather when I heard my own name. A woman standing next to me had read my name tag and shrieked, "Oh my God, that's you!" I shushed her so I could hear what Kyle said about me. He told the crowd how I had been hit just before we submitted the permit applications, and how I had continued to advise

Brad from the hospital and started working again before I had medical clearance. He broke down in tears as he said that anyone else would have dropped out of the project, but that I never let go of the ball.

Then it was time to cut the ribbon. Kyle held the comically large scissors and at the last minute, he handed them to his mother. At that moment I was so glad I had given him the card; he was not only the real star of the day, but he was bearing the honor with a grace and humility that made me a little envious of Jenny.

I tried to get through the crowd to get on the first wheel car with Simon. I could see him scanning the crowd for me and he didn't want to get on without me, but they needed to keep loading the wheel. I couldn't elbow my way through the crowd; it still hurt to be jostled. The entire Husky marching band got on before I did; Brad and I made the second load. As the wheel spun silently skyward, the enormity of what we'd done filled my heart and I stared out the windows transfixed as Brad and Debbie chatted with the wheel's lighting engineer, who rode in the gondola with us.

Then there was the party on the outdoor deck where I had spent so many hours monitoring. I had to laugh, Brad always corrected me before when I called him my boss, he never liked that word, but that day, when they asked him who he was, he pointed at me, beamed, and said, "I'm *her* boss!"

The champagne mixed with the oxycodone and I was profoundly drunk for the first time in two years. The Ferris wheel spun silently overhead, its colored lights glowing in the early evening sky. I looked over at Simon and saw the same deeply satisfied look on his face. We did it.

The Unthinkable

My summer bike trip had been so fantastic, I couldn't bear the idea of letting the summer end without a final bike weekend. Kenn had just bought a new bike and I invited him to go to Nanaimo with me. We reserved hostel bunks and planned a weekend of riding the local bike trails and playing miniature golf in Parksville. With Kenn along, I wasn't likely to overdo it and reinjure my knee.

Days before departure, I bent to give Nimby a pat while I set his food dish down. What was that I felt? I touched it again and found a large mass outside his rib cage. He stopped and looked at me seriously; "Now you know."

I got online and cancelled our reservations, then called Kenn to tell him the trip was off. I left a message for Nimby's vet, a home-care vet who was often available odd hours. Dr. Fjeld came to examine Nimby and she wasn't terribly alarmed by the mass, but thought I should have it X-rayed. I was alarmed. A mother knows.

Nimby was so strong that I had to have Lisa, his new sitter since Karen moved away, come help me get him into his carrier. A few days later I listened, numb, as the doctor explained about spindle-cell tumors, one of the most aggressive kinds of cancer in cats. The tumor was at the site where he got his rabies shots. I had always opted for the one-year vaccine because it was less likely to cause tumors than the three-year vaccine. It still happened. He was only seven.

The radiologist strongly recommended surgical removal of the tumor. Nimby's vet didn't feel up to tackling this difficult surgery; she wasn't able to find a vet in town who did. I was told a board-certified surgeon was my only option. I could take Nimby north to

Vancouver or south to Lynnwood, or I could try to get Dr. Mark Davis, the traveling surgeon who served the smaller communities in northwestern Washington. My vet forwarded Nimby's records to him.

Dr. Davis stated with confidence that he thought he could get the whole tumor. His price was high but I liked him, and more importantly, Nimby curled up in my lap and purred while I had Dr. Davis on speaker phone—his voice made Nimby feel safe. By the time we were able to secure an operating room in a local clinic, a month had gone by since I found the tumor, and it was noticeably bigger.

I had to leave Nimby at the clinic by 8:00 on surgery day. Lisa came over to help me get him in his carrier, and the first time I dropped him in through the open top, he leapt out seemingly as he landed, so fluid was his evasion. He ran to the bedroom and under the bed—I had not thought to close the door. Lisa and I looked at each other in disbelief—this was *surgery day*, for crying out loud, we couldn't have a problem like this! I didn't think for a second that it would work, but I shook Nimby's can of bonito flake treats and he actually came into the kitchen. I felt terrible, but I nabbed him and dropped him in the carrier, and this time Lisa closed it against my arms before I let go and I extracted my hands one by one. Nimby yowled with indignation the whole way to the vet. I dropped him off as scheduled and went home until noon, but there was no way I was waiting at home while he was in surgery. I returned to the clinic.

Dr. Davis arrived at one o'clock. Alice came and knitted with me while I crocheted. At about 3:15 Dr. Davis came out and said Nimby was awake. He believed he got the entire tumor, 1.2 pounds of malignant tissue. As I signed Nimby's release paperwork, he tried to escape his carrier and upended it on the floor, doing a headstand in his "cone of shame." My heart nearly stopped! The staff whisked him back to check on his stitches and increase his sedation.

Nimby spent the night at the emergency clinic a few miles from my house. I borrowed Kali for the night for company. She was confused, wondering where her friend was, and I felt a little bad for using her that way. At 11:00 I went to the hospital and said good-night to Nimby. It was the first time I'd really seen him; half of one side was shaved down to pink skin and he had a four-inch incision on his side, belly to shoulder. He was miserable and the staff couldn't do much for him because he wouldn't let anyone near him. He let me clean the sprayed urine off his kennel wall. He didn't want to be touched, so I sat outside his kennel and sang his kitty songs to him until they made me go.

I didn't sleep at all that night; the rude neighbors upstairs had their obnoxious friend over, a young man who had previously been evicted as a renter from our complex, and they played loud music and made drunken "woo-hoo" sounds. On a Thursday night, no less. Sometime after midnight I banged on the ceiling with my broomstick and their guest went home. I still didn't sleep. Kali curled up at my feet with her tail switching, as restless as I was.

In the morning the clinic nurse said she didn't want to release Nimby until he ate a meal. He hadn't touched his food there. I assured the vet on duty that Nimby would eat when I got him home, I knew my boy that well. No matter what happened, whether he was sick or stressed, nothing ever blunted his appetite at home. The vet made me promise to call and report whether he actually did eat. The minute I released him from the carrier, he went to his dish and ate half a can of food and howled for more.

He had on a soft-cone collar that hung like a skirt, and he tripped on it as he got used to walking in it. I didn't have to give him any meds since Dr. Davis had packed the wound with nerve-blocking medication and he wore a Fentanyl patch on his shaved back foot, just like the ones I'd worn, secured with a neon-green bandage.

I wasn't supposed to let him jump, but within the first twenty-four hours he was up on the bed (reporting for morning hugdown), my chair, the bathroom counter, and his scratching tree. There was no stopping my little tough guy. He ate robustly and devoted a tremendous amount of energy to escaping his cone. He did escape it enough times that I put a hard cone on him while I sewed a collar inside the soft cone so he couldn't get it off. It took him two days to shake the hard cone and another three to shake the soft cone. He so resisted me putting it back on that I had to call Lisa to help me with it.

After five days, he had to have his wound checked and his Fentanyl patch removed. I didn't want to wrestle him back to the clinic so I asked Katy, one of our Animal Control Officers who was a veterinary technician, to come to my house. She came with her fiancé and a medical bag, and set about the first order of business—making friends with Nimby. Then she took her special rounded scissors and tried to cut the bandage off his foot. He immediately went feral, growling and hissing and resisting her every attempt. Katy directed me to "scruff" him, a technique I had seen other volunteers use with angry cats, but had never been taught to do myself. Katy showed me that all I needed to do was grab the fur behind his neck and hold on tight. Poor Nimby—he submitted to Katy, but screamed the whole time, I'd never heard any cat make a sound like it. That bandage was stuck on and it took about ten minutes to remove, during which Nimby got so stressed, I was afraid for him. The bare skin on his side was flushed dark pink, his eyes dilated and wild with fear. Finally we were done, and Katy congratulated us both for sticking it out. My hands shook from the stress of it all and my spine felt brittle from contorting on the floor. She said it was important to reward Nimby with a treat right away, and me too—she suggested a big glass of wine. A few days later when I went to the shelter, Emily said Katy had told her she'd never seen a mom who could stick it out to the end like I did. I told her that the alternative was packing him off in the car to the clinic; that would have been even worse, so I protected him from that.

I tried letting Kali back in, and after a few false starts in which she sniffed Nimby too aggressively and he snapped at her, they were finally okay together. I waited the full two weeks to take Nimby's cone off, and I was under unbearable stress the whole time because I could see how he suffered in it. The four-inch-long stitch line intimidated me, though; I couldn't let him reopen that wound. The morning of the de-coning, I got him up on the bed for morning hugdown and I unsnapped the collar inside the cone. Nimby immediately ran away with the cone flapping, but he was able to pull out of it and I picked it up and put it away, telling him all the while that he was done with it. He sat down to bathe and did not stop for over an hour. Then he took a long, relaxed nap.

After he woke from his nap, he announced that he wanted *out*. No gentle meowing at the door, he pummeled it with his paws and hollered. It infuriated him that Kali was free to come and go as she pleased.

Finally I dared to take him on a short walk. Winter had set in during his confinement and his skin flushed bright pink in the cold. He obediently followed me and came in when we were done with the walk. This became our daily routine until his fur started to grow back in a gray felt-like mat and I could let him out for short times. He was smart and mostly sat on his chair on the back porch, not straying far from safety. I could see the stripes and spots reappearing slowly as his fur grew back in and marveled at the complexity of DNA that could recreate his original markings.

A few weeks after surgery, I received a call from the oncologist, who had examined the tumor after it was removed. Her prognosis was bleak. The tumor margins were only half what they had hoped, and it was likely that the cancer would grow back with a vengeance. The second-growth tumors for this type of cancer are generally invasive and inoperable, and kill within three months. I was advised to consider radiation treatment or chemotherapy.

Radiation would require leaving Nimby in Pullman, 300 miles east, for 30 days of treatments. I could only imagine the psychological damage of such a thing; even if I could afford the cost, it was not an option I could live with. Chemotherapy would retard his bone marrow production and make him sick and anemic, confined indoors. I thought about it long and hard, even consulting Joanna Schmidt, a locally respected pet communicator, and I decided the only choice for Nimby was to let him be a cat for as long as he was able to, and then let him go. I believed that was the choice Nimby would make if he could tell us what he wanted.

Another Opening Day

Nimby recovered from his surgery and I lived day by day, celebrating each day we had together. Gradually life returned to routine, but I never took a day for granted. I loved our daily long walks through the condo complex together.

It pained me to no end that I had not been able to be the benefactor the Humane Society needed so badly in order to build a new shelter. We worked in third-world conditions out of two buildings in different parts of town, both unsuitable for shelter use. We had poor ventilation, old barred metal cages, and leaky roofs. One time I went to work with the cats and didn't actually get to visit anyone, because it was raining so hard, all I did was change the buckets on top of the cat kennels. I couldn't lift a full bucket, so I had to empty them every time they gathered a few inches of water. When it came time to go, I had to figure out how to get out of the flooded dirt parking lot without getting stuck. We needed a new building in the worst way; we just couldn't keep going on like this indefinitely.

One day I was called to a meeting of the Paws Awhile store volunteers in the basement of the Fairhaven Village Inn. We gathered our piles of Thea's home-baked treats on napkins and sat, expecting a typical staff meeting. Laura came up to the front—her presence a sign that this was a big deal meeting—and announced that our new building was going to be a reality. We had received a huge gift from an anonymous donor and she was willing to match public contributions up to the same amount. The final number was what we needed to build a state-of-the-art facility. We walked around after the meeting stunned, weeping and hugging one another.

With the donor matching, funds poured in from all

over. We raised the money while construction went on in our new lot in the Irongate industrial district. We were next to lumber and warehouse operations, but nothing nearly as loud as the airport, and our medical clinic was being built with sound insulation so recovering animals (to say nothing of their caregivers) could enjoy peace and quiet.

I got to tour the building during the winter when it was still being walled in. A proper vet clinic, animal care areas with directional ventilation systems to reduce the spread of disease, even a laundry room with four stacking washer-dryer units. A food prep room with a dishwasher ensured that we didn't have to stage food dishes on top of the washing machines any more. Security features, storage space, a separate small animal room so rodents didn't have to sit on top of cats—we were overwhelmed. Even the bathrooms (more than one!) seemed impossibly luxurious after the rickety, slow-flushing toilet and rusty sink in the old building. The cat kennels were what finally made me cry. No bars, they had clear windows, and separated litter box compartments so the cats could eat away from their litter boxes. Each kennel had three climbing shelves, and the kennels could be joined by removing wall panels so bonded pairs or litters of kittens could have a double suite. This was so much better than the barred cage Nimby had spent two months in before I came along.

My contribution, of course, was the bike rack. I had a local artist design a custom rack based on our logo. It cost as much as Nimby's cancer surgery, but it was worth it, and Kenn chipped in a generous chunk toward it. I hadn't planned to put my name on it, but everything else there had a donor name plate, even the individual cat kennels, and my friend Sylvia told me she would choke me if I didn't put my name on my bike rack. Dr. Ouellette said that the bike rack represented a level of emotional recovery that few of her patients ever reach.

I also have a brick in the walkway, dedicated to Nimby Tyson Noreen, WHS Class of '07. When I ordered it, I had no way of knowing if he'd be with us or not on opening day, so I chose an inscription that worked both ways.

I rode my bike by the construction site almost daily to see if the rack had been installed yet. I couldn't see from the road, and the site was gated to prevent people from coming in and getting hurt. Laura had asked that the volunteers not hang around at the construction gate, so I rode by without stopping and never got a good look.

About a month before we opened, I was shocked when Emily announced that she was moving to Montana to take an Assistant Director job at the Yellowstone Wildlife Refuge in Montana. Her dream job came along at the least opportune time, but she still had to take it. I struggled with the idea of her leaving; she was my best friend in the organization. Her farewell party was bittersweet. (It was a good move for her, though; she was promoted to Executive Director in less than a year.)

We couldn't have asked for a more perfect opening day. Bright and sunny, with a gentle breeze, a perfect June day. Folding chairs filled the parking lot, and crowds of people stood. It seemed like the entire county turned out for the big event. As well they should; this was a community project. Everyone gave what they could, from a five-dollar donation to a five-room medical clinic. My bike rack stood near the entry, dressing up the building with a festive splash of color. My friend Janet called it "building jewelry."

Finally, we met our anonymous donor, now unmasked as we pulled the covers off the signs to reveal the Curt Sorenson Center for Animal Care and

Adoption. Dorothy spoke briefly about this memorial to her late husband, almost drowned out by the thunderous applause. I had expected someone tall and imposing, with lots of gold and diamond jewelry. Dorothy was anyone's grandma, dressed nicely in jeans and a jersey cardigan with hand-stitched appliqués.

I realized later that day that it didn't matter whose name was on the building, as long as it came to be. I had wanted to be the county's benefactor, but it still happened, at about the same time as I would have delivered it. I wrote Dorothy a letter thanking her for her gift, and the contribution she made toward healing my anger over my paltry settlement.

In a way, this was bigger for me than Ferris wheel opening day. It felt like I had worked even harder toward this goal and the triumph was shared with the whole community.

Happy Days

Eight months had gone by since Nimby's surgery and I found no sign of tumor regrowth. His vet cautiously declared him clear. I still never took a day with him for granted. Every morning we did "hugdown," with me surreptitiously checking the tumor site for lumps, and celebrated another day together. In the afternoons, Nimby helped me with a giant wine bag sewing project for the Humane Society, happily rolling in my fabric and playing with the gold braid I used to tie the bags. "Go Sew" was the high point of Nimby's days.

We often had barbeques with Eric and Sarah, my friends two doors down, in the summer evenings. All five of our cats would play together out in the yard. When we played bocce ball, one game took an hour because the cats would pounce at every ball we tossed. We had to make up rules to deal with things like the cats' influence on a ball in play. When we played ladder golf, little Freya the Abyssinian turned it into a hilarious gymnastic event.

I felt safe enough to go on a bike trip for ten days. By this time Kali was a full-time resident. Nimby and Kali were so bonded that Eric, Sarah and I talked about it and decided they should live together. Eric and Sarah had three much younger cats and eight-year-old Kali felt under siege. The transition to my house was barely noticeable; she was there so much of the time already. There were some adjustment pains with the sleeping arrangements, but eventually Kali took my feet and Nimby slept up by my side. Mornings were delightful as they galloped around the house playing ambush games while the sun came up.

Leaving for a bike trip was much easier now that both cats would keep each other company. That was always the hardest part about leaving, separating the friends. It felt so mean. My cat sitter, Lisa, had even said she couldn't take any more jobs from me if I continued to separate the cats; it was too hard for her to watch them try to reach each other through the glass back door. We planned for Lisa to tend to the cats in the morning, then let them out for the day, and "Mama Sarah" would round them up before dark. I decided to ride up the Sunshine Coast north of Vancouver this year, ferry across from Powell River to Comox, and visit Renee before resuming my usual route back down to Nanaimo via Free Spirit Spheres.

The first night out was actually with Sarah, I had invited her to a Wailin' Jennys concert in Harrison Hot Springs in exchange for a ride to the ferry terminal at Horseshoe Bay. We visited Sarah's family in Abbotsford on the way up to the show, and we stayed so long that we arrived without time to eat before the show. I linked up with Jamie, who was there too, and we had ice cream cones for dinner while we waited in line at the door. After the show, Sarah and I struck out to find the only place open for food after 10 PM, a bar that served appetizers up to closing time.

The next morning we set out to have breakfast at a funky little place we'd seen the night before. It was a food truck with a wooden deck built on, and served an incredible variety of Indian and North American food. It was 9:00 and the place was supposed to be open. We waited half an hour until the owner arrived and apologized and said it would take another half hour to heat up the kitchen equipment. I needed to make the 1:00 sailing to Langdale so we decided to grab something at a Tim Hortons and turned back toward the hotel. As we walked down the beachfront sidewalk, we heard a plaintive cry from the bushes. We investigated and found a small white long-haired cat, starving and matted so badly that the mats had torn her skin in places. She was friendly and trusting, when I sat down on the grass, she climbed right into my lap and purred. I could barely feel her weight in my lap.

Sarah asked me to wait right there with the cat while she ran back to her car. Of course she was packing cat food. She opened a container of moist fish and offered it to the cat. The cat sniffed at it with interest and lapped a bit of the juice from the top but didn't eat any more. Sarah and I realized that this cat needed immediate help and we turned on our phone data plans to search the internet for a nearby animal shelter, international data rates be damned. There wasn't one in Harrison Hot Springs, so we phoned a local veterinarian. It turns out that there is a bylaw in that town that prohibits vets from taking in stray animals. Citizens are also not allowed to take them in; no law was going to stop us from helping that cat. Sarah knew of a BCSPCA shelter near her family home in Abbotsford. It was an hour in the wrong direction, but we called and made arrangements. They were closed to the public that day, but since we were tourists and couldn't take the cat with us across the border, they agreed to the intake.

In the car, we were struck by how docile and unafraid the cat was. I had started to call her Angel, because she was all white, and we modified the name to Weeping Angel after the nefarious living statues from Dr. Who, in keeping with Eric and Sarah's naming scheme. We kept calling her Angel for short, but it didn't feel so sappy now. Angel was alert and interested in the view out the window. I had no trouble containing her in my lap while Sarah drove. She smelled terrible, like unwashed fur and infection; I knew my shirt would reek long after we turned Angel in to the shelter. Never mind that.

I was grateful that I was with Sarah when we found the cat; we were of one mind and it never occurred to either of us that not helping her was even an option.

Not every friend would have seen it that way.

We wound our way through an industrial neighborhood to the shelter, and we phoned for someone to come out and open the gate for us. We brought Weeping Angel inside, to a building that reminded me of our own old shelter building by the airport. Shabby but cheerful, and there was a cat colony room with brightly painted climbing structures. These people did the best they could with what little they had, just like us.

All the Canadian money I had was a twenty-dollar bill, but I handed it over to help with Weeping Angel's care. Sarah emptied her pockets as well. We were horrified when they put Angel in a small, rusty wire cage, but they assured us it was just for her trip to the vet, which she would make right away. She would be housed in a proper kennel when she returned. The man who had opened the gate carried her out to a truck and drove off with her, leaving us to complete the paperwork. I excused myself to use the washroom and when I washed my hands, the water ran dark brown, then gray. I scrubbed like a surgeon, past the elbow. My red-and-white cycling top was stained brown from the dirty cat. When Sarah and I got back in the car, my top smelled just vile and we rolled down the windows.

Sarah drove north on Highway 1, straight to the ferry terminal, and I made the 2:00 sailing, one later than I had planned, but still not late enough to affect my arrival time, or so I thought. The thirty-five miles to Sechelt on the other side were incredibly hilly, with a 600-foot climb right out of the ferry terminal and another 300-foot hill not long after. I didn't get to my night stop until 7:00. The ride was so gorgeous, with snow-peaked mountains and views of shining water below, the beauty took the edge off my exhaustion.

The Upper Deck Guesthouse was delightful. It was the upper floor of a two-story building and featured a large rooftop deck with tables and chairs, lots of flowers, and maritime décor like buoys and nets tossed over the fence that surrounded the deck. Hugh, the manager, welcomed me warmly. Throughout the evening, he made the rounds of the guests and distracted us from our devices, introducing guests to each other and telling us something he knew we had in common to get us started talking. Before bed, he invited me to the common room to have tea and "read paper books." I chose a paperback from the large collection and enjoyed the companionable silence.

Around 10:30, I texted Sarah and asked if the cats had rounded up easily. Nimby was still outside! He refused to come in no matter what anyone did. They took Kali to their house so they could leave the kitty door open for Nimby to come back inside. Around midnight, Eric tried to grab Nimby off the steps and he ran into the woods. They gave up and went to bed. I stayed up all night imagining Nimby out there with the coyotes. I cried and prayed and felt helpless.

At 6:00 AM, Lisa texted me to say she'd come over early to see if she could find Nimby, and he had been asleep on my bed. I asked her to lock both cats in for the rest of my trip. I wasn't spending another night like that! My 38 miles through the mountains to Egmont were absolutely brutal after my sleepless night. According to my elevation mapping utility, I climbed a total of 4,000 feet in over-90-degree heat. That's an exhausting day for a healthy cyclist who got a full night's sleep. But the scenery brought to mind Alan Paton's words from *Cry, the Beloved Country*: "lovely beyond any singing of it."

The highway cut through wild mountain forests and shallow lakes, and I saw eagles, moose, rabbits, and an enormous coyote that might have been a wolf. My hotel room in Egmont was a serene refuge to catch up on my sleep. A luxurious queen-size bed, a large fan, a lovely bathroom, and a view that almost made me cry.

The balcony looked out on the marina, and across the Skookumchuck Narrows to snow peaks on the other side. A tide pool just below my balcony teemed with sea stars and anemones.

The service was less spectacular. The owner had clearly been in the business long enough to hate people. I couldn't blame her; I'd been there myself with my various service-sector jobs. A sign behind the counter read in block letters, "We don't lend tools so don't ask." When I asked for the wi-fi code, Val said you had to be staying more than one night to get it. I said there was no cell signal and I had to check in with my parents, and promised to use the wi-fi code only to do that. I said if she didn't let me check in, I'd given my mom the hotel's phone number and Hurricane Dorothy was going to make landfall in Val's bedroom at 10 PM. Val slapped a card down on the counter and scrawled the access code on the back, and said, "You better not stream any video. That's all you young people want to do, stream video." I almost giggled; Val and I were not far apart in age. But I wore a braid and she wore a beehive; I rode a bike and she drove an Oldsmobile.

Next I went to put in my laundry. It was already 5:00 and a note on the laundry room door said it closed at 6:00 sharp, no exceptions (in the now-familiar block letters). I didn't need to use the dryer, there was plenty of time to run the wash cycle, but I wanted to run down the road and get some dinner while the wash ran and I was worried that I might not get back in time. I went to ask Val if she could accommodate any wiggle room in the closing time. She said there was a restaurant one kilometer down the road and I could easily make it back in time. I asked if she would mind stuffing my laundry in the bag I left on the machine lid, and setting it outside the shed door if I was delayed. She said to make it back on time and we wouldn't have a problem.

I ventured out to the restaurant, which was over a mile away and up a hill that might as well have been a wall. I walked the bike up the hill and breathlessly ordered a meal for take-out. The food took half an hour to cook, and I arrived back at the hotel at 6:05 to find the laundry shed padlocked. Val, her husband and two other couples were having drinks together out on the store patio. I went and asked Val if I could please get my laundry out of the shed; it had to hang overnight and I wouldn't have anything dry to ride in the next day if I couldn't retrieve it. Val said I knew the shed closed at six and I should have been back on time.

I said, "That hill was like a *wall*, you'd know that if you'd ever gone up it under your own power and not in that beast of an Oldsmobile you drive!" Tired and sweaty from the dinner run, I peeled off my red taffeta overblouse to reveal a t-shirt underneath, and my long, red, angry keloid scar from shoulder to elbow. Val's friends gasped and one asked what happened.

I told her about my crash as succinctly as I could. They gushed their amazement at the fact that I was back on my bike, and suddenly the friends were all over Val to let me have my laundry. She buckled under the peer pressure and when I came back with my bag of wet clothes, her friends poured me a glass of wine and urged me to sit down. I began to see how my story could be used to my advantage in certain situations.

I could hardly bear to leave the serene harbor, but in the morning I went out the four-mile roller-coaster of an access road and got back on the highway to Earl's Cove and the ferry to Saltery Bay. It was a gorgeous ride through fjords on a small ferry, and a pleasant day's ride to Powell River from there. The terrain rolled gently, a welcome change from the steep hills of yesterday, and a frequent view of the water made the scenery plenty enjoyable, though less majestic. After a 90-minute ferry ride to Comox, Renee picked me up at the ferry dock and took me to her house, where I spent a pleasant three days with her and her family. I got to spend time with two of her sons and I was so impressed with the young men she'd raised. My jaw just about dropped when her youngest, Jake, said, "Thanks for making dinner, Mom," and carried his own dishes into the kitchen.

My first morning waking up at Renee's, I felt a little dizzy and shaky. I realized I'd missed my 4:00 pain pill, the one I always wake up for at 3:00 and force myself to wait to take. It was almost 9:00. I took the pill and waited for it to kick in, then went upstairs to greet Renee. I told her it was my first pain-free night since I got hit. She understood what a huge deal that was and gave me a hug, then went to take down the information from the mattress tag. After two more nights on that bed, I knew I had to buy that very mattress model. No more improvising with layered feather beds and magnetized pads (a gift from a friend), I would have a proper mattress that fit my new body.

I spent another three nights at Free Spirit Spheres, catching up with Rosey and Tom and watching some guys from Tumbleweed Houses, the Tiny Home building company, film a segment of a documentary about alternative dwellings that inspired their own philosophy. I discovered upon arriving that I'd left my off-bike pants, t-shirt and blouse hanging on hooks behind the door in my room at Renee's house. All I had to wear was my reversible travel dress. No matter, the dress was appropriate, and Rosey complimented "those cute dresses I wear." I showed her it was just one dress, worn inside out on the second day for a different look.

While at Free Spirit, Rosey told me about a sand castle exhibit in Parksville and encouraged me to go see it. I thought about the grueling ride back to Nanaimo and realized I couldn't possibly tromp around sand castles for an hour in the sun, then get back on my bike and hit the four-lane highway. But I really wanted to see the sand castles; I love sand art. I didn't enjoy that stretch along the four-lane and I didn't have to ride it! Vancouver Island is served by abundant buses and I could hop a bus past that stretch and get off on the outskirts of Nanaimo, right where the old railroad trail began. I'd already proven I could ride the distance—twice. I went to see the sand castles, had an ice cream cone, and then got on the bus.

I enjoyed the trail in Nanaimo because I wasn't stressed and exhausted, and arrived at the hostel fresh enough to enjoy exploring the town in the midsummer evening light. I decided to integrate buses more on my tours and be willing to bail and hop a bus when a day's ride proved more difficult than expected. Taking the bus was different from SUV support; I was using energy that was already being expended for a public bus route, whether or not I was on board. If it expanded my touring range in my new body, there was only benefit, no harm.

On the way home, I made a memory that kind of summed up everything good about bike touring and why I do it. I was at the Duke Point ferry terminal, awaiting the boat to Tsawwassen. I needed to use the washroom before eating lunch, and as I walked, in, I saw a young, tough-looking First Nations woman doing her morning routine on the road, her stuff spread all over the counter. Her phone was playing a video of Psy's "Gangnam Style," and she broke away from the mirror to dance with abandon in the middle of the sink area. I stood there feeling conspicuously fiftyish and white in my bike gear, and weighed my options: sidle by warily or back out and come back later. The beat sank into my bones and the choice was suddenly obvious—I joined her. She laughed with delight and we danced together to the end of the song, then I admired the intricate silver raven bracelet she wore. She showed me pictures of her kids and I told her about my trip. I don't know her name, but I will never forget her and the moment of connection we shared.

On the ferry ride home, I got bad news from Sarah. Weeping Angel had been doing poorly at the vet's and we had offered to pay for continuing care to make sure she got every possible chance. She was in kidney failure and they were asking for our permission to euthanize her. We gave it and I went to a quiet seating area to cry. That poor little cat. I had felt like we were destined to save her, we even found her a home with Sarah's family in Abbotsford for when she was released. At least she died knowing love and care, and maybe that had to be enough, knowing we brought her a bit of grace at the end.

I got home to find my clothes shipped from Renee's house, folded more neatly than I ever managed to do.

In August my parents came to visit. They got to see the new shelter, and Laura let me take them into the cat colony room, where they spent a happy hour with the cats. My dad bonded with Nala, a small gray-brown tabby, and it was hard to tear them away from each other. I loved telling him a month later that Nala had been adopted. I took them down to Seattle to ride the Ferris wheel, and we had six rides in a row, with Frank Sinatra playing on the sound system in the VIP car.

Best of all, they got to spend a lot of time with Nimby. He sat in my mom's lap, and my dad and I took him for lots of walks.

Sign of a New Challenge

After my parents left, I started a class in American Sign Language (ASL) at the community college. The campus is a mile from my house and I've always wanted to learn ASL. After using the manual alphabet to rehabilitate my hand, I decided to reward myself with a twelve-week course. I was a little intimidated by the fact that the teacher was Deaf[2]; not because I felt any discomfort with her "disability," (most Deaf people do not consider themselves disabled), but because of my own communication issues. As a child, I had problems with eye contact and using appropriate body language (I hugged my arms to my chest most of the time).

All my life, I've had to make conscious eye contact until I'm comfortable enough with a person for it to happen naturally, and I don't automatically look at people when they're speaking, especially in a classroom situation. I knew that Dawn might have to get my attention until I learned to be alert to visual cues in the way ASL demands. I wrote her a note explaining my issues the best I could, and asking her to be patient with me and not assume I was being rude. She responded warmly, and several times during class, she walked around the room, stopping to gently tap on my hand rather than clap her hands the way she would to bring the entire class to attention. The care she took to be subtle about this made me respect her and try harder to stay with the action.

The other challenge I discovered was that my left arm had been rehabilitated for large range of motion, but not the fine motion required by ASL. Dawn told me my awkward left arm gave me the equivalent of

---

2   Deaf is capitalized when referring to members of a deaf community that uses ASL and shares common cultural attitudes about deafness. Not all deaf people are Deaf.

slurred speech. She often gently turned my arm to put it in the correct position, then I would repeat the sign until I could do it naturally. My arm and shoulder ached for days after class, and just the effort to stay alert for two hours was enough to increase my back pain. I practiced a lot at home, using an online coaching program that had me translate sentences signed on video. I tend to learn to speak and read languages easily; understanding speech is much harder for me. I expected "reading" ASL to be easier, but I had the same challenges I did with spoken comprehension.

One woman in the class, Robin, had a birth defect; her left arm ended at the elbow with a thumb and two fingers. She had a new daughter-in-law who was deaf and used ASL; Robin wanted to learn to talk with her, and Dawn was very encouraging. After two classes, Robin seemed doubtful that she could overcome the challenge of her different limb, so I took her aside and told her about my own arm issues, hoping she'd feel less alone. I told her that ASL was physically painful for me, but I hoped it would restore my fine motor skills and become easier with time. Robin dropped out after three classes. I was sorry to see her go, especially since she really needed to learn to at least understand ASL to have a relationship with her daughter-in-law and stay close to her son.

Lauren's friend Ashley was in my class, and it was fun getting to know her better. Ashley was a stickler for practicing and tried to sign as much as she could of our out-of-class conversations. I liked that; everyone else seemed too self-conscious to try to practice with one another.

We changed teachers after six weeks, and our second teacher, Mike, was less comfortable in the written world than Dawn. He kicked off our training wheels and forced us to sign among ourselves. Any pre-class chatter had to be signed, and Mike would eagerly help us by filling in any signs we didn't know after we finger-spelled a word. We tended to sign as if we were speaking English, and Mike would repeat our sentences in correct ASL grammatical order. Mike encouraged spontaneous signing by teasing us so we'd try to respond. I rehearsed several likely comebacks and enjoyed my triumph the day he asked me to give him $20 and I signed, "In your dreams." The other students didn't respond as well to that teaching method, so Mike tended to pick on the few of us who made the effort to talk back.

My ASL study was interrupted by the events of the next chapter, and I haven't returned to it, but I want to some day. Something about gestural communication feels right to me. Maybe it's because it involves the whole body and requires appropriate facial expressions. I feel more alert to the nonverbal communication that goes on with my hearing friends after learning to sign with Deaf people.

Tragedy

In November, things were heating up at work. I had just taken on a new Seattle waterfront client and I looked forward to a busy winter. I was working at home on a Saturday when I got a phone call from Kathy, that my dad had collapsed while running and he was in a coma in the hospital. She told me to wait until we knew more, but by Sunday morning I couldn't stand it and Kenn booked me a flight.

It was the day of the Volunteer Appreciation Party, our first in the new shelter. I left Sylvia a tearful message explaining why I wouldn't be there. I emailed Ashley and asked her to explain my absence from ASL class to Mike.

My niece Sara picked me up at the airport and I was grateful for her confident driving in the snow. We stopped at a McDonalds where I got a late dinner and went on to my parents' house. The next morning we got up early and went straight to the hospital, where my dad was in the ICU. There was a hand sanitizing station in the doorway to his room where we were required to foam up coming in and out. We filed in one by one, waving our hands dry as we entered. My dad looked so fragile lying there in a cervical collar, a ventilator tube taped to his mouth. I realized that I must have looked exactly the same in the ICU. This was someplace I'd already been, it couldn't be that scary, right? And I'd be able to help him through the disorientation and understand what he was going through when he woke up. My experience made me useful, not helpless.

The neurologist came in and talked briefly with us. No one knew how long my dad had been down after he collapsed; his heart had stopped and he had some level of anoxic brain injury. His blood was being chilled to give his brain a chance to heal, just like mine had been. The plan was to keep him in the induced coma until tomorrow. They'd warm him up, then reduce the sedation to allow him to wake up. This all sounded hopeful to me; having been in the same position, I didn't find it as scary as the others did. I held my dad's cold hand, our matching black rubber Road ID wristbands touching.

On Monday morning, my dad was warmed back to normal temperature and we gathered around his bed as the nurse reduced the sedation to wake him up. My dad's eyes snapped open and his arms raised rigidly as his whole body shook in a grand mal seizure. Within seconds, the sedation was back on full and the seizure stopped, leaving him looking like he'd been dropped into the bed from a helicopter. This was not a good sign. My mom just about fell apart; I knew my dad wasn't aware during the seizure but it didn't make it any less disturbing to see.

The neurologist gathered us in a small room in the family lounge and told us this wasn't a good sign, but all hope wasn't lost yet; they would resume the chilled coma therapy until Friday and try again. My whole family was sobbing; I excused myself and ran to the bathroom where I threw up.

We developed a routine of eating in the hospital cafeteria. The food was dreadful and I quickly learned to stick with the prepacked salads, ask for soup samples, and avoid the hot entrees altogether, they were predictably terrible.

Every morning my mom dressed in her best clothes, to look nice for my dad in case he woke up. The rest of us threw on jeans and sweatshirts for the long day in the hospital. Ever the light packer, I had brought one reversible fleece sweater that I washed every other day after wearing it with both sides out.

Kenn was in Florida visiting his brother and due

to come home in a week. He left early and detoured to Minnesota, driving his van up and arriving Wednesday night long after my mom had gone to bed. I was so exhausted, I just said hello and turned in. He had to share the guest room with me, there was nowhere else to sleep. I stuffed in my ear plugs, but they were a thin defense against the roaring snores that started around 1:00. I dragged a blanket to the couch in the living room, where I lay with considerable spinal pain, then my mom's snoring cut through her closed bedroom door and my ear plugs. I started to cry and went back to bed, where I laid awake until things quieted down around 4:00.

We got up early to start our morning vigil. As the designated driver of my mom's Saturn Vue (a hybrid SUV/minivan), on icy November roads, I wasn't much good, but I was too exhausted to know it. I dropped my mom off with Kenn to help her and drove around several lots before finding a parking space. I walked back in the scouring cold wind, barely able to take a breath. Upstairs, I greeted my dad by saying, "I drove your car and I let the gas gauge drop to a quarter tank." If anything would wake him up, that would be it. My dad taught me to always fill up at the half-tank mark. I hate getting gas and usually let the fuel light come on before I go to the gas station.

I kept telling him he had to get better, that he was the one who gave me the strength to get back on my bike and I came all that way to return the favor.

Beth and John arrived from Florida and I spent most of the day in the family lounge, working on permit applications for my new client on my laptop while John worked on his beside me. It was hard to think about work, but once I got my head in the right place, it helped to have a distraction. A lot of my work involved standard forms that required gathering information from various reference web sites to fill in the blanks. The TV was usually blaring in the family lounge, and it drove me up a wall. As soon as the last actively watching person left the lounge, I turned the volume down for five minutes of silence before the next person turned it back up.

Kathy and I walked the hospital corridors regularly, struggling to keep up our exercise regimes despite the confinement in the hospital. We both suffered from a lot of back pain. I started taking as much oxycodone as I needed, regardless of my actual dose schedule, and chasing it with Tylenol.

On Thursday night, John suggested that we all go out to a swanky restaurant for a proper meal. He offered to treat. We went to Granite City, where John ordered bottles of wine. There was no alcohol ever in our house growing up, and my mom didn't drink, but John knew the rest of us needed to. As my mom's designated driver, I had to abstain, and the smell of wine all around me just about drove me mad. I'm afraid I wasn't a very good sport about it. My mom asked John for the maraschino cherry in his drink; John was drinking a strong whiskey cocktail and he gamely handed my mom the cherry. She popped it in her mouth and made a face and spit it out; it was steeped in whiskey. We all laughed, then half an hour later, John handed my mom another cherry and she fell for it a second time. We needed to laugh over *something*.

The days wore on in a new, terrible routine. Representatives from my parents' church came by and we all prayed together. I felt like a bit of a fraud, as I'm an agnostic. Not agnostic in the sense of you think Christianity might be true or not, but in the sense that *any* religion is real or not. I think if there is something, it's nothing like the Judeo-Christian concept of God, and it isn't separate from us. But it was a family cultural thing, and I'm pretty sure my dad participated for the same reason. He saw the value in the church culture, and in the moral teachings and all. I talked frankly with one of the church workers and we had a good, respectful chat.

I stayed in the room once when the nurses cleaned my dad's ventilator tube. I liked the nurse who handled him so gently, an older man who called my dad by name and talked to him as if he understood. My dad's body arched in the bed during the tube cleaning, and I had a memory of a dark agitation when that was done to me. Not a conscious thought, just a general *minding* what was being done. It wasn't so bad remembering my own experience, but it was intolerable to see my dad going through the same thing.

Friday morning came and we gathered in my dad's room with dread. We waited for the neurologists until 10:30. When they arrived, they sent us to the family lounge while they ran their tests alone. They came back and explained that there was minimal brain activity. My dad wasn't brain-dead, but there wasn't enough function for him to regain even the most basic consciousness. The head neurologist told us to take twenty-four hours to decide what we wanted to do.

We sat in stunned silence as the team turned to leave, then I said, "If he's not going to get better, I don't want him in there for twenty-four more minutes." My mom agreed and said she wanted to disconnect life support right away. They persuaded us to wait until after lunch. No one felt like eating, but we all forced one another to go through the motions for my mom's sake; she was diabetic and had to keep her blood sugar stable.

Like zombies, we went back to the room, where they told us about the disconnection process and how my dad would likely not go right away, it could take anywhere from an hour to days. When they took out the breathing tube, he started making a terrible, hoarse, tortured breath sound. This is "agonal breathing,"

breathing directed by the brain stem, and it's something you never see on TV, where the family holds hands while their loved one quietly slips away. It's nothing like that in real life and we weren't prepared for that. (You'd think that would be one of the things they'd tell us about beforehand.) The doctor said he could give my dad Ativan to control the breathing if we wanted him to, but it might hasten his death. We begged him to do it right away, I couldn't stand the sound, and who wouldn't want to hasten death if life was like this? Every noisy breath reminded me of lying in the ditch with collapsed lungs.

Out in the hall, Sara and Jenny were having a full meltdown. I realized that living as close to my parents as they did, they had kind of had two sets of parents. Jordan, my brother-in-law, tried to comfort them when he could clearly use comfort himself.

Seeing my dad like that, going through my own worst-case scenario, put me over the edge. I called my nurse practitioner back home, knowing her clinic was still open, and asked for something, anything, to help me not feel this way. She prescribed a low dose of Xanax and phoned it into the pharmacy my parents used. I couldn't go get it until the family was ready to go. We waited a few hours and it became clear that nothing was going to change any time soon, so we went home.

My mom's neighbors, Don and Gerri, cooked us a lovely Italian dinner that night. I couldn't go to the pharmacy until after dinner, and I drank a bit too much wine with dinner—I was afraid they wouldn't let me have the pills. I agreed not to take any until morning. At least the wine numbed me a bit. Just sitting with Don and Gerri helped reorient me in the world a little, but it was all so unreal.

I barely slept that night, between the wine and my nerves. In the morning I didn't feel like eating anything. I asked Kenn if he could drive because I didn't know how the Xanax was going to affect me and I didn't want to wait to take it.

Within minutes of taking the pill, my appetite returned with a vengeance. I wolfed a breakfast bar in the car and actually tasted it. Unbelievably, I felt better. We arrived to find that my dad had been moved from the ICU to a hospice suite on another floor. Outside the room, a table had been set up with coffee and tea service, a bowl of fruit, and a variety of snacks. A tent card said, "For the comfort of the Noreen family." I was so touched by that bit of consideration.

A doctor arrived, a woman with curly blonde hair and blue eyes. She looked familiar. She introduced herself as Dr. Anne Whitney, daughter of my dad's running friend, Jim Whitney. Of course—Anne and I played together as children while our dads ran their races. We were never close friends, but I always liked her. Dr. Whitney said she had requested my dad's hospice care duty and asked for our permission to serve as his doctor, saying it would be her honor. My mom agreed, and Dr. Whitney and her nursing team cared for us all as compassionately as they could.

The church team came back to pray with us. We formed a circle around my dad's bed, holding hands, and Reverend Sartain led the prayer. My dad's breathing was much quieter, but he still vocalized a bit on every exhalation. When Reverend Sartain said, "Paul was a true believer," my dad made a sound like "huh-uh," and it was all I could do not to laugh. The timing was so perfect.

We kept vigil in the bigger, more comfortable hospice room for two more days. Then I had to make a decision. I was missing a lot of work, losing about $300 a day by being gone. It had been a very light summer and I needed that money. My cats had a great sitter but I needed to get back to them at some point. Dr.

Whitney said it could be days yet. All of us were wearing on one another's nerves. There was nothing more I could do. Impossibly, on Monday morning I said goodbye to my dad and left in Kenn's van for the three-day trip home.

Riding in a van on icy roads for twelve hours a day was about the last thing I was fit to do. Fortunately, the Xanax put me in a haze where I felt distanced from what was happening. The first day on the road, we made it to Billings, Montana, only a few hours from where Emily now worked. If I'd been there for a different reason, I might have tried to meet up with her. We stayed in a motel with a swimming pool and I enjoyed a good stretch in the pool before bed. It was below zero outside and the condensation formed hard ice on the pool room windows. Between my ear plugs and the Xanax, I at least had no trouble sleeping.

In the van about halfway across Montana, I got the call from my mom. My dad had gone while she was taking a break. Their friends Doug and Betty were with him. It didn't feel like anything had changed, really. I had lost my dad the minute he fell on the running path.

We spent the next night in Missoula, where Kenn and I met in college. We tried to stay in the old Red Lion hotel, but it had changed to a Doubletree Inn. I didn't care, Doubletree was fine with me, but Kenn had a sentimental attachment to the Red Lion so we went to their other location in town near the hospital. I wanted a swim, but the pool was closed and the hot tub was also outdoors. Billowing steam marked its location on the opposite side of the parking lot. In mid-November, with deep snow and ice? I might have tried it before I got hit, but not now.

The next day we powered all the way to Bellingham, getting in around 10:30 at night. The cats were thrilled to see us, and full of beans from being confined for so many days. The poor kids didn't get much playtime, I went straight to bed with Nimby curled at my side and Kali pinning down my legs.

Because my dad wanted to be cremated, and everyone was so scattered around the country, we decided to hold his memorial service in January so we could all plan ahead. The original date my mom set was the 18th. I vetoed that immediately. No way was I doing that the day after my birthday. We chose the 11th.

Now there was nothing left to do but get on with the stark reality of living without him. I returned to my ASL class the week after I got home. I wasn't ready, but I'd already missed so much, and I hadn't practiced while I was out. When I walked back in the room, Mike signed, "How is your dad?" I signed, "He died." Mike signed, "I'm sorry," with such sincerity that I cried. The last two class sessions were pretty much lost on me; I was literally just going through the motions.

Happy Hellidays

Thanksgiving came just three days after my dad died. In a way, it was good, because it meant I got a few days off where my clients were off too. Kenn brought the usual dinner from his friend's restaurant in Mountlake Terrace. I went through the motions. The cats and their happy antics made it bearable.

Friday morning I was back to work, making up for lost time. I had a Seattle waterfront client who needed to obtain permits in time for the anticipated seawall replacement work, when the pier would be closed anyway. It was the perfect time for them to do their own renovations. I had to work hard in order to get the applications in on time.

The following week I had to make a trip down to Seattle to visit the new client's pier. It was a cold winter day with an icy wind that cut through my wool dress coat. There was no rail on the end of the pier where we were, and plywood sheets covered open pile ends. In the back of my mind, I wondered if I should be wearing a life jacket. I was too numb to care; I just tried to make nice with my new client, who I genuinely liked. I had parked my car in their on-site garage, too close to the support pillar. I had been able to slither out with my smooth wool coat acting like a spatula, but getting back in was another story. I had to get in on the passenger side and climb over the shifter, no easy task with a spine that's been fractured in several places. I was vaguely conscious of the fact that I would laugh at that incident someday.

I drove home in a trance. I shouldn't have been driving at all, I was medicated and not even partly there. As I pulled in to Bellingham, the song "Under Pressure" came on the radio. I turned it up until the car shook with it. Then suddenly I pulled over and sobbed, screaming and pounding the steering wheel. I sat there, on the shoulder next to the community college play field, until I was spent.

I had to write a Biological Evaluation for my client; it's a report used for compliance with the Endangered Species Act. One component of a BE is the noise analysis in which I have to determine the distance that sound travels from the project site to the point where it no longer affects fish behavior. This is done using a logarithmic math formula. Usually I do noise analyses pretty effortlessly; it was my specialty when I was at my old company. I taught everyone else how to do it. I even studied acoustical science on my own to better understand the principles, confirming my suspicion that the formula was a flawed model at best.

This time I could not wrap my head around the noise analysis no matter how hard I tried. Bear in mind that this was during a time when people are normally out on bereavement leave, and there I was at my desk. I asked Brad for help, and he tried to cajole me into realizing I could do it. I couldn't do it. Finally I sent him the report minus the noise analysis and told him I just couldn't manage it. I hated to admit that vulnerability, but I hated too that he thought I could just power through it at a time like this.

The conflict over the noise analysis made me decide to see my trauma psychologist, Dr. Ford, the one I had seen for a few months after my crash. Dr. Ford was aghast that I was working at all. He said taking time off to heal was essential to my mental health. Not only was I in mourning, I was under severe post-traumatic stress with delayed processing of my own issues. It was going to take time to process what I had seen in the hospital. I told Brad I was going on limited duty for a week.

I went to the gym to take care of my body. I was having the highest pain levels since I was hit, and I had to get back into my exercise routine. I went to my beloved stationary bike and programmed in my usual workout, not bothering to switch the display to French or Spanish as I normally did. I started my iPod and pedaled until the rhythm set in, my breathing deepened, and then I started sobbing. Something about that first surge of endorphins made me lose it. I managed to finish my seven miles, crying the whole way. I shut everyone out around me, ignoring the stares and the wide path people took around the bike.

Downstairs in the shower area, violent bangs startled me from barbells being dropped on the floor above. My normal response to being startled is outrage; I can't use an alarm clock for that reason. Starting the day angry is no way to live; I use a graduated light alarm when I have to. At the gym, the bangs made me want to curl up and hide. I managed to finish my shower and get out of there. I had to take Xanax in order to be in that locker room for the rest of the winter.

In December I had to go down to the Corps of Engineers office for an interagency meeting. Normally we'd have had the meeting at the pier office, but my Corps reviewer graciously scheduled the meeting for me while I was in Minnesota. The other team members groused about having to go to the Corps compound and I explained why the meeting was there and that they should thank our reviewer for her hospitality.

I drove down the morning of the meeting, leaving the house at 7:00 so I had plenty of time to make the 10:00 meeting. It was still dark when I pulled out and I watched the sun come up over the mountains as I drove south. I arrived at the Corps compound at 9:15, needing to use the bathroom so badly, I was sweating. I drove around looking for the entrance gate. Each time I turned in off East Marginal Way and found a dead end, I had to get back out on the busy four-lane road. The majority of traffic on East Marginal Way consists of semi trucks, generally barreling along at about 45 miles per hour. Finally I saw a gate with a security booth and got in line behind two other cars. My turn came and I showed my ID and stated my business. The guard said I needed to be in the guest lot across the street and gave rather involved directions to get there. I asked if I could use a restroom before I went back out in search of parking. He said there was one inside the building I could use after I park. In pain, I backed up and drove back out, noticing a Port-a-Potty along the way where construction was going on. I pulled over and ran inside before anyone could stop me.

I could not find the alleged visitor lot to save my life. The smell of the hand sanitizer from the Port-a-Potty permeated the car, so strong it made me dizzy. I went up and down East Marginal Way three times before I pulled back up to the security gate and asked the guard to repeat his directions. I was sure he could smell the hand sanitizer and had seen me use the Port-a-Potty.

This time I found the lot and couldn't believe I was expected to park there. It looked like a police impound lot, with cracked pavement and loose gravel strewn about, few pedestrian exits through the high chainlink fence, and a general creepy feeling. I checked my path to the gate to make sure no shady characters lurked along the way. Now that I was done driving, I popped a Xanax and crossed busy East Marginal Way at the crosswalk to get to the Corps building, waiting until I was sure the trucks were stopped, then running as the crossing light countdown reached twelve seconds. It was 10:10 and my phone lit up with texts from Kyle asking where I was. I felt battered and wished for a rest, but there was nothing to do but keep walking toward the building.

I produced my passport for federally-issued ID and was escorted back to the meeting room, where they had started without me. Before I went in, I ducked into the bathroom to wash the Port-a-Potty sanitizer off my hands. I could still smell it in my nostrils as I walked to the one remaining open seat at the table, and felt sure the others could smell it too. We were working out the mitigation approach for a pier project and we had to get creative with ideas, since opportunities on our site were so limited. Normally in meetings, I have a hard time staying with the discussion and my happy place beckons irresistibly. When I felt the Xanax kick in, I was suddenly present at the meeting and everything else fell away. I asked appropriate questions to guide the discussion. Laura from the Department of Fish and Wildlife provided the comic relief, and the meeting was actually productive.

As I walked back to the parking lot, I imagined my dad watching me in the meeting and wondered how he'd feel about what I do. I guessed that he'd have been bored three minutes in and moved on to see what Kathy and Beth were up to. As a child, I had been told that the dead "watch over" the living from heaven. I didn't believe that any more, but childhood conditioning is hard to break. I pictured him always with Fud, our giant male tabby cat who was my best friend as a child, but always Dad's cat.

The Xanax helped me that day, and it seemed to enhance my pain relief, but as time went by, I found it was hollowing out my brain like a melon baller. My short-term memory was shot and I was always in a mildly nervous state, trying to remember what I was supposed to be doing. It also seemed to trigger hot flashes, severe ones that drenched me and then started again twenty minutes later. I backed it off and then stopped taking it. It took weeks to recover from the effects and I was still anxious much of the time, I just didn't dare keep taking it for fear of losing my livelihood.

I always write a holiday letter to enclose in my

cards, but this year I just didn't feel like it. I told Dr. Ford that I had always written the letters for my dad. He suggested that I write it for my dad again now, then he asked me to read it out loud to my dad in his office. It was an agonizing exercise, but I did it, and it was a good letter. It even made Dr. Ford tear up a little.

I needed to go in to Village Books to get my annual moon calendar; I love the ones they sell there. Walking into my dad's happy place was hard. I walked around tearfully until I came to the Giving Tree, where you pick an ornament and buy a book for the child described on it. I took one for a seven-year-old girl and got Pickles the Cat, one of my favorite books as a child. The gifts are supposed to be anonymous, but I wrote on my ornament, "With love from Paul Noreen." Dr. Ford said that was an outstandingly appropriate, meaningful, and healthy thing to do, and he felt much better about my progress.

Christmas passed without much celebration. The recent birth of my grandniece, Molly, relieved us a little, but she lived in Florida and I couldn't afford to go see her. I'm still the only one in the family who hasn't met her.

Memorial

My dad's service was in January, and Kenn came along. Well, Kenn bought his own ticket and booked me as a companion fare, so to say he "came along" isn't quite fair. I flew out of Bellingham and met him at the Seattle airport. As I prepared to leave, I said good-bye to Kali first. She scuttled away, knowing what was happening, then I went to Nimby, who stretched out on the floor and reached back for me with his front legs, the way I love. I started to run my hand down his entire body and stopped near his shoulder. It was unmistakable, the tumor was back. I had to catch the plane—my vision swam with tears as I left. Eric and Sarah drove me to the airport and I was too dispirited to say much of anything.

When I arrived in Minnesota, I called Nimby's vet and made an appointment for the day after I was scheduled to get home, the day before my birthday. It was all I could do to hang on for the week I was there.

At the service, I saw relatives I hadn't seen in years; some I didn't recognize. My cousin Sherri seemed offended that I didn't know who she was, but the last time we saw each other, we were awkward teenagers. The beautiful woman she'd become should have been pleased that I didn't recognize her. I was a little dismayed that she had no trouble recognizing me.

Seeing Ralph out of context was odd; he belonged in Washington with me. He was an enormous comfort, though. He nattered at me about coming to visit. I knew that leaving for an overnight to Bainbridge Island was out of the question until Nimby's situation was resolved, however that happened.

Liz, my best friend from high school, came to the service and I was so grateful to have her there. Another friend of ours, Nancy, was there too. My dad had been a mentor to her when she was going through difficult times, and lots of other people came to tell us how my dad had helped them. It was good to see he'd made a real difference to so many.

In a trance, I went to lunches with family friends and relatives. Jenny cut my hair, as she had recently graduated from cosmetology school. She did a great job. Finally it was time to go home. My mom was still fragile and begged me to stay longer. I needed to get back to Nimby.

Kitty Hospice

Nimby's appointment was the day after I got back from my dad's service. Kenn came up to help me get him to the vet. Nimby was still unbelievably strong, nineteen pounds of solid muscle, and getting him into a crate with my arms was no easy task. The first surgery had left him with two fragile artificial ribs; it was dangerous to struggle with him. I needed a quick capture.

This time the first trap attempt was successful. Nimby was taken completely by surprise and he yowled in outrage for the first few miles before settling into sullen silence. I talked to him and sang his kitty songs, grateful to not be driving for once.

The vet who was so good with him before, Dr. Coyne, did the exam and she sent him upstairs for an X-ray. Preliminarily, she thought the mass wasn't adhesive and could be removed with another surgery. It was a lot smaller than before, and the surgery would be less of a strain on Nimby's body. The X-ray results came back and my hopes were dashed. The mass had penetrated the chest wall. It was too late for surgery. There was nothing left to do but take him home and let him be a cat for as long as he could. Dr. Coyne's own dog had the same type of cancer and she hated giving me that news, but it helped to know that a vet had made the same choices for her own animal.

My fiftieth birthday passed pretty much unnoticed. I took Nimby for a long walk around the complex and made sure he had a good day. From here on in, I wanted every day to be a good day until it couldn't be any more. I was going to cram as much quality into his life as I could.

I withdrew from volunteering to focus my attention on Nimby. I also quit going to trivia; I needed to spend my evenings at home with the cats. For the rest of the winter, we did have lots of good days. We spent our days in the sewing room when I wasn't busy working. I took him on walks whenever the weather allowed. He played with his friends and enjoyed his life. Every morning he played "troll" with Kali while I laid in bed. He laid across the bedroom doorway on his back and Kali would run toward him and jump over him. She could clear him easily, but she never did; she always jumped low enough for him to swipe her down with one paw. She would roll to the floor with mock histrionics, acting as if his attack were completely unexpected. Nimby joy-rolled triumphantly. When I got up, Nimby reported for Morning Hugdown, then he clamored for breakfast, reaching up to the counter and yelling at me to serve it up faster. He was positively bursting with life. I found myself feeling happy even as my heart broke for what was to come.

In February, Kali came in from her morning rounds limping badly. She favored her right rear leg and seemed to be in pain. I got in with the vet right away and she diagnosed a torn anterior cruciate ligament (ACL). There were some claw wounds around her hips, indicating that she'd been attacked from behind. Later, a neighbor confirmed that it was another neighbor's cat who had regular dustups with all five of the colony—Eric's, Sarah's and my cats. Kali had tried to run up a tree and Jasmine had grabbed her and tried to pull her down. Poor little Kali had to stay inside for ten days and take anti-inflammatory medicine. She proved ridiculously easy to give pills to, compared to the fight Nimby put up. The flap on my kitty door broke, so I had to lock the panel anyway until the new one came. Nimby was confused by the whole door scenario and Kali had cabin fever; she often pawed at the door while Nimby sat outside on the back porch.

The stress of dealing with two infirm cats was incredible. I was told Kali needed expensive surgery for her knee, after which she would be confined to a knee-high kennel for six weeks to keep her from jumping. That would just have to wait until Nimby was gone; managing that while he was sick would be too much. Kali recovered quickly and didn't seem to be in any pain, so the vet concurred.

In March Nimby started losing weight rapidly and the tumor became a visible bulge. Lisa encouraged me to keep a daily record of his condition so I would know whether changes represented a trend or just a bad day. Looking back at that journal brings back so many memories.

By April it was day by day, every morning I would feel incredible relief that today was not the day. I alerted the home care vet to be on call, knowing it wouldn't be long. I still took bike rides and came home to find Nimby waiting for me in the bushes. He ran out to greet me and play on the stairs like he always had. Once in a while he would run up the stairs and stand there befuddled, like he couldn't remember why he was there, and he wouldn't respond to my high-five games through the rails. This happened more and more often, and it just tore my heart to pieces. I would pet him and tell him it was okay, let's go in now and get treats.

Every morning Nimby followed me across the drive to the sidewalk on the other side, the first stretch of our walk to the mailbox. He pranced across the drive, his tail erect, Large and In Charge. I called him my Lion-Hearted Boy and my heart swelled with pride for my little fighter. He followed me to the Shouty House, a lower-floor unit where three adults and three children kept up their Jerry Springer shrieking theatrics 24-7, scuttled past the blast zone, and holed up behind the bushes along the next building to wait as I went around the bend to the mailbox. He wasn't up to the walk behind the 3-story building where there were daylight basement units and people left their windows open for their cats to come and go. He knew he couldn't defend his Top Cat status any more and he had the sense to hang back. Eventually he even avoided the Shouty House. I couldn't blame him; I'd go another way if there was one.

Kenn came up most weekends to spend time with Nimby. We took quick trips up to Canada for provisions, what I called my "Canadimoddities," and devoted most of our time to walking with Nimby and giving him lap time. He seemed to really enjoy Kenn's visits and pull out a little extra energy for them.

One weekend Nimby just couldn't keep up, he was clearly losing ground. Kenn left in tears, knowing it was the last time he'd see him. The next day, Nimby was on the back porch and I happened to see a raccoon approaching him. Nimby stood still and locked eyes with the raccoon, knowing if he turned his back, the raccoon would attack. The raccoon kept coming toward him. I stepped outside and grabbed Nimby when the raccoon was only about six feet away, tossing him inside, sliding the door closed behind me and locking the kitty door almost in a single motion. Nimby hissed and spit in outrage. I said, "Not like that, Boo. You will *not* go out like that. You will live until Mommy pays Dr. Fjeld $300 to kill you properly." And I went to cry where he wouldn't see me doing it.

I realized that Nimby was getting too frail to be outside without supervision. Nimby *would* rather die than be locked inside all the time. It was almost Time. Most nights he sank into the comfort of my folded winter duvet, stretching happily when I checked on him during the night. One night he was wakeful and restless, and I could tell he was uncomfortable. The next morning I called Dr. Fjeld. She arranged to come at 11:00. I opened the door for Nimby to do his morning rounds, thinking he wouldn't bother because it was raining. Nimby took off on his route and didn't come back for his usual 10:00 nap. It was pouring rain and I couldn't find him anywhere. I called Dr. Fjeld and said he was AWOL. She laughed and said that was exactly like Nimby, and should we wait? I said no, he couldn't have another night like last night. She rescheduled for late afternoon.

Nimby did come back around lunch time and settled in for a restless nap on his window perch. I wanted to stay with him but knew it would agitate him, so I talked to him for a while, then let him be. I told him what was going to happen that afternoon and why, and that it was going to be all right. I told him he was my best friend in all the world, of all time, and my love would be his forever. I finally cried in front of him. I had tried so hard to stay upbeat while he was sick.

I stared blankly at the pieces of a jigsaw puzzle until Dr. Fjeld arrived. Kali curled up in my lap and I talked to her about what was happening.

I put on Nimby's favorite Wailin' Jennys CD, *40 Days*, and Dr. Fjeld spent a few minutes petting Nimby and assessing his condition. She was shocked by how thin he was and agreed with me that it was Time. While she petted him, she quickly injected him with the sedative that would make him unaware of the rest of the proceedings. He hissed and walked toward the bedroom but never made it under the bed; he dropped in his tracks in under a minute. This was the end of Nimby's conscious life.

I sat in my living-room chair, shattered, as Dr. Fjeld laid him in my lap. His breathing was deep and loud as his body fought to keep breathing under the heavy sedation. I petted him and talked to him while Dr. Fjeld prepared the IV. Kali jumped up on the end table and watched quietly, her eyes fearful. I petted her too and tearfully explained what was happening. I told Nimby to go find his grandpa.

Dr. Fjeld gave the final injection and Nimby's

breathing slowed, then stopped. She verified that his heart had stopped and then sat quietly with me until the CD finished its last song. Kali tore around the house, her eyes dilated. There was a manic, angry quality to her run, it was nothing like her playful "psycho runs." Eventually she quieted and I didn't see where she went. Nimby stayed warm in my lap. Handing him over to Dr. Fjeld was the hardest thing I ever did. Tears streaked her face too and she handled him with love and respect.

Then they were gone, and I went to look for Kali. She was curled in a tight ball at the foot of my bed, and when I touched her, she let out a keening wail and curled up tighter. I petted her and sobbed until we both fell asleep.

Picking Up the Pieces

Kali stayed curled up on the bed for the better part of two days. I made lists of all the things I had let go while Nimby was sick, like getting a haircut, and numbly went about doing tasks. I had only served existing clients over the last six months and made no effort to drum up more business; that would have required leaving Nimby's side. My bike trip was scheduled for late July. I'd had to book my overnight stays back in February and I'd had to estimate when I would be free to go. It had felt like betting against Nimby, but I knew how badly I was going to need that trip. Nimby died on May 28. I had almost seven weeks before I pushed off.

Kali was finally an only cat, a role she had pretended to covet. Kali didn't know what she wanted without Nimby to compete with for it. She seemed cut adrift, needy and unhappy. I decided to give it until I got back from my trip, then reassess how she was doing and decide whether or not to get her a new friend. Meanwhile, I couldn't sit down anywhere without her being instantly in my lap. In bed, she clung to me and followed me to the bathroom when I got up. I hated to leave her alone when I went out for the day or the evening, and often asked Sarah or Lisa to visit her if I was going to be long.

One morning I tried to put away the extra set of dishes I'd bought when Kali moved in. It just made me too sad to see them empty on the floor. Kali had used Nimby's dishes and forced him to eat from the smaller ones that were just her size. Kali melted down when I picked up the metal frame that raises the dishes a few inches off the floor. She mewed and paced, her tail flicking in distress. I set the dishes back down and held her and cried. One morning a few days later, she came and tapped my side with her paw while I sat at my desk, the way she usually asked for attention, and I followed her to the kitchen. She paced around Nimby's dishes, mewing frantically, as if to ask where he was. I filled the dishes with food and water and it soothed her a bit.

I went down to Seattle for a day to visit the clients I hadn't seen while Nimby was sick. Everything felt empty and wrong. Seattle pulled out its worst traffic in my honor and I wondered how I used to live that way. I didn't bother to ride the Ferris wheel. The weeks before departure crawled by.

It was time to take Kali to the doctor and deal with her knee issue. I arranged an X-ray to see if she still needed surgery. I was told her ligament was damaged, but surgery wouldn't help because she had severe degenerative arthritis in her tiny hips. The poor girl was only nine years old. I studied up on diet and lifestyle changes to make her more comfortable and she responded right away. She especially liked the self-heating blanket; it used a space blanket inside a fleece sleeve to reflect her own body heat back at her. I ordered it in a leopard print that resembled Nimby's fur.

I needed a weekend warmup ride to get Kali used to the idea of me being gone. She'd gone through many bike trips in her time, but never as my only cat. The warmup ride also serves as my dry run; I forget something, discover a mechanical issue, or make one mistake on the warmup every year that I would have made on the big trip otherwise. For me, the warmup ride was a hedge against Murphy's Law.

I planned to go to Victoria and ride the Lochside and Galloping Goose trails. I took the ferry on a Friday morning, sitting in on my 11:00 conference call from a bench at the ferry terminal. We boarded while I had the conference on mute. The background noise was so loud, I could barely follow along. Once when it was my turn to say something, a loud horn blast nearly deafened the people in the conference room back on Pier 57. Mercifully, the signal cut out just before the vessel left the slip and I didn't try to get back on the conference.

The warm, sunny day reminded me that summer had started while I was on hospice duty and I was joining the season already in progress. I rolled off the ferry at Saanich Point onto the Lochside Trail, reveling in the fresh island air and the sun on my skin. I greeted my beloved landmarks along the trail, the remote control airplane park, the trailside produce market, the boardwalk across the slough. Victoria came into view and I was almost sorry to be arriving so quickly.

I checked in at the hostel and was assigned a bunk in the upstairs dorm nearest the showers. The dorm was much lighter and airier than the ones downstairs. My bunkmate greeted me from her yoga mat on the floor by the window. She stood without touching the floor with her hands and I marveled that she looked older than me but radiated a youthful energy. She told me her name was Joy and I almost said, "Of course it is." Joy returned to her yoga and I set out to rustle up some dinner at my favorite grocery store, The Market on Yates. Seeing my familiar haunts cheered me. This had been a part of my life I lived without Nimby; he wasn't conspicuously missing here. For the first time in weeks, my world felt normal.

The next morning I got up early and went to the bus stop ahead of time to make sure I got on the right bus. Another crystal summer day. A woman at the bus stop made small talk and asked if I'd seen the strawberries at the farmer's market. I said I hadn't gone, but I'd noticed that all the berries at the grocery store were from California. The woman said that was because most of the good local berries got shipped to

China, and if I wanted to get some, I needed to hit the local farm stands. I thanked her sincerely for the information and she passed me a ripe red berry that almost filled the palm of my hand. It burst with flavor; it was the first food I really noticed enjoying since my dad died.

The bus was a double decker and I would have loved to go upstairs, but I wanted to keep an eye on my bike. The ride lasted an hour, tooling through small towns and eventually winding out into the country on a hilly two-lane highway. I wasn't sure where to get off, and the driver wasn't sure where to tell me to, so I got off at the same place I had two years ago. I knew this put me ten kilometers from the trail head, but it was familiar and I wanted the day to go smoothly. I stopped at the little convenience store by the road to use the washroom, and the owner was a delightful British man. We chatted a bit and I bought a bunch of imported British candy.

I texted Renee to announce my presence on the island, however far south, and started off on the trail. The woods formed a canopy over my head and a cool breeze blew gently through the trees. The smell of juniper was intoxicating. I had only done this trail once, but I greeted every familiar sight like an old friend. I was aware of my heart working and my muscles stretching and contracting—I felt *strong* for the first time since I'd been hit. I remembered the trail being strenuously long. This time it went way too quickly. I was dismayed to reach my lunch stop a full hour before I had expected to. I was plenty hungry and ready to eat, I just didn't want the day to go by so quickly.

As I got close to town, I noticed a black cat sprawled on the trail, asleep in the sun. I stopped and said hello, and suggested that she might like to stretch out in a safer place. She purred and joy-rolled on the pavement.

A man with a little girl came by and the girl greeted

the cat like an old friend. Her father told me the cat slept out on the trail like that all the time. I let the little girl have her time with her friend and rode on.

Back at the hostel, I showered and walked across the street to the Indian restaurant for a delicious meal, texting with several friends between bites. It was almost like eating with other people. I was by the window and could see the boat traffic in the canal under the blue steel Johnson Street Bridge. I went back to the hostel after dinner and found Joy with her friend Leigh upstairs. Both women were displaced while their apartment building was being fumigated, and enjoying big savings by staying at the hostel on their hotel allowance. Leigh was a pretty 60ish woman who loved to tell stories, and I suspected she enjoyed plenty of booze as well. She was off work and not driving; I didn't begrudge her that.

We talked a long time and Leigh said she was in the Jazz Festival going on that weekend; her church choir was going to be part of an all-music service the next morning. Leigh invited a bunch of people to come. Downstairs in the kitchen, I asked another of our roommates if she was going. She said no, church wasn't her thing. I thought about it for a bit; church is definitely not my thing, but I do like gospel music, and Leigh had invited me to come. One of my bike-trip ethics is that if a new friend invites you to participate in her local culture, you do it if you can. It would mean a later departure than I wanted, but I decided to attend Leigh's church in the morning.

Leigh was dressed and gone when I got up. I had breakfast and struck out for the old stone-and-brick United Church on Balmoral Road. I locked Silver in the playground behind the church and went inside carrying my bags, as the surrounding neighborhood looked like the kind of place where you don't leave your valuables unattended. I found a seat and set my panniers next to me on the pew. I looked up toward the front and the choir was already seated in folding chairs on wide risers. I picked out Leigh, looking lovely in a white skirt and pink blouse. She saw me and stood up, grinning and waving. I was so glad I had come. I was the only one there from the hostel dorm.

The music was worth coming for. Jazz pianist Leslie Rose was there, and those stodgy-looking elderly Canadians got down and rocked like the church from the Blues Brothers. It was fun to be welcomed into their community, and a joy to join in singing "Peace Like a River."

I hugged Leigh good-bye and rode Silver back toward the Johnson Street Bridge to get back on the trail. Since I was already behind, I stopped in Chinatown and had an Evil Orchid bubble tea, a purple concoction with passion fruit juice. I remembered Karen calling me two years before to put Nimby on the phone. Reminiscing here, with some distance, I could enjoy the happy memory with less pain. Now my visit to Victoria was complete.

On the trail through a residential neighborhood, two women were riding behind me and talking loudly. I pedaled faster to stay ahead of them; they seemed to match my pace exactly. They were having the typical vapid conversation of two friends meeting in their own neighborhood. There was nothing wrong with it except for the fact that I couldn't tune them out. As I rode, I nicknamed them the Chatty Cathies and tried to remember that this was their place and I was a guest in it, and I should accept them as part of my experience. Try as I might, they drove me crazy. I finally put on a burst of speed and got a decisive lead. Soon they were out of earshot and after a while, I even dared to make a pit stop without fear of them catching up. I was so far ahead of schedule by then, I made it to the ferry I'd originally planned to catch.

I didn't want the weekend to be over, but I was ready to see Kali. I had Lisa let her out in the morning because I knew I'd be home in plenty of time to bring her in for the night. She was no worse for the wear, glad to see me but not traumatized by my being gone for two nights. I couldn't believe it was still another month before my big trip.

At the chiropractor a few days later, I told Dr. Nelsen (Dr. Lisa to me) that I felt really strong on the trail. She stopped and said, "You used to use that word a lot—strong. I've been waiting four years to hear you say it again." Her eyes filled with tears and I gave her a hug.

The Incredible Journey Begins

The time drew near to leave on my big trip. I could hardly stand the wait. I went back to volunteering, that helped a little. I worked on my big sewing project for the Gala, cutting out fifty wine bags this year instead of forty. I didn't look forward to sewing without Nimby. I could barely breathe in my sewing room.

The day before departure, I carefully opened the wooden box that contained Nimby's ashes and was relieved to see them contained inside a plastic bag. I pressed out the air, tied it closed, and stowed it in an orange nylon stuff sack. I did the same with Miranda's and Sadie's ashes, labeling each with the cat's first initial in black Sharpie. Sadie's ashes were noticeably darker than Nimby's and Miranda's. Sadie was a black cat, but that wouldn't matter. I wondered if it had to do with temperature or something like that. The ashes of all three cats weighed about four pounds.

I put the two ash boxes and the urn back on the shelf where they normally sat, and stowed the stuff sack at the bottom of my bike bag. The heaviest items should be on the bottom for good load balance, but I also wanted them not to be disturbed during the ride, and I hoped that if the customs officers went through my bags, they wouldn't bother going all the way to the bottom. I had researched the legality of transporting animal remains across the border, and nothing was said about ashes. They were sterile and posed no risk to the environment; in fact, the calcium would be beneficial to the estuary where I planned to scatter them. Renee lived close by the park and told me many people used that place to scatter ashes of all species, including human; her own father's ashes had been scattered from a boat in deeper water there. I decided to adopt a policy of don't ask, don't tell.

It had bothered me for years that I still had Miranda's ashes; she had been gone more than ten years. It's important to me that the ashes be returned to the life cycle. Sadie's ashes added to the pressure. I didn't own land to scatter them on, and I didn't want them anywhere in my condo complex anyway. The wetland out back meant nothing to Miranda but had been Sadie's and Nimby's happy place. It was also where my neighbors went to do drugs and I knew those guys urinated back there. It's a ratty urban wetland, not a good final resting place. At the rate Bellingham is developing, there will probably be a strip mall there before the decade is out.

My friend Beth in Eugene offered me a place in her personal cat cemetery. I considered it, but Beth has been talking about moving closer to town as she and Rich get older and I didn't want strangers moving into their house and deciding to dig up that part of the yard for any reason. It troubled me that I hadn't returned my cats' physical remains to the earth. I had finally found a suitable place to scatter their ashes, and with the addition of Nimby to the shelf, I felt a sense of urgency about it.

I had wanted to take my dad's ashes on the new bike trail between Minneapolis and Duluth, to the place on the shore of Lake Superior where he wanted to be scattered. The rest of the family didn't like that idea. This gave me a chance to take the cats on a final journey, and my dad in spirit. I lit the candle I'd designated as his and invited him to join us on our quest.

The forecast had degenerated steadily the week before departure, a surprise for July. I finally left with wind and rain slapping at the yellow rain covers on my panniers. I rode through town through clouds so dark I used my lights, reaching the train station an hour early. I locked up against the platform fence and went inside to warm up with a coffee. The train was running a few minutes late but I rolled Silver out on the platform early, always nervous about the handoff to the baggage claim agent and the subsequent hustle to the train car with my panniers. As I waited, I recognized an old man in a yellow rain slicker—Yono, my favorite customer from Paws Awhile. I called out to him, he turned to walk up to the fence and we hugged, our wet rain jackets clinging together. I almost always see Yono walking near the station either coming or going from a bike trip. The store had closed its doors a month earlier so this was a joyful reunion indeed. Yono was a world traveler himself and we had spent many happy hours at the store, commenting on interesting customs we had seen.

The train finally came and the announcer said it was a full train, so please be prepared for a seat mate. Somehow I managed to get a seat to myself—perhaps my dripping rain gear discouraged people from sitting next to me, maybe it was the one bulky pannier I didn't put on the baggage shelf but kept down by my feet so I could access its contents. This year I carried a small tablet computer with e-books and a few movies loaded on it. It made for a lighter load, more headspace in my bags, and a lot more entertainment potential. Plus, I could easily research route changes and local attractions online without having to rent a hostel computer terminal. The rain made the view hard to see, so I pulled out my tablet and read one of the books I'd downloaded.

The long line for customs in Vancouver was made even less pleasant by the dripping of the rain off the eaves that didn't extend all the way over the platform. I put my rain covers back on my panniers and hoped I wouldn't have to take all that apart at the counter. The counter agent waited impatiently while I maneuvered the bike up to her station, pushing it flat against the counter so other people could sidle by. It's really not a bike-friendly process.

The agent asked me about my travel plans, making me recite specifically where I was staying each night. She asked me three times if I was traveling alone; the repetition rattled me and I felt compelled to explain that I planned to see friends along the way. She asked Renee's last name and I blanked—then it came to me and I blurted it with relief, realizing how much it sounded like I made it up on the spot. The agent stared me down for a few seconds, then said I could go. It was all I could do not to blurt out, "I have three dead cats in my bike bag." I didn't know what would happen if the ashes weren't okay, would they confiscate them? I was prepared to turn back and take them home with me if I had to; I was terrified to have them taken away. As I stepped out into the big station atrium, I felt the flop sweat trickle down my back.

I had left a day early because of the long trip to the ferry; I wanted to actually see the town of Sechelt this year so I planned to spend the night at the hostel in Vancouver and catch an early bus to the ferry terminal. To pass the time in Vancouver, I decided to check out the Fly Over Canada flight simulator ride at the Convention Center. A friend had told me it was worth the trip.

After a quick lunch of a Thai chicken wrap and a berry smoothie at McDonald's, I rode along the Seawall trail from the Science Center to the Convention Center, a delightful tour around the city's perimeter. My bike seat started rocking on its ancient seat bolt, a problem I'd been having since I replaced the seat six weeks ago. My bike being thirty-three years old, it has an old-style bracket that is harder to tighten than the modern ones, especially with the original aging bolts. I had tried to swap the seat post when I replaced the seat, but couldn't get a precise fit for my now non-standard frame. The timing for this loosening couldn't be better; I was a block from Reckless Bikes, where I buy a new novelty bike bell every year. The people at Reckless Bikes offered me the use of their tools, and shooed me away when I looked for a tip jar to deposit a $2 Canadian coin. There was a collection jar to help out a seriously ill coworker by the door. I dropped the Toonie in that jar and rolled Silver on out.

Purely by accident, by using the wrong exit from the traffic circle in front of the bike shop, I discovered a new east-west bicycle route through the city on Hornby Street. It was a miniature street separated from the main street by a curb, to the right of the parking lane. Separate traffic lights for bikes with a bicycle stenciled on the light lens indicated when it was safe to go. At the first intersection, I didn't know about the lights and went on the regular green, nearly getting clipped by a silver Mercedes. He stopped just as I noticed the red bicycle light and I shouted, "Sorry, I'm new here." He rolled down the window and said, "Look for the special bike lights, and welcome!" *So* Canadian!

The rain finally stopped and the sun tried to poke out of the clouds. I was still wet and cold, but this was much better. On the Convention Center pier, I decided to check my bags at the Pacific Place Hotel for $10 rather than have to haul them around with me. I knew I couldn't take them on the simulator ride, but I did not know they offered free bag checking there. First I went to the food court across the street, had a quick lunch, and checked on my bike on the way back down the pier. Silver looked vulnerable without her bags, but she stood in the rack unmolested.

I walked down the long pier past an unbelievably large cruise ship. Window washers worked above me to prepare for the voyage; I counted seven stories of passenger cabins up to the top where the washers were.

What a behemoth—I allowed myself a minute to feel superior for my green mode of travel. The pier was inlaid with bricks imprinted with the names of the provinces from west to east, and smaller bricks bore the names of towns in their relative locations within the provinces. At least they gave us a geography lesson on the long walk. This would be much more fun to do with a friend, I thought. I snapped a photo of the brick labeled for the town of Bella Bella, to send to my friend Bella later when I had wi-fi.

At the end of the pier, I rode the escalator to the ticketing area. Bass notes boomed from the theater and the excitement of the waiting crowd crackled in the air. I bought my ticket for $20 and joined the line that looped around the building. An older woman tired and fell while we stood waiting. An attendant rushed to bring her a chair and asked if anyone else needed one. I felt too foolish in my bike gear to ask for a chair, but my spine was screaming. I tried stretching in place. After about twenty minutes, I heard someone call, "Do we have any parties of one?" I raised my hand and was beckoned to the front of the line to fill the one remaining seat on the next ride. Suddenly I didn't mind being alone.

We were herded into a square room with screens on all the walls for a short movie. I figured that was a holding area to entertain the people for the last miserable stretch of the line. The movie featured a bunch of images from pre-settlement Canada to the modern age, with loud music and flashy special effects. I did kind of enjoy it once I found the very edge of a seat; benches were provided for elderly and disabled people but the majority of the people stood. In my bike gear, I didn't feel I could scout out a priority seat, but I was okay filling in the last bit of space. That is an awkward problem on the road; I need facilities for disabled people but I don't look like one, and my willingness to assert myself depends on how uncomfortable I am at the time. Often my reluctance to ask catches up with me later in the day when I hit my pain and fatigue limit too early.

The movie ended and we queued up in two lines by party size, then we were assigned to numbered circles on the floor. After a short video on how to stow our bags under the seat and buckle up, we were herded into the theater. The seats looked like airplane seats *should* look, large and comfortable, with net bags below for loose items. This was important because the floor retracted as the ride began, and we were suspended in three rows with the half-sphere of screen in front of us.

The eight-minute movie began, flying over Canada from east to west like the sun. Images of Toronto flashed by, then the vast natural beauty of Canada, over mountains where cold mist was blown on us as we went through clouds and over ridges where powder blew, down into canyons where we were misted again as we passed through waterfalls. The seats tipped slightly with the turn of the camera. It was so realistic, I actually pulled my feet up when we swooped low over a bunch of kids playing hockey on a frozen lake. When I recognized Vancouver, I knew we were almost done, and I could hardly bear it as the flight rose into the pulsing northern lights to its end. I stepped outside blinking in the light—sunshine, finally—and texted Kenn that I could hardly wait to show him the ride. Then I sat down on the deck and watched the barges and float planes in Coal Harbor, and realized that I was on the first day of my journey. Hardly wait to ride again indeed, I was just getting started on an adventure that would make Fly Over Canada look tame.

The Incredible Journey Continues

The next morning, I hurried through breakfast and broke camp at the hostel, riding downtown for the bus to the ferry terminal. My face was swollen from allergies (a hostel pillow will do it every time), and I took a Benadryl with breakfast. I could barely drag myself along, but I knew I had to get on the bus as fast as I could. The rain had returned and the drop in air pressure didn't help with mental clarity. Less than a mile from the hostel, I nearly rode into an oncoming rider as I drifted to the left. I braked to a stop and said, "I'm so sorry." The woman, forced to stop as well, scolded me, "It's just like the road, ride on the right. How hard is that?" I said, "I said I was sorry."

She continued to scold and I interrupted, "Look, I apologized twice, it's *your* problem now," and rode on. Good grief, I was in the wrong but that woman was a crank. I thought of the nice man in the silver Mercedes and wondered if that woman was really Canadian or a visiting Yank like me. Aware that I was in a compromised state, I rode more slowly and carefully.

My head cleared gradually as I made my way around the seawall trail. I had imagined that the bus stop came sooner than it did. I had to ride all the way to the Hornby bypass to get to the bus lane on Georgia Street. On the Hornby bikeway, my seat bolt came loose again. I considered riding back to Reckless Bikes, but it was 9:00 on Sunday morning and I doubted they were open. I rode on, looking for bike shops along the way and gingerly leaning forward to keep from rocking backward and injuring my lower back. The seat got looser as I rode and I stood on the pedals to avoid lurching back. My choices were to stay in Vancouver until the bike shops opened or get on the ferry, where the nearest bike shop might be a three-day ride away.

All I needed was a hardware store, and I thought there was a bike shop in Horseshoe Bay next to the ferry terminal, so I kept going. I didn't want to lose half the day and reach Sechelt at 7:00 like last year.

The bus came almost instantly and I left Silver out on the rack in the rain while I carried my dripping bags inside the bus. I got one of the last available seats facing forward. The next lot of passengers stood in the aisle as the windows fogged over so I could barely see my bike out the front. The ride took forty-five minutes. The rain had stopped for a bit and I walked Silver up and down the streets of Horseshoe Bay, looking for the shop I thought I remembered. If it had been there, it wasn't there anymore. I walked Silver to the loading area and waited for the ferry.

On the vessel, I planned to ask a crew member if there were tools available, but after the busy loading procedure, I couldn't find a single orange vest on the auto deck. I went upstairs to eat lunch and come up with a plan. In the cafeteria area, I noticed a group of older people wearing name tags with a tour company logo. Nearby, a group of Asian people chattered in Chinese, also wearing name tags. Of course, tour buses crossed on the ferry. I didn't see anyone who looked like a driver and figured the drivers must be in their buses enjoying a break from their passengers. And I would bet my Nanaimo bar they were carrying tool kits.

Sure enough, the first bus I walked up to had a driver inside, reading a book. I knocked on his door and he opened it, startled. I apologized for bothering him, explained my bike trouble, and asked if he had any tools. Yes, he did, and he grabbed a black pouch and followed me to my bike. As we trekked across the vehicle deck, a few other people asked if they could help, and I had half a dozen assistants by the time we reached the bike rack. One person held a flashlight on my work, no small help on the dark vehicle deck with the big rolling doors closed. I selected an adjustable crescent wrench and tightened the bolt on each side, then mounted the bike to check the angle before tightening it all the way. It tended to move during the last turns of the wrench so I overcorrected a bit. Then I asked who was a good arm wrestler. A man stepped forward and I asked him to give the wrench a good hard clockwise tug.

I thanked them all and started to dig around in my bag for my tablet to take back upstairs, but these people didn't want to leave me that quickly. I answered questions about my trip and realized how badly they wanted to claim a tiny piece of my adventure for their own. I rewarded them by telling them about my journey with the ashes, and how I made it past customs. They were enthralled. I could have gilded the lily by telling them about my crash, but enough was enough. My story was cool and interesting enough without all that.

Coming off the ferry in Sechelt, I remembered the 600-foot hill followed by the 300-foot hill, and I headed straight for the bus. A light rain fell again. The driver teased me a little for bypassing the hills, but he admitted he wouldn't do those hills in the rain either. The bus ride took a surprisingly long time, winding through the neighborhoods of Langdale and Lower Gibsons before arriving at the Sunnycrest Mall in Upper Gibsons. Sunnycrest felt like a bit of a misnomer on this gloomy day.

I surveyed the pickings and chose the sushi restaurant for lunch. It proved to be a very good choice and I struck back out for Home Hardware as the rain picked up. I bought a miniature adjustable crescent wrench for $12; it would let me tighten my seat bolt enough to hold it at least a few hours. I didn't end up needing it, but the peace of mind was worth a few extra ounces of weight. The rain settled into a steady mist as I pressed on toward Sechelt.

I remembered the ride to Sechelt as being long and very hilly. I was surprised how quickly I reached the point where I could see the town at a distance around the bend of the shoreline. The stretch between that vantage point and Sechelt was indeed hilly, but I didn't have to walk up any hills like I did last year. I realized I'd spared my legs 900 feet of climbing and it was four hours earlier in the day than last time I'd come this way. I got into Sechelt with hours to spare before dinner.

I didn't find Hugh, the manager, anywhere around, so I called his cell number that was posted on his door and left a message saying I was waiting to check in. I went back down and carried my things upstairs to the deck and took over one of the outdoor tables. I stowed my food in the fridge and fixed a cup of rooibos tea in the kitchen; they were expecting me, after all. No reason not to make myself at home.

Hugh came out from his home attached to the deck about an hour later, groggy from sleep. He'd suffered a severe migraine and was clearly still exhausted, but he grabbed my linens and showed me to my room. I had booked a bunk, but another guest in that room had extended her stay and he put me in a private room for the same price as the bunk I'd booked. No complaints here!

I decided to go out and explore the town to give Hugh some time to collect himself before he had to prepare my room. I knew all too well what it was like to be pushed into things when you weren't up to it. I would have had to make my own bed in the dorm, so I offered to make my own now, but Hugh wouldn't hear of it. By the time I got back from exploring and a memorably terrible dinner of "spicy buffalo poutine" at McDonald's (after which I discovered the restaurant strip), Hugh felt much better and we had a nice time catching up on each other's past year. I met the other guests and we stayed up late in the community room, talking and making friends. I thought another woman looked familiar; it turned out she was my roommate there last summer and we hadn't spent much time getting acquainted—she had been asleep most of the time I was there. She took professional cooking classes at the community college and stayed in the hostel to avoid the long drive home during the week.

In my room, which had an Orient theme, I found a Japanese scroll with a picture of a cat on it rolled up on the shelf in the wardrobe closet. I unrolled it and hung it inside the closet, then placed the ash bag on the shelf below. It seemed a good place for the cats to spend the night. This was my last chance as their mother to care for them physically, and I wanted to treat them well up to the last minute.

The private-room bed meant I didn't have to blow up my backpacker pad. I realized that I only had one night left on my trip where I'd need it, and nine more nights in between when I didn't. My knee was sore from riding with the extra weight and I'd strained it a little while riding with the rocking seat. I decided an upgrade to a private room in Nanaimo my last night out was worth the opportunity to jettison over a pound of pack weight.

While buying instant ice packs for my knee at Shoppers Drug Mart, I'd found the Canada Post office and I knew where to take my pack to mail it. The next morning I did just that. It cost $40 including the mailing box, and I tossed in a small but heavy padlock I wouldn't need for a hostel locker too, since I'd have a private room with a locking door. The weight reduction and headspace this opened up in my pack was most welcome.

Because of my sore knee, I decided to portage past the steep hill on Redrooffs Road by bus. I remembered walking up it for literally miles last year, and I didn't want to spoil the trip so early on by irritating my knee into a full-blown injury. The bus driver was delightful; we had a long talk about his adult daughter who was just recovering after being incapacitated since childhood by an undiagnosed illness. The diagnosis would have been devastating if it had been made early, but after years of living with an unexplained disability, it meant they finally understood what was happening and she could manage her condition and have a life. I marveled again at how little we know about the people we interact with daily, and how many people out there are quietly living with horrific problems.

I still had quite a haul to get to my night stop at Ruby Lake Resort, where I would stay in a safari tent before pressing on to Egmont down the roller-coaster road. Ruby Lake offered swimming and I didn't want to have to miss that. The road to Ruby Lake was a gloriously winding mountain highway, and the only stops were down 400-foot hills that pitched down toward the coast. Madeira Park offered a low point, only a 300-foot ascent back up to the highway, so that was my scheduled lunch stop.

The woman at the café remembered me from the summer before and we had a fun chat. After lunch I went across the street to the IGA to stock up for the evening, knowing there wasn't a general store at Ruby Lake Resort, just one world-class Italian restaurant with limited hours. Most of their travelers arrived by car, and for them a fifteen-minute drive to a grocery store was almost as good as having a store on the premises. As a bike traveler, I had to ask questions and plan for such things in advance.

After pushing up the hill to get back to the highway, I started to feel ready to reach my destination. My knee was complaining a little, but not enough to alarm me. I had an extra instant ice pack to use on it that evening. Normally I reject chemical stuff like that, but the ice packs degrade to a mix of water and uric acid, they're pretty harmless as such things go. I arrived at an entrance road to Ruby Lake Resort; I knew the office was farther down the road. About a mile down a screaming downhill, to be exact, which was nice going down, but I dreaded hauling back up it.

I stopped at the office and a young lady handed me a map to my safari tent. I followed the map along a side road, up a hill so steep that my feet slid on the pavement as I pushed the bike, and along a dirt road a fair distance. I saw numbered tents and cabins, but they didn't appear to follow the sequence shown on the map. I stopped and checked my phone for signal; three bars meant I could call the office for help. The young lady said to come back down and she'd show me the right way to go. Exhausted from the climb and cranky, I said, "No, I rode my bike thirty-five miles to get here and hauled up a *huge-ass* hill, and someone can come and show me—"

Just then a golf cart came into view and a nicely dressed woman called my name. She was Jessica, the concierge I had been told would escort me to my cabin. She apologized for being out when I arrived and guided me to a different tent than the one circled on my map, closer to the washroom building and the main road through the resort. I was behind the amphitheater where they held folk music festivals, deserted now but fun to explore.

The safari tent was like a childhood dream. The cabin-sized canvas tent held a double bed, an electric fireplace, a table, and a burlwood chair with a writing surface that I used that night to write in my trip diary. The deck looked over the narrow slough that extended from Ruby Lake, at the bottom of a steep ravine. Ancient shelf fungus decorated the old-growth trees. As soon as Jessica left me to get settled, the sound of bird calls became almost deafening. Some of the birds were like nothing I'd ever heard before, wild cackles and shrieks. I learned later that some of the calls came from the aviary near the washrooms, a huge pen that held turkeys and peacocks.

I was sweaty and exhausted, and starting to chill a little, as the day's sunshine started to give way to new rain clouds, but I was determined to swim in the lake. That's what I came here to do, and by God, I was going to swim. I put on my swim suit with a pair of shorts and coasted back down the long hill to the dock. There were already about a half dozen people sitting on lawn chairs on the dock. I said hello and walked into the lake wearing my net water tennies.

The water wasn't so cold... until I got waist-deep, the bottom dropped off, and I was dumped into what felt like liquid ice. Pain shot through my arm as the chill hit the metal plate, which can't retain warmth like bone can. I pride myself on my cold-water tolerance and I stuck it out, paddling around until I got used to it and the arm pain subsided to a dull ache like brain freeze. A cyclist rode by and shouted to me, asking how the water was. I called back that it was refreshing and encouraged him to pull over and take a dip in the lake. He rode on and I felt alone with my wonderful secret.

Even the dry people on the dock didn't know how good the water felt. I swam out a way and looked around through my swim goggles—a forest stood underwater! Ruby Lake was a dammed reservoir and the skeletons of the original forest still stood rooted in the ground. I was terrified and fascinated; the water was so deep! I am only afraid of water I can't see to the bottom of; this water showed me a lot more than I had expected to see and I was still a little creeped out. I paddled back to the shallows and floated on my back for a while before reluctantly getting out. I sat on the bench at the shore, dripping until I was dry enough to pedal

Silver back up the hill and work up a fresh sweat for the shower.

I did a load of camp laundry in the shower—you dump your dirty clothes on the shower floor, pour some biodegradable camp soap concentrate over the pile, turn off the water and stomp on it until everything is sudsy, then pick up, rinse, and wring each item while standing under the spray. I hung the wash out on my deck and used my Rick Steves gripping rubber clothes-line to prevent my clothes from blowing down the ravine.

I dressed in my nice convertible pants, adjusted to Capri length, a plain tan tee, and my red taffeta over-blouse for dinner at La Trattoria. Yet again, I coasted down the long hill to dinner. I locked Silver to a fence surrounded by free-range chickens as sleek and fat as spoiled pets, which I was pretty sure they were. I took my tablet inside and got a deck table overlooking the lagoon. An enormous St. Bernard-border collie mix pa-trolled the grounds and I asked the server if he was okay in a wildlife refuge like that, and she said yes, he never scared the birds and seemed to understand his guard duty very well. Later, when I walked the board-walk across the lagoon, the dog pushed past me, intent on his job, with no interest at all in being petted.

Thanks to a staffing issue, my server was also the chef that night. I was amazed how well she held down the fort. My dinner arrived in good time, sturgeon with prawns and asparagus pesto. The greens were ridicu-lously fresh; I'm guessing they were grown on-site. I wolfed down the entire dinner and the server invited me to have a slice of local cherry cheesecake she baked herself. Of course I had to, with a cup of coffee to take the edge off the generously filled glass of pinot grigio I had with dinner. I did, after all, have to make it back up that hill on my bike.

I took my time this time, and the sun was almost

down when I got back to my safari tent. I moved my clothesline inside in case it was a dewy night. I placed the bag of ashes on the mantel of the electric fireplace and said, "Look, Manda, foomp!" Miranda had loved the gas fireplace at our old house, and it made a "foomp" sound when I turned it on. If she wanted a fire, she meowed at the fireplace, not me, until I made it go foomp. I looked everywhere for the switch on this one, but never found it.

Instead I turned on the blue-shaded mood light and laid on the bed to watch the movie "The Way," with Martin Sheen, written by Emilio Estevez. The movie is about a father's journey on the Camino del Santiago de Compostela, a 400-mile trail from France to Spain, with his son's ashes. It inspired this journey and it felt right to watch it on my tablet in my safari tent. The night fell around me and the exotic bird calls continued. It was a noisy forest. The movie made me cry as it always does, and I spent some time just sitting with the ashes when it was over.

In the morning I moved the ash bag out onto the tree stump that served as a table, and had my breakfast on the deck enjoying the view. There wasn't any coffee service, but I made an adequate cup of coffee by running hot water from the washroom tap and mixing a packet of Starbucks instant. With a cut-up apple and a muffin I'd bought back in Madeira Park, it was a perfect breakfast. I hated leaving the tent, but my next stop was Egmont and I planned to get there early and actually see the Skookumchuck Rapids this time.

It was only an eight-mile ride to Egmont, four on the highway and four on the hilly access road. My odometer said I must be getting close when I noticed a large log building on my left. The Egmont Visitor Center had still been under construction when I was there last year. Here it was, open for business. I decided to pop in and look around. A woman about my age was working the counter and we said hello and she left me alone to look around. I admired some Native button-craft pieces, red felt decorated with beads and buttons to make animal scenes. I told the lady that there was a time when I would have been able to buy them, and I wished I could buy them now, because I liked to support places like this that usually paid a fair price to the Native crafters.

We got into a chat about the times and the economy, and Sam introduced herself. We couldn't stop talking, it was like my first time at Renee's, one topic just led to another. We hit all the unsafe topics—politics, religion, and our families. Sam bought me two cans of iced tea and some chips so I wouldn't leave and try to find lunch. Finally it got to be 1:00 and I told Sam I wanted to check in at the hotel and hike the trail to the rapids. I asked her if the trail was worth it and she reluctantly admitted it was. She invited me to stay at her house instead of the hotel, and I almost did. I kind of wish I had, but I paid in full for the room in February, it was nonrefundable, and I did love my balcony view. Now I have a reason to go back next summer.

So I headed down the screaming-steep hill to the hotel below, and checked in with Val. She had greeted me warmly when I made my reservation by email, but didn't seem to remember me in person. The first thing I did was throw my laundry in the washing machine so I could retrieve it before striking out on the trail. Then I greeted my old room and stepped out on the balcony to soak in the view. The cats should be out here; I unpacked quickly and set the ash bag on the glass table. Maybe somehow their spirits could absorb the serenity. Being a scientist, I viewed their earthly remains as just that, minerals that should be returned to the earth so they can become part of more living things.

But carrying the ashes on my bike, I was rebonding with my lost friends and I talked to them as I rode.

You never stop being a mother, after all. I thought of Kali back home alone and sang her kitty song, Mary Lambert's, "*She keeps me warm.*"

Aware of the time, I heated a bowl of ramen noodles in the microwave and ate as much as I could. They were really terrible, but the alternative was cured-meat sandwiches on white bread dripping with mayo, an allergenic cocktail that would leave me floating face-down in the Skookumchuck Rapids if I made it that far. I supplemented the meal with a Snickers bar and laced on my water tennies. The trail was supposed to be flat and easy, it should be more comfortable to walk in those than my cleated sport sandals with stiffened soles. I grabbed my laundry and tossed the wet things in the bathtub to hang out later.

Walking back up the hill to the trailhead was challenge enough. I caught my breath at the top and cast a longing glance at the visitor center; I could spend the rest of the afternoon chatting with Sam, but I wanted to see the Rapids, so off I went. For about two miles, the trail was indeed wide, smooth, and well-groomed. The second half was a tangle of tree roots and rocks, going up and down like random staircases but never significantly changing elevation. I saw the richness of the old-growth ecosystem; enormous fungal colonies on fallen logs, new trees sprouting from the soil formed by decomposition, exotic mosses I'd never seen before. I snapped many photos before the clock on my phone reminded me that the Rapids were peaking. I didn't want to miss that, so I pressed on.

I arrived about half an hour past the tidal peak, but the Rapids were still going strong. I'm a good swimmer and generally don't fear water, but this water possessed a wild energy and I knew it could pulverize me in seconds. I watched with the crowd of about thirty other people, mesmerized. A few had thought to bring folding chairs. I found a flat rock and sat, my lower back reminding me painfully that I'm more of a chair-with-a-back person these days. The noise was incredible, you had to shout to be heard.

I stayed half an hour, until the water started to slacken and the Clamp seized my back. The water was still going plenty fast, but the glassy hump of wave closest to me had relaxed to a foamy plume, and I was getting hungry. I started the walk back. About this time I realized how inadequate my water tennies were for the roots-and-rocks stretch. My feet bent painfully, unprotected by the aging jogging-shoe soles. By the time I gratefully stepped out onto the flats, my feet were in full revolt, fighting for attention with my back pain. I kept walking because I had to.

Finally the coffee house a short distance from the trailhead came into view. I climbed the steps to the counter and ordered a berry smoothie for $6, and a raspberry bar for tomorrow's breakfast for $5. What the market will bear indeed. To be fair, that smoothie was huge and full of good things, and it gave me $10 worth of refreshment.

I stood up from my stool at the counter and realized my legs had set like concrete while I sat. Painfully, I pressed on to the trailhead. The steep hill back into town was hard to negotiate. I walked backward down it most of the way, my muscles and feet objecting to every step. I felt like a wuss; who breaks down after an eight-mile bike ride and a six-mile hike? And my day was far from over. I had laundry to hang up and dinner to scout out. I had to go back up another hill-like-a-wall to get to the café where I planned to sit down to a proper dinner.

Somehow I did it all, moving like a zombie, and I made it to the café and ordered a hard cherry cider with a Moroccan chicken dish for dinner. I drained the cider in a few gulps and got another. I thought of the Yiddish word *mechayeh*, a relief like a cool breeze on a blazing-hot day. The cider was a *mechayeh* indeed.

Late that night, I woke up with leg cramps and felt the Clamp's familiar steely grip on my spine. I got up to take a pain pill. The marina was surprisingly noisy, with people walking about and talking with no thought to "indoor voice." I stepped out on my balcony and sat beside the ash bag, drinking in the summer night. The pill kicked in and I felt a deep contentment and knew I'd return to this moment many times.

Sam didn't work until ten the next morning, and I needed to get to the ferry at Earls Cove for the early sailing, so I took the postcard provided in the hotel's guest information binder and wrote her a note. I had brought a beaded necklace along that I'd made before I left, thinking I'd give it to someone along the way, and wrote to Sam, "I made this for you, I just hadn't met you yet," and added all my contact information. I dropped the note and the necklace on a bench by the door, hoping she'd see it on her way in and no child of a tourist would nab it before she got there.

I rode on along the roller-coaster road, stunned by the beauty of the small lakes and old-growth forest. A father and two children walked along the road, chattering loudly in Spanish and carrying swim gear toward a pond with a floating dock. I greeted them in Spanish and they waved and shouted back. The driveways to the homes along the road all had landmarks in their entries, one had a teakettle painted white hanging in an archway, others had brightly painted derelict boats. It was a tradition on the Sunshine Coast to mark your entry so your friends could find you. "Turn left at the white teakettle" made more sense than an address in this mountainous maze.

I reached the highway quickly and coasted the six kilometers to the terminal. Yesterday's sunshine was long gone and the clouds hung low. As I sat on a bench in the boarding area, a light rain started to fall.

Several motorcycles waited at the front of the line and I heard one man say it took him about an hour and a half to ride from Gibsons. I turned to him and said with a smile, "It was a two-day ride for me. You suck!"

He laughed and asked if I enjoyed the ride. I said, "Oh, yes. I even made a new friend along the way." He said, "Then *you* suck, you had a better time." We laughed and chatted pleasantly until the small ferry arrived.

The auto deck only held about two dozen cars, but there was a proper bike rack near the bow. I dutifully hitched up Silver in the rain, then asked a crew member if it would be okay to park in a more sheltered place. A raised area under a ramp to the upper deck held a picnic table for the crew's lunch area, and the crewman gestured for me to park Silver there. She rode dry as the rain picked up to a downpour.

I went upstairs and perused the small food counter and gift shop; I selected a crossword puzzle book, a 100-piece jigsaw puzzle of the large ferry Coastal Renaissance to do in Eve and leave behind as a gift, and a small paper cup of Island Farms ice cream with a wooden paddle rubber-banded to the lid.

The sailing took about an hour and I rode off the boat into more rain. The requisite long hill at every ferry landing awaited. I did not remember this 550-foot ascent from last year; I must have either been numb by that point or much more refreshed. The climb actually seemed to help, though, the stiffness in my legs relaxed as my muscles warmed up. I pedaled slowly and steadily, barely faster than a walking pace. The rain fell steadily and I checked my rain covers to make sure they were secure. The problem with rain covers is that they fit the bags perfectly when filled almost to capacity; the actual stuffing that goes on during an extended tour stretches the rain covers. They're held on with elastic, and if you can't actually stretch the cover enough for the elastic to grip, they let water in and they can pop off in a stiff wind. Fortunately, my jettisoning the backpacker pad back in Sechelt eased the bulge and I had good coverage.

I had about thirty-five miles to ride to get to the ferry terminal in Powell River. The ninety-minute sailing began at 5:00 and I had plenty of time to get there. I planned to have lunch at Skeeter Jack's, a very nice roadside café along the way. I didn't remember how far down the road it was, so I kept an eye out to make sure I wouldn't miss it through the curtain of rain.

Watching for Skeeter Jack's became increasingly difficult as the rain fell harder. The last thing I remember being able to see by the side of the road was a driveway with a toilet marking the entry, a pair of rubber hip boots stuffed into the bowl feet-up.

The rain fell harder than I've ever seen it, and I've seen thunderstorms in Montana, Minnesota and Missouri. The drops hit so hard that a layer of froth four inches high formed above the pavement. The water level rose quickly on the shoulder until my pedals almost reached the surface on the downstroke. I had zero braking power. A ringing in my ears proved to be my bike bell, pelted with heavy drops. My rain jacket clung to my soaked skin, the water-resistant fabric penetrated completely. There was nothing to do but keep going, no shelter nearby. At least there were hardly any cars; the drivers all pulled over to wait out the storm. I turned on my flashing head and tail lights, for what little good they would do. When one car passed me and doused me with a rooster-tail of water, I just laughed, it couldn't make me any wetter.

Finally a dip in the road with a guard rail indicating a creek crossing jogged my memory—there was a rest stop here with a washroom building. I dismounted and backtracked to the gravel parking lot, now swirling in mud, and found the log structure. I rolled my bike inside with me and stood there dripping for a bit, marveling at the size of the puddle that gathered on the floor under my bike. I sat on the lid of the pit toilet until the roar of rain on the corrugated metal roof dulled and I could hear individual drops again. I had no idea how much time passed; I felt drowsy as I rolled Silver outside. The stream had risen to a churning rapid, spilling several feet past its banks. At least it wasn't covering the road yet, though the shoulder was now strewn with rocks.

No sooner had I topped the first big hill after the rest stop than the rain started up again in all its fury. Doggedly I pedaled on until a familiar lighted sign announced that I had finally reached Skeeter Jack's. I pulled Silver into the covered outdoor eating area and water flowed from her bags in a river toward the parking lot. I was sure my stuff must all be soaked. I pulled off the rain cover on the bag that held my wallet and my tablet; the tablet had stayed dry in its neoprene case but I could see my paper guide sheets were wrinkled and the ink had run to the edges in rivers of color.

I went inside and stood on the mat, and the woman at the pie counter laughed heartily, then came to my aid. She took my sodden rain jacket and hung it over a chair, training a large floor fan at it. I slogged into the washroom and stripped completely, wringing out my clothes over the sink piece by piece. Even my fleece sweater was soaked through and I wrung cups of water from it. I had truly never been this wet without being fully submerged. I tried squeezing my wrung-out clothes in paper towels to extract more water.

Putting them back on was like layering on three wet bathing suits. I struggled to adjust everything that clung in the wrong places, then I went back out to inform my host that the washroom floor would have to be squeegeed before anyone could safely go in there. I offered to do it myself but she shooed me to a table and directed a fan my way to dry me off as I ate.

I had a season of Republic of Doyle loaded on my tablet and put on my headphones to enjoy an episode over lunch. I ate slowly, starting a second episode and staying the entire forty-five minutes before I finally collected my things and pressed on. The rain had stopped for a bit, and I was deeply chilled from the fan and *still* wet. The cool breeze cut through my sweater and jacket and my teeth chattered as I kept pedaling to warm my body. I knew the dangers of hypothermia and that I was in big trouble.

I considered going back to Skeeter Jack's and buying a new dry sweatshirt to warm up in, but cotton wouldn't be much help once it got wet, and I decided to keep going. After a few miles of vigorous pedaling, my teeth stopped chattering and I just shivered a bit. The rain started again as I rolled into Powell River around three o'clock. Two hours until the ferry sailing. I remembered a café from last year and parked Silver under the eaves rather than using the uncovered bike rack out on the sidewalk. I was sure no one would mind in this weather. I asked the server for a towel to put on my chair and ordered a pot of hot lemon herbal tea. I sat drinking my tea for an hour before using the washroom, with the now-familiar wet swimsuit feeling, and walked through the rain to the ferry terminal.

The vessel was an enormous Queen class ferry, the Queen of Burnaby. I found a padded vinyl seat in the passenger lounge and fell asleep almost immediately. When I woke up to the announcement that we were pulling into port, there was a huge puddle at my feet and I was *still* wet.

Renee waited by her truck in the parking lot, wearing one of her festive homemade play dresses. She hugged me, wet clothes and all, and we got my bike into her truck and she turned on the heat for the short ride to her house. A hot shower in her luxurious bathroom, followed by dry clothes (I actually had some in my pack!) and a home-cooked meal with wine, and I was practically purring. We went downstairs to watch a few episodes of The West Wing, one of my favorite shows, and I fell asleep with Renee's mop-dog Mojo in my lap.

The next morning I was so stiff, I had to hold onto the wall to stay upright. The chill had done a number on my muscles. Renee suggested that I go to the aquatic center on the edge of town and sit in the hot tub. It was about a five-mile ride. It would give me a chance to give Silver a good checking out after her day in the rain. I thought I might scream as I lifted my leg to mount the bike, but I assured Renee that I was fine and didn't need a ride in the truck. Thank God I was here for three days, I would need that to recover.

I struck out using Renee's directions and found the Aquatic Center tucked out of view at the intersection where Renee said it would be. It was a beautiful concrete-and-glass building with heavy wood trim, and the inside surprised me—the facilities in large suburbs of Seattle weren't this nice, and this was a small town.

Canada places a high priority on community recreation facilities. A regular half-Olympic-size pool took up about half the space, then a shallow wave pool with several play features, then a large hot tub that would seat about twenty-five adults took up the back by the window.

The locker room featured hanger bars with hooks to keep dry clothes off the wet surfaces, and a spin dryer to wring out wet swim suits. I had my quick-drying microfiber towel; it was about half the size of a standard bath towel, so there was no hiding behind it or wrapping it around me sarong-style. I carried it out into the pool area and eased into the warm bubbles of the hot tub. A man about my age introduced himself as Peter and told me he was there with his ninety-three-year-old mother, who was swimming laps. Peter was an avid cyclist and a leader in the local cycling community, so we talked for a good hour before he had to go tend to his mother. I'd had plenty of heat, so I moved into the warm shallow children's pool. The gentle waves were fun to swim into, so I paddled around happily for a while before returning to the hot tub for one last soak.

Back at Renee's, her husband Ken cooked outside on the grill and we enjoyed an evening of music and conversation on the back deck. Their son Jake joined us for some of it, and we bonded over our love of Dr. Who. Jake headed off for work at the local grocery store, a jaunty Dr. Who-style bowtie completing his stockman's uniform.

The next day, my last full day there, it was time to do the errand I came to do. I stalled for time, riding around town on a hunt for a brand of soap Renee needed in order to make the home-brewed laundry detergent that I used. She hadn't been able to find the soap locally and I was determined to get it for her. I came up empty after many stops, and finally it was time to ride to the pavilion at the estuary where the Courtenay River joined the Salish Sea.

I arrived and found two women with two young girls having lunch at the picnic table. This wouldn't do; it hadn't occurred to me that I might not have a private moment in which to do my ritual. I sat on a log near the water and waited about half an hour for them to leave, trying to ignore the backache that started after five minutes. A light rain started to fall and they finally got up and piled into the car. Another car drove up, but I was determined to start, no matter who was around. I put in my iPod and started the song I'd played many times after Miranda died, Mary Chapin Carpenter's "Ten Thousand Miles," which uses the words of the folk ballad "Fare Thee Well," (*If I had a friend on all this earth, you've been a friend to me...*). I held Miranda's bag of ashes in my hands and focused my attention on recreating her presence in my mind. I remembered how she came to me as a spunky alley kitten in Tacoma, moving with me four times, and our joyful routines in every home. I remembered her friendship with Patty the horse next door in Edmonds, and how I called her home from Patty's stall every night and she jumped from the top of the paddock fence across the ditch, her legs splayed comically, before she trotted to me and rubbed up against my legs.

The song came to a close and I stepped down to the water's edge, leaning out over the deepest water I could reach, and sprinkled the ashes. A pile settled on the bottom and a cloud of dissolving light material spread out in the water, forming a plume that flowed out gently with the tide.

I returned to the log, aware of a couple staring at my tear-streaked face. I took out Sadie's ashes, held them, and turned on her song, "Flip Fantasia" by US3. The song expressed her goofy, happy nature perfectly. This long skinny black stray I had rescued from a home with four other cats who beat up on her—too late, it turned out. The irritable bowel disease she had contracted from stress there had laid the conditions for lymphoma. I only got to enjoy Sadie for two and a half years before she died. And I spent enough money at the vet to buy a boat, but I wouldn't have taken back a minute of my time with her. Like with Nimby, I had declined treatment that I thought was too extreme, and she had lived happily and comfortably for nine months after her diagnosis. I scattered her ashes about a foot from Miranda's, and the clouds that rose from their ash piles mixed in the water.

Now for the hardest one of all. I openly sobbed as I turned on Nimby's song, "Follow the Day," by Polyphonic Spree. Nimby, the best friend I ever had in this world. I remembered the day I went to meet "Tyson" at the Whatcom Humane Society, the way he trilled "Schrrrrraaaaaam" when I walked in and looked ever so pleased with himself when I tried to place that crazy sound. He yowled impatiently as I looked at all the other cats, determining by elimination that he was the only cat my home was ideally suited for, and I asked to spend some time with him in the Get Acquainted Room.

I waited in the tiny windowless cinderblock room for him and when the attendant brought him, I sat on a plastic bench. Before I was even down, his claws were hooked into my jeans and he was in my lap. As soon as I sat back, he drilled his enormous tabby head between my breasts and purred ridiculously loudly. This went on for twenty minutes. I petted him and he kept purring and head-butting my chest. Finally I said, "Would you like to finish getting acquainted at home?" And I had my new best friend.

I found my human friends at the Humane Society as well; what Nimby added to my life went so far beyond his feline companionship. He gave me strength for my recovery, then demonstrated an even greater courage dealing with his own disease. The heart of a lion indeed. As his song ended, I got up and scattered his ashes, the heaviest bag of the lot. I took photos of the plumes in the water and the beautiful resting place in the gentle rain. One more step remained; I returned to my log and listened to the Wailin' Jennys cover of Julie Miller's song "By Way of Sorrow."

> *You have come by way of sorrow,*
> *You have come by way of tears,*
> *But you'll reach your destiny,*
> *Meant to find you all these years,*
> *Meant to find you all these years.*

I don't think I've ever cried so hard in my life.

I rode around in the rain for a bit before returning to Renee's. We had a lovely dinner of Indian butter chicken and went downstairs for another West Wing marathon. I was grateful that Renee and Ken understood what the day had meant and didn't expect much from me socially. Renee wasn't feeling very well either; she had been exposed to a sneaky food allergen. Later she told me she was grateful that I hadn't expected much of her socially that night. It was good to cuddle with Mojo and reflect on the day.

The Incredible Journey Comes to an End

I hadn't anticipated how hard it was going to be to leave the ashes behind. I had come all this way to deliver them safely back to the earth; now I had to move on too. During the ride, I had felt the cats' presence strongly and I knew that didn't have to change, they would always be part of me. But my job of caring for them physically was done. I thought of the Dar Williams song,

> *You'll fly away, but take my hand until that day*
> *So when they ask how far love goes*
> *When my job's done you'll be the one who knows*

I didn't have to leave first thing in the morning, so we started the day with a visit to the Comox Farmer's Market. Renee and Ken introduced me to several of their friends at the stands and in the crowd. The Farmer's Market was a fun way to get acquainted with the local agricultural products and handcraft specialties. They weren't so different from those of my own region, heavy on the season's berries, local honey, and lavender.

After the market, I did need to get on the road; I was expected at Free Spirit Spheres that afternoon. It was a pleasant ride along the coastal highway of just the right length, thirty-eight miles. Enough to have a good day's ride without spoiling my evening by being too tired to enjoy it. I had to pass the ash site on my way out of town, and I wanted to visit the place one more time. Traffic on Comox Road was heavy, I wasn't able to turn left without stopping and waiting ten minutes for a safe moment to dart across, my heart pounding as the oncoming car nearly clipped my back wheel.

It was a sunny day and several cars were parked at

the pavilion. Three women walked up and down the beach, collecting trash. They left the few fish carcasses alone; those were naturally occurring. I stepped across the same large fish skeleton that had been there yesterday to reach the water's edge. I stopped, appalled to see the ash spots on bare ground, the water a foot away. I had thought it was close to low tide when I scattered the ashes because of the fish skeleton so far up the beach, and a few other signs I knew to look for.

The trash ladies reached the place where I stood and I protectively placed a foot between each ash spot so they wouldn't step directly on my cats. I went back to my log and thought about what to do. I could go to a store and get a pail and shovel and move the ashes out into deeper water. They would dissolve in the salt water within three weeks, and that calcium would do a lot more good in the intertidal zone where shellfish grew. I decided to leave them where they were. The trash ladies were a fair distance away by now, so I went back to say good-bye. I promised to return every summer if I could, and told them I hoped it would be a very long time before I had to bring Kali with me.

Riding away was so hard! I had the distraction of getting safely back across the highway to help me break away, but as I got farther down the road, I obsessed over whether or not to go back and move the ashes. I had been lucky to scatter them without drawing any negative attention; surely digging up part of the beach wouldn't go unnoticed. In three weeks it wouldn't matter; how many crews of trash ladies and exploring children would there be in that time? Soon I got far enough away to let the matter rest. I realized I was crying as I rode.

I kept crying all the way to Union Bay, where I hoped to enjoy a favorite lunch spot. I went into the convenience store to find the lunch counter closed down. That was disappointing, and I was really hungry.

The lady at the counter reminded me that there was a Subway a few miles down the road at the Denman Island ferry terminal. I remembered the place; it would do for lunch. I went on and had my sandwich there. After lunch I noticed how strong I felt. I was fully recovered from the chill in the rainstorm and it had toughened my legs, my sore knee forgotten. It was hard to keep my speed down, but I didn't want to ride so fast, I wanted to be out on the road longer. The rolling hills felt like nothing, I just pedaled steadily uphill and enjoyed coasting down the other side.

There was an ice cream stand not much farther down the road from the Subway, and I stopped there for a cone, more out of a love of routine than actual hunger. Last year it had been raining when I passed by; this year I wanted to enjoy my cone in the sun. I sat next to an older couple and complimented the woman's cat necklace. She lit up and told me all about her cats and the cat rescue work she does in Comox. I told her I was a cat volunteer too, and we chatted like old friends for an hour before we went our separate ways.

Too quickly I reached the grocery store in Bowser, the nearest town to Free Spirit Spheres. I got a few things for a light dinner, knowing Rosey's snack basket would more than cover my carbohydrate needs. The ride to Free Spirit was over before I was ready. Still, it was good to see the familiar gravel driveway.

The porch of Tom and Rosey's house was littered with shoes of all sizes, and the racket from inside told me the grandchildren were all downstairs. I knocked on the door and Tom answered, breathless from playing with the young ones. We walked back to Eve together, with the ease of a happy routine. I mentally greeted all the familiar art objects along the walkway. Tom stopped at the trailer to show me the new washrooms, a private one for each sphere. I could leave my personal items there now during my stay, that was nice. The new washrooms smelled just like the original ones, like fresh new wood. Sometimes I smell my newish bathroom vanity at home and it takes me right back to the washroom trailer at Free Spirit.

I parked Silver near the picnic table in her usual place and Tom carried one of my panniers up the steps for me as we did the paperwork and caught up on the last year. After he left, I said, "Hi, Eve, it's so good to see you again," and flopped down on the bed.

Rosey arrived with the snack basket and we planned to get together one of the evenings I was there. With the visiting relatives, it would take some juggling and I didn't want to intrude on her family time. I was grateful that she thought it was important too.

That evening I hooked my iPod up to the sound system and played the cat songs again, ending with By Way of Sorrow, and cried as if I would never stop. I cried for the cats, I cried for my dad, I cried for the way I felt cut adrift since Nimby died, I even cried for what I'd lost in the crash, a luxury of self-pity I'd never allowed myself before. I had hoped to resolve a bunch of issues on the road, how to restore my income to a realistic level, and whether I should try to stay in my condo with the noisy rude neighbors, or move to a rental and try to save up for a better re-entry to homeownership.

My journey was almost over and I didn't have any answers. But Eve calmed me and told me what I already knew; there were no easy answers. The journey itself was what I needed, and I would just have to deal with whatever came after it day by day. For now, I could let out the sorrow of the last year in a place where it wouldn't crush me.

The next day I rode to Qualicum Beach and planned to swim at the Ravensong Aquatic Center there. I found the place and admired it, but it was too nice out to go indoors to swim. I decided to swim at

Qualicum Beach, in the same waters where Miranda, Sadie and Nimby rested. The water was shallow a long way out, and consequently warmed by the sun. I had left my water shoes back at the Spheres but I didn't need them. After I crossed the rocks, I took off my bike shoes and enjoyed the thick layer of soft sand. I paddled around happily for at least an hour, marveling at the profusion of live sand dollars on the bottom and avoiding stepping in the fragile eelgrass beds. It was such a comfort knowing this sacred water was where my cats' bones would find new life.

I could hear the kids playing in the yard as I walked Silver back along the path toward Eve. I spent a quiet evening reading and doing my ferry puzzle, and walking around the grounds thinking about things. Rosey came by with her granddaughter, delivering baskets to the other guests. They sat down at my picnic table and another guest joined us, asking the little girl all kinds of questions that were appropriate to ask a six-year-old. I'm always so impressed with people who know how to talk with kids. I'm terrible at it. Rosey's granddaughter didn't seem to notice, she asked me plenty of questions of her own. I felt a warm contentment to be there, grateful that I seemed to be all cried out. It was like I had to let go of all that sorrow in order for anything else to fit back inside.

My last full day, I decided not to leave the compound. I would simply enjoy Eve and the grounds and demand nothing of myself. I was napping when I heard Rosey come by with her granddaughter and she called "Hello!" I thought she was calling up to another guest; surely she would call me by name. I fell back to sleep before I could hear her call my name. Later I bumped into her again by the washroom trailer and she said she had tried to visit. I explained about my nap and we laughed, and she asked if she could come by with wine later that evening. I was thrilled that she wanted to and agreed to stay up as late as it took for the grandkids to fall asleep.

Rosey arrived with wine at 9:30 that evening. It was a warm night and I left the door and windows wide open to let in fresh air. It also let in moths; by ten o'clock the sphere was alive with a squadron of white and brown moths flapping at the low mood lights. First we did our best to chase them out, laughing as we were already a little tipsy, and then I closed the door. I think it was close to midnight when Rosey nodded off to sleep at the table in mid-sentence. I gently woke her up and walked with her as far as the washroom trailer; her home was just a few steps farther down the path.

The next morning I woke with a heavy heart, knowing I had to pack up and go. When I opened the door, Rosey was walking down the path wearing an art t-shirt featuring the brush-stroked figure of a woman on a bicycle, her ponytail streaming in the wind. I grinned and she told me Tom was wearing his bike shirt too today in my honor. Never one for a short checkout, Tom and I sat in his new office sphere, high in the fir tree next to the house, talking about architecture and the difference between Tiny and traditional space use philosophies.

I told Tom how poorly I fit into my 560-square-foot cottage in Ballard, and he explained that the cottage was a small traditional house, not a proper Tiny Home. Traditional homes are built for separation of activities and presentation of things, while Tiny Homes integrate space to be used for multiple purposes. A workspace might fold away to provide a dining area, for example. Beds are typically folded up during the day or placed in a small loft; there is no need for an entire room with free-standing furniture to hold clothing. Clothes are kept in closets and drawers built under the stairs or elsewhere, using what would otherwise be blank wall space, and people dress in the main living area. I began to see how a Tiny Home might be ideal for me. Bike touring had taught me how little stuff I really need. Show me another woman who can pack for two weeks in seven cubic feet!

There was one piece of my life dilemma solved on the road, my next housing stop. I was tired of sharing walls with inconsiderate and downright dangerous people. A nicer condo was not the answer and a traditional house was out of reach. I had already opted out of a lot of the consumer culture; I brewed my own laundry soap and I shunned all disposables like paper towels, using washable wipes instead, even using a washcloth on the head of my Swiffer mop rather than buying mop refills. Going Tiny was a natural next step. My limited income would go a lot farther and my world would get bigger, not smaller.

Leaving Tom and Rosey was bittersweet. They had outgrown their small land parcel and weren't able to expand to accommodate more spheres, so they were looking for a new place to move and expand the resort. It would still be on the island, that much was certain, but this might be my last time at this location. I was glad I hadn't asked to scatter the cat ashes in the pond there, now that I knew they were moving. The estuary was a better choice, it gave them access to the whole world as their physical remains worked their way back into living things. And what cat wouldn't want to be buried in a bird sanctuary?

The ride to Parksville was pleasant and effortless, even euphoric. I stopped at the sand castle festival and enjoyed this year's music theme, especially the sculpture dedicated to Nanaimo native Diana Krall. After a soft-serve cone, I felt plenty strong enough to ride on to Nanaimo, but chose to take the bus past the busy highway section. Why spoil a perfect day with an avoidable mishap? I knew all too well how quickly and completely life could change in a split second. I got off at the Woodgrove Centre and scouted the Wal-Mart store for Renee's soap. Unbelievably, they didn't have it. I located the trail behind the mall and enjoyed a long, gently downhill-sloping ride back to the hostel.

As I sat in my private room that night, a floor fan combating the summer heat and drying my laundry strung merrily from the closet bar, a brochure for nearby Gabriola Island opened out on the bed, I thought about how this trip had been a coming of age in my new normal world. I had maintained and grown old friendships and made a new friend, reconnected with the land I love, found new places to explore, and most importantly, I had carried my three best friends to a safe and suitable resting place. These past few days, my body was alive with energy. Not free of pain, but transcending it somehow. The end of this trip wasn't the end of anything. Yes, things were kind of a mess all around back home, but life was about finding your way. I knew what I was made of and looked forward to knowing who I would become, flying on Silver wings.

Afterword

I don't know how Jaycee Dugard came out with her book about her abduction less than a year after her return. I imagine she kept a diary in her head all the time she was gone, and she was able to simply brain-dump. Either that, or she had help. (And since I mentioned her, I should also mention that her book is remarkable and she's become a hero of mine.) It took me four years to finish this book, and of course even more changes have happened since then. The first draft ended at the Ferris wheel opening, with a Pollyanna ending about how I was no longer limited by what happened to me. As I worked on the revisions, that ending started to annoy me more and more. *Of course* I'm limited by what happened to me in some very significant ways. I've just found it in myself to keep moving ahead anyway and realize that my human potential isn't any less because of it, and it might even be greater because of what I've learned.

At the end of my bike trip last summer, I felt like I'd learned some important lessons about life and I'd reached a good ending point for the story I wanted to tell. I've already started my second book, about my relationship with Stuff and how it led me on the path toward the Tiny Home movement. Rosey was right, at some point I would remember that I'm about more than this one huge thing that happened to me. At some point, I would turn my energy from surviving back to living.

Lots of people comment that I was brave to get back on my bike. I tell them it wasn't bravery that made me do it, it was healthy anger. No 23-year-old kid has the right to take from me what I love. Not like that, in a moment of thoughtlessness. He didn't *mean* any harm, careless people never do, but he treated his own gift of life casually and it collided with mine. Because of legal considerations, I wasn't able to print his real name in this book, but it's a matter of public record.

If you are a cyclist, I can't urge you strongly enough to meet with your insurance agent and make sure you're properly covered. You can't depend on the other guy! If I had the policy then that I have now, I'd be living in a new house and I would be able to live comfortably working part time. Most importantly, I'd be able to compensate my family for flying out here many times and caring for me. I'm not the only one who was rendered broke by this. If you are not a cyclist, I'd still urge you to review your insurance coverage. The attitude in our culture is that insurance is a bother, and you should pay as little as possible for it. The fact is, insurance covers the cost of any expensive mistakes you might make. Could you live with yourself if you caused harm to someone and couldn't compensate for the damage done? Good liability coverage can make a terrible situation less so.

There are so many small stories that didn't get told, so many people whose friendship matters to me but who didn't get mentioned. I have no doubt that for months after I fire off the final file to Kate Weisel, I will be smacking my head over people and stories that didn't make it in.

Thanks to many generous donations to my Kickstarter campaign, I can give 10% of my profits to the Whatcom Humane Society. They saved the lives of two of my best friends, Nimby and Timbits, Kali's new friend.

Yes, Kali adjusted to a new friend and it's wonderful to see her with her pepper back. There will never be another Nimby Tyson Noreen, but this giant clown makes me laugh and floods my brain with oxytocin every time I look at his handsome and slightly insolent black face.

I hope that whatever problems you're facing, my story helps you find your fighting spirit. I hope that as my own challenges mount, seeing my book on the shelf at Village Books gives me more than vain pleasure, that I never lose the mantra I received that fateful night at the Northwest Washington Fair—"You just found out what you're made of. Now I get to know you while we find out who you're going to become." You're made of more than you think. I wish you a gentler process of finding that out than I had.

Acknowledgments

There are too many people to thank for helping with my recovery, it would take another book to call you all out. I'm restricting this page to the people who helped with the actual book.

First of all, Mom! For bailing out my Kickstarter campaign at the 11th hour.

Writing a book with real people in it is messy and hard. This book might never have seen the light of day without the help of Dr. Bella DePaulo, host of the blog on Psychology Today, *Living Single*. She did the job of an editor without asking for anything in return. (Any mistakes that remain are my own, not hers.) I didn't dare give up on this project for fear of letting her down. Thank you, Bella, for your helpful critique and for believing in me and my story.

Thanks and boundless hugs to Jill Bates for her read-throughs with both endings, and for being my most faithful cheerleader. Her friendship has been a touchstone in my life, always reminding me what I'm about and helping me to get over myself.

Thanks to Kenn Rich, for enabling my writing habit by covering my payments when I forgot to work. Also for being a steadfast friend and an excellent Andrew.>:)

Thanks to Taimi Dunn Gorman, for helping me through the publication process and introducing me to Kate Weisel, book production specialist. Some writers would rather see a struggling author learn the hard way like they did. Taimi generously offered a hand up.

Thanks to Rosey Cowan and Tom Chudleigh of Free Spirit Spheres on Vancouver Island, for sharing so much of themselves with me. Going to Free Spirit

Spheres was a goal I picked out of thin air. Who knew there really was a pot of gold at the end of the rainbow?

Bottomless thanks to Andy Clay, for sharing her story, for her generous heart, and for the words that have inspired my life since she spoke them.

CPSIA information can be obtained
at www.ICGtesting.com
Printed in the USA
FSOW02n1738010715
8431FS